Ancient Rome

Ancient Rome

From Romulus to Justinian

THOMAS R. MARTIN

Yale UNIVERSITY PRESS/NEW HAVEN & LONDON

Published with assistance from the
foundation established in memory of
Calvin Chapin of the Class of 1788, Yale
College.

Yale University Press books may be
purchased in quantity for educational,
business, or promotional use.
For information, please e-mail
sales.press@yale.edu (U.S. office)
or sales@yaleup.co.uk (U.K. office).

Designed by Mary Valencia.
Set in Joanna type by Integrated
Publishing Solutions.
Printed in the United States of America.

The Library of Congress has cataloged
the hardcover edition as follows:

Martin, Thomas R., 1947–
  Ancient Rome : from Romulus to
Justinian / Thomas R. Martin.
    p. cm.
  Includes bibliographical references
and index.
  ISBN 978-0-300-16004-8 (cloth : alk.
paper) 1. Rome—History. 2. Rome—
Civilization. I. Title.
  DG209.M38 2012
  937'.63—dc23   2012011010

ISBN 978-0-300-19831-7 (pbk.)

A catalogue record for this book is
available from the British Library.

This book is dedicated to the students who have studied ancient Roman history in my courses and to Blaise Nagy, *magnus amicus et perfectus magister*, who encouraged and inspired me to persevere in this project.

Iuppiter, te hoc ferto obmovendo bonas preces precor, uti sies volens propitius mihi liberisque meis domo familiaeque meae mactus hoc ferto.
—Cato, *De agri cultura* 134

CONTENTS

ACKNOWLEDGMENTS

For their patience, advice, and concern in bringing this project to completion, I want to record my deep gratitude to Jennifer Banks (Senior Editor), Piyali Bhattacharya (Editorial Assistant), Susan Laity (Manuscript Editor), and Margaret Otzel (Editor) of Yale University Press, and express my warm thanks to Suzie Tibor for her thorough art research, Gavin Lewis for his expert and insightful editing, and Anne Salloom for proof reading. The anonymous reviewers also deserve warm thanks for their thoughtful insights and constructive criticisms that helped improve the text at many points. As always, for her acute insight and endless support I owe to my wife, Ivy Sui-yuen Sun, a debt that can never be fully repaid, or even adequately expressed.

NOTE ON CITATIONS TO SOURCES

The term "primary sources" as used here (and commonly in classical studies) refers to ancient texts, whether literary, documentary, epigraphic, or numismatic. To help readers find the passages in primary sources that are embedded in the text of this book, citations will be presented, whenever possible, using the standard internal reference systems of those sources that are conventional in modern scholarly editions of those sources and are used in the most useful translations. So, for example, the citation "Livy, *From the Foundation of the City* 5.54" means that the passage is Book 5, section 54 of that work by Livy. This will enable readers to find the passage in question in any modern edition or translation that includes the internal reference system.

"Secondary sources" accordingly refers to postclassical or modern scholarship about these sources and the history that they describe. The embedded citations of secondary sources contain only the name of the author or a short title, with the relevant page numbers or, in the case of catalogued objects such as coins or inscriptions, the number of the object. Full bibliographic information on secondary sources, as well as on modern translations of primary sources, can be found in the Suggested Readings.

1

Introduction and Background

This overview of the history of ancient Rome covers the period from the foundation of Rome by Romulus (so legend said) in the eighth century B.C., through the Roman Republic, to the establishment of what we today call the Roman Empire, finishing with the rule of Emperor Justinian in the sixth century A.D. Roman history emphatically did not come to an end with Justinian's reign, but that period will provide the chronological stopping point for this book. This reflects the (for Romans) regrettable circumstances that made Justinian the last ruler to try to restore the territorial extent and glory of the later Roman Empire, which had shrunk by that emperor's time to a fraction of the size and might that it had reached at the height of Roman power nearly half a millennium before Justinian's time. Geographically, the narrative covers the enormous territory in Europe, North Africa, and western Asia (the Middle East) that the Romans ruled at that earlier high point in their power.

As a brief survey, this book necessarily omits a great deal of information about ancient Rome and pays more attention to some topics than others. For example, a fuller survey would describe in more detail the history of the Italian peoples before the traditional date of Rome's foundation in 753 B.C., whose deeds and thoughts greatly influenced the Romans themselves.

Likewise, a longer book would explore the history of the Roman world after Justinian, when the emergence of Islam changed forever the political, cultural, and religious circumstances of the Mediterranean world that the Roman Empire once dominated. The books listed in the Suggested Readings section provide further discussion and guidance on many topics that receive little or no coverage here.

In my experience teaching Roman history for nearly forty years, if readers are willing to do the hard work required to participate in the fascinating and still-ongoing conversation about interpreting what Romans did and said and thought, the best thing that they can do for themselves is to read the ancient sources—more than once! For this reason, citations in parentheses direct readers to ancient sources quoted in the text, most of which also appear in the Suggested Readings section. In this way I hope to encourage readers to read the primary sources for themselves, so that they can experience the contexts of the evidence, discover what in particular interests them in the ancient texts, and on the basis of their further reading arrive at independent judgments on the significance of events and persons and ideas in Roman history. In the service of this same goal, the first two sections in the Suggested Readings are devoted to currently available translations of ancient sources that are either explicitly mentioned in the text or lie behind discussions in the text, even if the particular sources are not mentioned there.

In any case, to follow the rest of the story the reader needs to know in advance some basic facts of Rome's history: its main chronological divisions; the main sources on which our knowledge of it is based; long-term themes with which we will be concerned; and something of the Romans' "prehistory"—the Romans' Italian forerunners, and the neighbors whose early influence helped set the direction of Rome's cultural development, the Etruscans and the Greeks.

THE PERIODS OF ROMAN HISTORY

This book follows the usual three-part chronological division of Roman history—Monarchy, Republic, and Empire (on which terms see below). It is important to make clear, however, that categorizing Rome's history under these three periods is an anachronistic practice. For the Romans, there was only one significant dividing point in their history: the elimination of the rule of kings at the end of the sixth century B.C. After the monarchy was abolished, the Romans themselves never stopped referring to their political system as a Republic (*res publica*, "the people's thing, the people's business"), even during the period that we call the Empire, which begins at the end of the first century B.C. with the career of Augustus. Today, Augustus is called the first Roman emperor; the Romans, however, referred to him as the *princeps*, the "First Man" (of the restored and continuing Republic). This is the political system that is usually called the Principate. The Romans certainly realized that Augustus's restructuring of the Roman state represented a turning point in their history, but all the "emperors" (in our terms) who followed him continued to insist that their government remained "the Republic."

The three time periods do not receive equal treatment in this book. The history of the Monarchy is presented much more briefly than the histories of the Republic and the Empire. This reflects above all the relative lack of reliable evidence for the time of the kings of Rome (although the evidence for the early Republic is hardly much better). The Republic and the Empire, on the other hand, receive roughly equal coverage. Only limited space is devoted to wide-ranging explanations of events and people in ancient Rome and judgments concerning the significance of Roman history for later times. This does not mean that I do not have strong opinions about these issues or that I believe the story "speaks for itself." Here, my goal is to present the story in such a way that it encourages readers to take on the difficult job of deciding for themselves why the Romans acted and thought as they did, and what meanings to attribute to the history of ancient Rome.

In the first of the three customary periods of Rome's political history, a series of seven kings ruled from 753 to 509 B.C., according to the traditionally accepted chronology. These dates are in fact only approximate, like most dates in Roman history until at least the third century B.C. (and in many cases for later centuries as well). The Republic, a new system of shared government replacing a sole ruler, extended from 509 to the second half of the first century B.C. In this overview, the end of the Republic is set in 27 B.C., the date when Augustus established the Principate (the government that modern historians call the Roman Empire).

The period of the Empire then follows. The last Roman emperor in the western half of the empire (roughly speaking, Europe west of Greece) was deposed in A.D. 476; this date has therefore sometimes been taken to mark "The Fall of the Roman Empire." However, the narrative here takes the history of the empire roughly a century beyond this "Fall," reaching the reign of Justinian (A.D. 527–565) in the eastern empire.

As far as the people of the eastern section of the empire were concerned, Roman imperial government continued for another thousand years, with Constantinople as the capital, the empire's "New Rome." The last eastern emperor was killed in A.D. 1453, when the Turkish commander Mehmet the Conqueror captured Constantinople and what little was left of the territory of the eastern Roman Empire. Historians today call the empire that Mehmet founded the Ottoman Empire. Since the Ottomans took over the remaining territory of the Eastern Roman Empire, this date might qualify as a better choice for the Roman Empire's "Fall" than A.D. 476. It is worth remembering, however, that Mehmet publicly announced that as a ruler he was building on (and aiming to outdo) the legacies of Alexander the Great, the Macedonian conqueror, Julius Caesar, and Augustus, whose accomplishments he had read about in Greek and Latin historical sources. Mehmet in fact proclaimed that his title was "Caesar of Rome." In other words, the first Turkish emperor was not seeking to end Roman history, but to redefine and extend it. In Russia, the idea soon began to be expressed that its empire was the "Third Rome." In the same spirit of emulation of the remembered glory of ancient Rome, around this time Frederick III proclaimed that he, too, was a Roman emperor, like his predecessors who had ruled the central European territories long known as the Holy Roman Empire. It is clear, then, that the memory of the glory of ancient Rome proved so seductive to later rulers that its history lived on in influential ways even after the empire's "Fall," regardless of how that concept is understood or what date historians give to it.

SOURCES AND EVIDENCE

The sources of information for Roman history are varied. There are first of all the texts of ancient historical writers, supplemented by the texts of authors of other kinds of literature, from epic and lyric poetry to comic plays. Documentary evidence, both formal and informal, survives as inscriptions carved, inked, or painted on stone, metal, and papyri. Archaeological excavation reveals the physical remains of buildings and other structures, from walls to wells, as well as coins, manufactured objects from weapons to jewelry, and traces of organic materials such as textiles or food and wine preserved in storage containers. Roman art survives in sculptures, paintings, and mosaics. In sum, however, despite their variety, the sources that have survived are too limited to allow us a view of the events, ideas, and ways of life of ancient Rome that is anywhere near as full as the panoramic reconstruction of the past that historical research on more recent periods can achieve.

In addition, in Roman history (as in all ancient history), the exact dates of events and of the lifetimes even of important people are often not accurately recorded in our surviving sources. Readers should therefore recognize that many dates given here are imprecise, even if they are not qualified as "around such and such a year." Indeed, it is best to assume that most dates given here, especially for the opening centuries of Roman history, are likely to be approximations at best and subject to debate among professional historians.

For all these reasons, Roman history remains a story characterized by uncertainties and controversies. Readers should therefore understand that the limited interpretations and conclusions offered here should always be imagined to be followed by the thought that "we might someday discover new evidence, or use our historical imaginations to arrive at new interpretations of currently known evidence, and then change our minds about this particular interpretation or conclusion."

The evidence for the early history of Rome is the most limited of all. The two most extensive narrative accounts of Roman history under the Monarchy and the Republic that have survived (at least in part) were not written until seven centuries after the city's foundation. In addition, the manuscripts on which we today depend for these texts are missing substantial parts of the original narratives. One of these primary ancient sources is the *From the Foundation of the City* by Livy (59 B.C.–A.D. 17), a Roman scholar with no career in war or politics who narrated Rome's history from its earliest days down to his own time.

The other extended narrative covering the early history of Rome is by Dionysius of Halicarnassus, a Greek scholar who lived in Rome as a foreigner making his living as a teacher. He wrote his history, *Roman Antiquities*, at about the same time as Livy, toward the end of the first century B.C. These authors tended to interpret the long-past era of early Rome as a golden age compared to what they saw as the moral decline of their own times, a period of civil war when the system of government known as the Roman Republic was being violently transformed into a disguised monarchy under the rule of Augustus, the system of government today known as the Roman Empire. When, for instance, Livy in the preface to his Roman history refers to this era—his own lifetime—he sadly calls it "these times in which we can withstand neither our vices nor the solutions for them."

The surviving textual sources become more numerous for the later history of the Republic; in addition to Livy and Dionysius (and to name only the best-known that are readily available in English translation), there are Polybius's *Histories* on the late third and early second centuries B.C., including famous descriptions of the Roman army and what modern scholars sometimes call the "mixed constitution" of the government of the Republic, seen as a combination of monarchy, oligarchy, and democracy. For the late second and first centuries, there are vivid narratives and personal reflections on and by major historical figures in Sallust's *War with Jugurtha* and *Conspiracy of Catiline*, Julius Caesar's *Commentaries on the Gallic War* and *Commentaries of the Civil War*, Cicero's *Orations* and *Letters*, and Appian's *Civil Wars*. Plutarch's *Parallel Lives* offers numerous lively biographies of the most famous leaders of the Roman Republic, from Romulus to Julius Caesar.

The textual sources of our information about the Roman Empire, despite being more extensive than for earlier periods, are also incomplete. The best known ancient authors whose works provide much of what we know about this period of history include Suetonius's *Lives of the Twelve Caesars* (biographies of Julius Caesar and the Roman emperors from Augustus to Domitian); Tacitus's narratives of imperial history in the first century A.D., the *Annals* and the *Histories*; Josephus's *The Jewish War*, an eyewitness account of the rebellion of the Jews and of the Roman military action that led to the destruction of Jerusalem in A.D. 70; Cassius Dio's *Roman History*, which narrates Roman history up to the early third century A.D.; Ammianus Marcellinus's *Roman History*, narrating the history of the fourth century A.D.; and Procopius's narratives of the reign of Emperor Justinian and Empress Theodora in the sixth century A.D., *History of the Wars* and *Secret History*, the former account full of praise and the latter fiercely critical. Orosius's *Seven Books of History against the Pagans* gives a Christian version of universal history, including the Roman Empire up to the early fifth century A.D.

By the time of the later Roman Empire, a great preponderance of the surviving evidence pertains to the history of Christianity. This salient fact reflects the overwhelming impact on the Roman (and later) world of the growth of the new faith, and it necessarily influences the content of any narrative of that period.

The ancient authors' points of views on Roman life and government during the period of the Empire vary too widely to be clearly summarized without distortion, but it is perhaps fair to say that over time a nostalgic sense of regret for the loss of the original Republic and its sense of liberty (at least for those in the upper class) gave way to a recognition that an empire under a sole and supreme ruler was the only possible permanent system of government for the Roman world. This acceptance of the return of monarchs as Rome's rulers nevertheless also reflected, for many Romans, anger and regret at the abuses and injustices committed by individual emperors.

Figure 1. This Renaissance-era manuscript of Tacitus's *Annals* is better preserved than most of the manuscripts on which we rely for texts of ancient authors. Tacitus's emphasis on politics in his narrative of the history of the early Roman Empire inspired a lively debate among Renaissance political theorists about the relative merits of a republic versus a monarchy. Beinecke Rare Book and Manuscript Library, Yale University.

THEMES OF ROMAN HISTORY

In my experience, a preliminary "flyover" helps readers who are new to ancient history comprehend the more detailed narrative that follows. All the terms used here will be explained subsequently at the appropriate places.

The ethnic and cultural origins of the ancient Romans reflect both their roots in Italy and also contact with Greeks. The political history of Rome begins with the rule of kings in the eighth century B.C.; the Romans remembered them as founders of enduring traditions in society and religion, but the limited information available from the surviving sources makes it difficult to know much in detail about this period. The Romans also reported that the monarchy was abolished at the end of the sixth century B.C. in response to the violent rape of a prominent Roman woman by the king's son. The kingship was then replaced by the Republic, a complicated system of shared government dominated by the upper class.

The greatest challenge in studying the Roman Republic is to understand how a society based on a long tradition of ethical values linking people to one another in a patron-client system (a social hierarchy with mutual obligations between those of higher and lower status) and with a successful military could eventually fail so spectacularly. From its beginnings, the Republic had grown stronger because the small farmers of Italy could produce an agricultural surplus. This surplus supported a growth in population that produced the soldiers for a large army of citizens and allies. The Roman willingness to endure great losses of people and property helped to make this army invincible in prolonged conflicts. Rome might lose battles, but never wars. Because Rome's wars initially brought profits, peace seemed a wasted opportunity. Upper-class commanders especially desired military careers with plenty of combat because, if they could win victories, they could win also glory and riches to enhance their status in Rome's social hierarchy.

The nearly continual wars of the Republic from the fifth to the second centuries B.C. had unexpected consequences that spelled disaster in the long run. Many of the small farmers on whom Italy's prosperity depended were ruined. When those families that had lost their land flocked to Rome, they created a new, unstable political force: the urban mob subject to the violent swings of the urban economy. The men of the upper class, on the other hand, competed with each other harder and harder for the increased career opportunities presented to them by constant war. This competition reached unmanageable proportions when successful generals began to extort advantages for themselves from the state by acting as patrons to their client armies of poor troops. The balance of ethical values that Roman mothers tried to teach their sons was being shattered in these new conditions, and lip service was the only respect that traditional values supporting the community received from nobles mad for individual status and wealth. In this superheated competitive atmosphere, violence and murder became a means for settling political disputes. But violent settlements provoked violent responses. The powerful ideas of Cicero's ethical philosophy went ignored in the murderous conflicts of the civil war of his own times. No reasonable Roman could have been optimistic about the chances for an enduring peace in the aftermath of Julius Caesar's assassination. That Augustus, the adopted son of Caesar, would forge such a peace less than fifteen years later would have seemed an impossible dream in 44 B.C.

History is full of surprises, however. Augustus created what we today call the Roman Empire by replacing the shared-government structure of the Republic with a monarchy, while insisting all the while that he was restoring Roman government to its traditional values. He succeeded above all because he retained the loyalty of the army and exploited the ancient tradition of the patron-client system. His new system, the Principate, made the emperor the patron of the army and of all the people. Most provincials, especially in the eastern Mediterranean, found this arrangement perfectly acceptable because it replicated the relationship between the monarch and his subjects that they had long experienced under the kingdoms that had previously ruled them.

So long as there were sufficient funds to allow the emperors to keep their tens of millions of clients across the empire satisfied, stability prevailed. The rulers spent money to provide food to the poor, build arenas and baths for public entertainment, and paid the soldiers to defend the peace internally and against foreign invaders. The emperors of the first and second centuries A.D. expanded the military by a third to protect their distant territories stretching from Britain to North Africa to Syria. By the second century, peace and prosperity had created an imperial Golden Age. Long-term financial difficulties set in, however, because the army, now focused on defense instead of conquest, no longer fought and won foreign wars that brought money into the treasury. Severe inflation made the situation worse. The decline in imperial revenues imposed intolerable financial pressures on the wealthy elites of the provinces to ensure full tax payments and support public services. When they could no longer meet this demand without ruining their fortunes, they lost their public-spiritedness and began avoiding their communal responsibilities. Loyalty to the state became too expensive.

The emergence of Christians added to the uncertainty by making officials suspicious of the new believers' dedication to the state and its traditional religion. This new religion started slowly with the mission of Jesus of Nazareth, and evolved from Jewish apocalypticism to an institutionalized and hierarchical church. Christianity's believers disputed with each other and with the authorities. Their martyrs both impressed and concerned the government with the depth of their convictions during persecutions. People placing loyalty to a new divinity ahead of traditional loyalty to the state was unheard-of and inexplicable for Roman officials.

When financial ruin, civil war, and natural disasters reinforced each other's horrors in the mid-third century A.D., the emperors lacked the money, the vision, and the dedication to communal values that might have alleviated, or at least significantly lessened, the crisis. Not even persecutions of the Christians could convince the gods to restore divine good will to the empire. It had to be transformed politically and religiously for that to happen.

The process of once again reinventing Roman government began at the end of the third century. The subsequent history of the late Roman Empire was a contest between the forces of unity and the forces of division. The third-century A.D. crisis brought the Roman Empire to a turning point. Diocletian's autocratic reorganization kept it from falling to pieces in the short term but opened the way to its eventual division into western and eastern halves. From this time on, its history more and more divided into two regional streams, even though emperors as late as Justinian in the sixth century A.D. retained the dream of reuniting the Roman Empire of Augustus and restoring its glory on a scale equal to that of its Golden Age.

A complex of forces interacted to destroy the unity of the Roman world, beginning with the catastrophic losses of people and property during the crisis, which had hit the west harder than the east. The fourth century A.D. introduced a new stress with the pressures on central government created by the migrations of Germanic peoples fleeing the Huns. Too numerous and too aggressive to be absorbed without disturbance, they created kingdoms that eventually replaced imperial government in the western empire. This change transformed not just western Europe's politics, society, and economy, but also the Germanic tribes themselves, as they had to develop a stronger sense of ethnic identity to become rulers.

The economic deterioration accompanying these transformations drove a stake into the heart of the elite's public-spiritedness that had been one of the foundations of Roman imperial stability, as super-wealthy nobles retreated to self-sufficient country estates, shunned municipal office, and ceased guaranteeing tax revenues to the central government. The eastern empire fared better economically and avoided the worst of the migrations' violent effects. Its rulers self-consciously continued the empire not only politically but also culturally by seeking to preserve "Romanness." The financial drain of pursuing this dream of unity through war against the Germanic kingdoms in the west ironically increased social discontent by driving tax rates to punitive levels, while the concentration of power in the capital weakened the local communities that had made the empire robust.

This period of increasing political and social division saw the religious unification of the empire under the banner of Christianity. The emperor Constantine's conversion to the new faith in the early fourth century A.D. marked an epochal point in the history of the world, though the process of Christianizing the Roman Empire had much longer to go at this date. Moreover, this process was far from simple or swift: Christians disagreed, even to the point of violence, over fundamental doctrines of faith, and believers in traditional Roman polytheistic religion continued to exist and worship for centuries more. Christians developed a hierarchy of leadership in their emerging church to try to prevent disunity, but believers proved remarkably recalcitrant in the face of authority. The most dedicated of them abandoned everyday society to live as monks and nuns. Monastic life redefined the meaning of holiness by creating communities of God's heroes withdrawing from this world to devote their valor to glorifying the next. In the end, then, the imperial vision of unity faded before the divisive forces of the human spirit combined with the mundane dynamics of political and social transformation. What remained was the memory of the past, encoded in the literature from classical antiquity that survived the many troubles of the time of the later Roman Empire.

GEOGRAPHY, ANCESTORS, AND CULTURAL INFLUENCES

To understand the people and the events of this history, we must begin, as always in historical study, with the geography and environment in which it took place. The location of Rome provides the fundamental clue in solving the puzzle of how this originally tiny, poor, and disrespected community eventually grew to be the greatest power in enormous regions surrounding the Mediterranean Sea. Rome's geography and climate helped its people, over a long period of time, to become more prosperous and powerful. Their original territory, located on the western side of the center of the north-south peninsula that is Italy, provided fertile farmland, temperate weather with adequate rainfall, and a nearby harbor on the Mediterranean. Since agriculture and trade by sea were the most important sources for generating wealth in ancient times, these geographical characteristics were crucial to Rome's long-term growth.

The landscape of Italy is diverse: its plains, river valleys, hills, and mountains crowd into a narrow, boot-shaped tongue of land extending far out into the waters of the Mediterranean. At the north, the towering Alps Mountains divide Italy from continental Europe. Since these snowy peaks are so difficult to cross, they provided some protection from invasions launched by raiders living north of the Alps. A large and rich plain, watered by the Po River, lies at the top of the Italian peninsula just south of the Alps. Another, lower chain of mountains, the Apennines, separates the northern plain from central and southern Italy. The Apennines then snake southeastward, down the middle of the peninsula like a knobby spine, with hills and coastal plains flanking the central mountain chain on the east and west. The western plains, where Rome was located, were larger and received more rainfall than the other side of the peninsula. An especially fertile area, the plain of Campania, surrounds the bay of Naples on Italy's southwestern coast. Italy's relatively open geography made political unification a possibility.

The original site of the city of Rome occupied hilltops above a lowland plain extending to the western coast of the peninsula. The various Italian peoples neighboring Roman territory were more prosperous than the first Romans; archaeological investigation has revealed that the earliest Romans lived in small huts. Their settlement, gradually extending over seven hills that formed a rough circle around a low-lying central area, had an advantage, however, because it controlled a crossing of the Tiber River. This setting on a crossroads encouraged trade and contact with other people crossing the river as they journeyed up and down the natural route for northwest-southeast land travel along the western side of Italy. The harbor at Ostia, at the mouth of the Tiber River only fifteen miles west of Rome, offered opportunities for contact with people much farther away, profit from overseas trade, and fees and other revenues from seaborne merchants stopping there—Italy stuck so far out into the Mediterranean Sea that east-west ship traffic naturally relied on its harbors. In addition, the large and fertile island of Sicily right off the "toe" of the Italian peninsula also attracted sea-going merchants who could from there easily travel up and down the western coast doing business. In short, geography put Rome at the natural center of both Italy and the Mediterranean world, giving it, in the long run, tremendous demographic

Map 1. Italy Around 500 B.C.

and commercial advantages. Livy summed up Rome's fortunate location with these words: "Gods and men had good reason to choose this site for our city—all its advantages make it of all places in the world the best for a city destined to grow great" (*From the Foundation of the City* 5.54).

Demography (the statistical study of human populations) rivals geography as a tool for understanding how Rome grew powerful in the long run. History shows that the larger a population, the greater its chances to gain prosperity and power, including ruling other, smaller populations. Nature gave the Romans the means to grow in population and wealth that the Greeks could never equal: Italy's level plains were better for agriculture and raising animals than was the heavily mountainous terrain of Greece. Italy could therefore house and feed more people than Greece. Of course, in the beginning, the Romans amounted only to a tiny community surrounded by frequently hostile neighbors. The base of Roman history is the story of how they expanded their population from that puny start to the tens of millions (the exact number is controversial) of the time of the Roman Empire.

The later Romans had many legends about their ancestral origins as a small population fighting the odds to survive in a hostile world. They highly respected that distant past as the source for the traditions and values by which they guided their lives. It is therefore frustrating to report that little reliable evidence survives to tell us about their ancestors. Linguistic investigation has shown that the Romans descended from earlier peoples who spoke Indo-European languages (of which English is one modern example). The Indo-Europeans organized their societies according to rankings of people in a hierarchy of status and privilege, with men as political leaders and the heads of families. These "proto-Romans" had migrated to Italy from continental Europe at an unknown date many, many centuries before the foundation of Rome. The Romans' ancestors had therefore lived in northern and central Italy for a very long time before the foundation of Rome. Some Romans at least believed that their ancestors had a more romantic identity: Dionysius reports that the Romans were descended from heroic Trojans who escaped their burning city at the end of the Trojan War, emigrating from Troy to Italy four hundred years before Rome's foundation.

Our main evidence for the Romans' immediate ancestors comes from archaeological excavation of graves dating to the ninth and eighth centuries B.C. Since we do not know what the people buried in these graves called themselves, scholars have usually referred to them as Villanovans, a term taken from the modern name of the location of the first excavation. In fact, there is no reason to think that these peoples, who lived in various different communities, thought of themselves as a unified group. What archaeology does reveal is that they farmed, raised horses, and forged metal weapons and many other objects from bronze and iron. Since bronze is a mixture of copper and tin, and since tin was only mined in locations far from Italy, these Roman ancestors engaged in long-distance trade.

By the eighth century B.C., the Romans and the other peoples of central and southern Italy had frequent contact with Greek traders voyaging to Italy by sea, and this originally commercial interaction had a significant impact on Roman society and culture. Many Greek entrepreneurs settled permanently in southern Italy in this period, seeking riches as immigrant farmers and traders. Many of these risk-takers succeeded, and numerous cities mainly populated by Greeks became important communities in Italy, from Naples to the southern regions of the peninsula, as well as nearby Sicily. The diverse population of that island also included Phoenicians originally from the eastern Mediterranean coast.

The Romans' contact with Greek culture had the greatest effect on the development of their own ways of life. Greek culture reached its most famous flowering by the fifth century B.C., centuries before Rome had its own literature, theater, or monumental architecture. When the Romans eventually began to develop these cultural characteristics, they took Greek models as inspiration. They adopted many fundamental aspects of their own ways from Greek culture, ranging from ethical values to deities for their national cults, from the models for their literature to the architectural design of large public buildings such as temples. Nevertheless, Romans had a love-hate relationship with Greeks, admiring much of their culture but looking down on Greece's political disunity and military inferiority to Rome.

The Romans also adopted ideas and cultural practices from the Etruscans, a people located north of Rome in a region of central Italy called Etruria. The extent of Etruscan cultural influence on Rome is controversial. Scholars have often thought of the Etruscans as the most influential outside force affecting the Roman way of life. Some have even speculated that Etruscans conquered early Rome, with Etruscan kings ruling the new city during the final part of the monarchy that was its first government. In addition, since early scholars rated the Etruscans as more culturally refined than early Romans (mainly because archaeologists had discovered so many Greek painted vases in Etruscan tombs), they assumed that these supposedly more sophisticated foreign rulers had completely reshaped Roman culture. More recent scholarship suggests that this interpretation is at the very least overstated. The truth seems to be that the Romans de-

Figure 2. Paestum was one of the numerous Greek cities in southern Italy and Sicily that had magnificent stone temples of the gods. The state of preservation of Paestum's three adjacent temples rivals that of any site in Greece. Courtesy of Dr. Jesus Oliver-Bonjoch.

veloped their own cultural traditions, borrowing whatever ways appealed to them from Etruscan and Greek culture and then adapting these foreign models to Roman circumstances.

Our knowledge of the Etruscans' origins remains limited because we only partly understand their language. We do not know to what group of languages it belonged, but it was probably not Indo-European. The fifth-century B.C. Greek historian Herodotus believed that the Etruscans had originally immigrated to Italy from Lydia in Anatolia, but Dionysius of Halicarnassus reported that Italy had always been their home, the predominant view today.

The Etruscans were not a unified ethnic group or political nation; they lived in numerous independent towns nestled on central Italian hilltops. They produced their own fine art work, jewelry, and sculpture, but they spent large sums to import many luxury objects from Greece and other Mediterranean lands. Above all, the Etruscans had close contacts with Greece and adapted much from Greek culture to their own way of life. For example, most of the intact Greek vases found in modern museums

Figure 3. A painting from an Etruscan tomb depicts dinner guests reclining in the Greek fashion and being attended by servants. The bright primary colors of scenes painted in Etruscan tombs reveal the characteristic style of Greek painting, of which few examples have survived in its homeland. AlMare/Wikimedia Commons.

were discovered in Etruscan tombs, where they had been placed to accompany the dead by the Etruscan families that had purchased them. Magnificently colored wall paintings, which still survive in some Etruscan tombs, portray games, entertainments, and funeral banquets testifying to a vivid social and religious life.

The Romans adopted certain ceremonial traditions from the Etruscans that persisted for centuries, such as the elaborate costumes worn by magistrates, as well as musical instruments and procedures for important religious rituals. It is no longer seen as accurate, however, to think that Romans also took from the Etruscans the tradition of erecting temples divided into three sections for worshipping a triad of main gods. It was a native Roman tradition to worship together Jupiter, the king of the gods, Juno, the queen of the gods, and Minerva, the goddess of wisdom, deities whom they and the Etruscans had taken over from the Greeks. On the other hand, the Romans did learn from the Etruscans their ritual for discovering the will of the gods by looking for clues in the shapes of the vital organs of slaughtered animals, a process known as divination. The Romans probably also adopted from Etruscan society the tradition of women joining men for dinner parties, which the Greeks restricted to men only. Tomb paintings, for instance, confirm what the Greek philosopher and scientist Aristotle reported: Etruscan women joined men at banquets on an apparently equal footing (Athenaeus, *The Learned Banqueters* 1 23d = *Constitution of the Tyrrhenians* fragment 607 Rose). In Greek society, the only women who ever attended dinner parties with men were courtesans, hired musicians, and slaves.

Other Roman developments that some scholars attribute to Etruscan influence were in fact characteristic of various societies around the Mediterranean at this time. This fact suggests that these characteristics were part of the shared cultural environment of the region and not specifically Etruscan in origin. Thus Rome's first political system, the monarchy, resembled Etruscan kingship, but this form of rule was so common in the world of the early Mediterranean, indeed the norm, that it was not something the Romans could only have learned from their near neighbors. For the same reason, the organization of the Roman army—a citizen militia of heavily armed infantry troops (hoplites) fighting in formation—could reflect Etruscan influence, but other Mediterranean peoples organized their militaries in the same way. The Romans adapted their alphabet (which forms the basis of the English alphabet) from the Etruscan alphabet, but that alphabet was in turn based on a version of that kind of writing system that the Greeks had created as a result of their contact with the earlier alphabets of eastern Mediterranean peoples. Finally, scholars have claimed that the Romans learned from the Etruscans how to conduct long-distance trade with other areas of the Mediterranean, which promoted economic growth, and sound civil engineering, which supported urbanization. But it is simplistic to assume that cultural developments of this breadth emerged as the result of a single superior culture "instructing" and "improving" another, less developed culture. Rather, at this time in Mediterranean history, there were similar sets of cultural developments under way in many places.

Cross-cultural contact with their neighbors had a significant influence on the Romans. However, the Romans did not take over the traditions of other cultures in some simple-minded way or change them only in superficial ways, such as giving Latin names to Greek gods. Rather, as always in cross-cultural influence, whatever people take over from other people they adapt to their own purposes—they change it to suit themselves and in this way make it their own. It is more accurate to think of cross-cultural contact as a kind of competition in innovation between equals than as a "superior" tutoring an "inferior." Cultural development is a complex historical process, and historians only reveal the poverty of their own understanding if they speak of one ancient culture's dominance over another or the corruption of a "primitive" culture by an "advanced" one. The Romans, like other peoples, developed their own ways of life through a complex process of independent invention and adaptation of the ways of others.

2

Roman Values, The Family, and Religion

The Romans' ways of life—especially the traditional values of Roman society, the nature of the Roman family, and the religious ideas and practices of Roman public and private life—provide the basic context in which the people and events of Roman history must be studied if we are to try to understand the Romans on their own terms. The Romans self-consciously saw themselves as interconnected in their personal lives with other people in complex ways. They believed strongly that eternal, and in some cases even divine, values defined proper behavior, and that their society's social and political institutions put these values into action. Romans looked through the lenses, as it were, of their ancestral values, family structure, and religion to make sense of the events of their history. We as modern readers of ancient history should try to do the same, to the extent that it is possible for people today to enter into the ideals, assumptions, emotions, and ways of life of people from long ago. This is not to say that the Romans' values and beliefs alone determined what happened in their history, but alongside geography, demography, and other factors that will appear in the course of the narrative, the way that the Romans looked at themselves and their place in the world played a crucial role in their destinies as a people.

ROMAN VALUES

The values that Romans believed they should live by primarily concerned their obligations to the gods and other people, and the respect and status in society that they won or lost according to how well they behaved, as judged by others. Of course, broad generalizations cannot cover the full range and subtlety of Roman values, or account for changes over time, or fully explain how the situations of women, children, and men differed. Still, a general description of the attitudes and behaviors that Romans saw as proper human conduct is necessary to understand fundamental and enduring aspects of Roman society: the patron-client system, the distribution of power in Roman families, the lives of women at home and in society, the nature of education, and the role of religion in the state and the family.

The upper class defined the system of values guiding Romans' private and public lives under the Roman Republic. When men from Rome's social elite originally created the Republic, their goal was to make rule by one man impossible by creating a system of power sharing for themselves, but not for everyone. Therefore, they aimed to keep the reins of political power out of the hands of the majority of the population, because poorer citizens might well prefer to live under a king who would win their support by giving them financial benefits that he would force the wealthy to provide from their own fortunes. At the same time, since the upper class was too small to rule and defend Rome by itself, it was necessary to make compromises giving some role in governing to other citizens of lesser social and financial status. Without their cooperation, Rome could not field an effective army. The political history of the Republic is fundamentally the story of the always tense and sometimes violent struggles over sharing the ruling power in the state. The most destructive of those disputes came in the later Republic when members of the upper class and their supporters fought literal battles among themselves to decide who among them was entitled to what level of power. Keeping in mind the result of these civil wars in the late Republic that pitted citizen against citizen, we should perhaps ask ourselves whether this destructive violence had roots in Romans' failing to follow their traditional values. It seems equally possible, however, that it was caused by some irresolvable tension in those values that stemmed from the overwhelming importance to Romans of earning individual status as their reward for service to the community.

Romans believed that their ancestors over the generations had handed down the values that should guide their lives. They therefore referred to their system of values as the "way of the elders" (mos maiorum). The Romans treasured the antiquity of their values because, for Romans, "old" meant "good because tested by experience," but "new" meant "potentially dangerous because untested." "New things" (res novae), in fact, was the Roman expression meaning "revolution," which they feared as a source of destructive violence and social disorder. The central values that Romans believed their ancestors had established covered what we might call uprightness, faithfulness, respect, and status. These values had many different effects on Romans' attitudes and behaviors, depending on the social context, and Roman values often interrelated and overlapped. The most important values for individuals concerned their relationships with other people and with the gods.

The value of uprightness defined how a person related to others. This value had an originally masculine sense, as the Latin word designating it, virtus, comes from the word for a manly man, vir. (The English word "virtue" comes from these Latin words.) In the second century B.C., the poet Lucilius listed what he saw as the moral qualities of a man with virtus: he could tell good from evil, he knew what was useless, shameful, and dishonorable, he was an enemy of bad men and bad values, he was a friend and protector of the good, he placed his country's well-being first of all, then the interests of his family next, and his own interests last of all (quoted in Lactantius, Divine Institutes 6.5.2). It was also the duty of a man with uprightness to take care of his body and exercise to stay strong and healthy so that he could support his family and fight for his country in war. Heroism in battle was the supreme achievement for the "upright" man, but only if his valor served his community rather than just his own individual glory. Women also were expected to display uprightness in their lives, but for them this did not include military service, which remained always a male responsibility. Uprightness for women required strict adherence to all the values that governed women's relations with their families, the world outside the family, and the state. Above all, a woman was supposed to marry, produce children, and train her sons and daughters from an early age in the ethical values of her community.

The value of faithfulness (fides) had many forms, for women as well as for men. Most of all, faithfulness meant keeping one's obligations regardless of the cost, or of whether the obligation was formal or informal. To fail to meet an obligation or to fulfill a contract offended the community and the gods. Women demonstrated their faithfulness by remaining virgins until marriage and monogamous as wives. This expectation did not apply to men, and discreet sexual relations with prostitutes were not considered disgraceful for them. Men demonstrated faithfulness by never

Figure 4. A silver coin minted in 47 B.C. shows on its front side a profile of Fides, the Roman value of faithfulness, as a divine being; the other side depicts a cavalryman dragging a captive by the hair. Among their other functions, coins were the most widely distributed works of art in the Greek and Roman worlds; deciphering the messages communicated by their compact images presents an important challenge for historians. Courtesy of the American Numismatic Society.

breaking their word, paying their debts, and treating everyone with justice (which did not mean treating everyone the same, but rather justly according to whether the other's social status was superior, equal, or inferior to one's own rank in society).

The English expression "showing respect" provides the best approximation to another complex Roman value, "piety" (*pietas*), which meant being devoted to the worship of the gods and the support of one's family. The English translation tends to make this value sound purely religious, but in fact it was just as much social. Women and men alike met the demands of *pietas* by respecting the superior authority of the elders, the ancestors of their families, and of the gods. To show respect for the gods, performing religious rituals properly and regularly was crucial. The divine favor that Romans believed protected their community demanded that people faithfully and piously worship the gods. Respecting oneself was also part of this value. Self-respect meant many things. Most importantly, it meant never giving up, no matter how difficult or painful the situation. Persevering and doing one's duty under all conditions were essential Roman behaviors. Respecting oneself also meant limiting displays of emotion and maintaining self-control, a value called "gravity" (*gravitas*). So strict was this expectation of "gravity" that not even wives and husbands could kiss each other in public without seeming emotionally out of control.

Status in the eyes of others, or "dignity" (*dignitas*) was the reward that a Roman gained for living these values. It came from the respect that a person earned, and indeed expected, from others in return for behaving according to traditional ways. Women earned respect most of all by bearing legitimate children and educating them morally, earning the rewards of reputation and social approval. A Roman mother deserved and expected great respect. Men's rewards included public honors, meaning above all (for men wealthy enough for government, which brought no pay) election to official positions in the Roman state. Soldiers in Rome's citizen militia expected public recognition of acts of military bravery. The effect of social status was so powerful for Romans that a man who had earned extremely high status by his actions and self-control could receive so much respect that others would obey him even though he held no formal or legal power over them. A man reaching this pinnacle of prestige was said to possess the moral power over others of "authority" (*auctoritas*). That meant people would do what he recommended not because any law required them to, but from their respect for his supreme example of living the values they believed their ancestors had passed down to them as the ideals of a Roman life.

Finally, Romans believed that family status affected values. The more upper-class a person's family, the more strict and complicated were the personal values that the person had to follow. Being born to a prominent family was therefore a two-edged sword. It automatically entitled a person to greater social status, but at the same time it imposed a harsher standard for measuring up to the demands of the Roman system of values. People born to families without prestige were believed to have a lesser ability to behave well, or at least that was the view of the upper class. This social elite's overtly superior attitude toward ordinary people contributed to the constant tension between them and everyone else in society.

In theory, wealth had nothing to do with moral virtue, and Romans told their children stories of poor but virtuous Roman heroes. The most famous such model was Lucius Quinctius Cincinnatus in the fifth century B.C. By saving Rome from annihilation after leading its army to a swift victory over invading foreign enemies, Cincinnatus had achieved so much status that he could have ruled Rome by himself. His faithfulness to Roman values, however, led him to return to his poverty-stricken family on his pitiful dirt farm, happy in having done his duty and having been faithful to his country (Livy, *From the Foundation of the City* 3.26–28).

As over the centuries the Roman Republic came to control a territorial empire, however, money became overwhelmingly important to the Roman social elite because they could increase their status by lavish spending on public buildings and entertainments for the community. In this way, wealth became necessary for status. By the second century B.C., ambitious Romans needed to have money, lots of money, to buy respect, and they became more willing to trample on other values to get it. In this way, the Roman value system did not always harmonize. Following one value to its logical conclusion could put it in conflict with others. This paradox— values that may be good in themselves can demand unjust behavior from an individual when taken to an extreme—exists in any system of human values that strives to balance the interests of the individual and those of the community. Maintaining balance among competing values promotes peace and social stability; stressing one particular value so strongly that it obliterates others opens the way to unrest and dictatorship. Romans in the late Republic were going to learn this lesson the hard way.

The relationships defined by the Latin terms "patron" (*patronus*, "protector") and "client" (*cliens*, "follower") provided a web of reciprocal obligations among people that linked Romans to each other up and down the social scale. The patron-client system emerged from the differences in social rank that defined individual males and their families, including (at least in practice) their female family members. A patron was a man of superior social status who was obligated to provide "kindnesses" (*beneficia*), as they were called in the official terminology of the system, to those people of lower status who paid him special attention. These people became his clients, who in return for his kindnesses owed "duties" (*officia*) to their patron. This relationship was therefore reciprocal (each side had obligations to the other) but asymmetrical (the parties involved were not social equals). Patrons could in turn be the clients of those of higher status than themselves, just as clients could be the patrons of those below them in the social hierarchy. The same person, in other words, could be both a patron and a client.

The Romans defined the patron-client relationship as a type of friendship (*amicitia*) with clearly defined roles for each party. A sensitive patron would show respect by greeting a client as "my friend," not as "my client." A client, on the other hand, would show respect for his patron by addressing him as "my patron." Despite the veneer of friendship, the patron-client relationship was not at all casual. In fact, this interlocking network of personal relationships obligated people to each other under the law. The Twelve Tables of 449 B.C., for instance, Rome's first set of written laws, declared any patron who cheated his client to be a criminal outlaw.

The duties of a client included supporting his patron financially and politically. Tradition held that a client in early Rome, for example, had to help provide dowries (valuable wedding presents) for his patron's daughters. In political life, a client was expected to aid in a patron's campaigns for election to government office, or when one of the patron's friends competed for an elective post. Clients could be especially helpful in swinging the votes of ordinary people to their patrons' side. A client could be also called upon to lend money to his patron when the latter had won the election and needed money to pay for the public works expected of him as an official, who, as usual in Roman government, received no pay. Furthermore, because by the time of the later Republic it was a mark of great status for a patron to have numerous clients surrounding him all the time like a swarm of bees, a patron expected his clients to gather at his house early in the morning and accompany him on his way to the Roman Forum, the political, legal, and business center of the city. A member of the Roman social elite therefore came to need a large, fine house to accommodate his throng of clients at the morning greeting, as well as to entertain his social equals at dinners. A crowded, well-appointed house was a mark of social success. This was one of the reasons that, over time, money became supremely important to upper-class Romans: they needed to spend large amounts to be seen as splendid patrons of hordes of clients.

Patrons also needed money to be able to provide their clients with an expensive range of kindnesses. Under the Republic, a patron might help a client get started in a political career by supporting his candidacy for office, or by providing financial support from time to time. By the time of the Empire, the patron was supposed to provide a picnic basket of food for the breakfast of the clients who clustered at his house at daybreak. A patron's most important kindness was the obligation to support a client and his family if they got into legal difficulties, such as in lawsuits over property ownership, which were common. People of lower social status were at a disadvantage in the Roman judicial system if they lacked influential friends to help them in presenting their case. The aid of a patron skilled at public speaking was particularly needed because in court both accusers and accused either had to speak for themselves, or have friends speak for them. Rome had no state-sponsored prosecutors or defenders, nor any lawyers for hire. Prominent citizens with special knowledge of legal history and procedure were Rome's legal experts. By the third century B.C., these self-educated experts, called jurists, played a central role in the Roman judicial system. Although jurists frequently developed their expertise in law by serving in Roman elective offices, they operated as private individuals, not officials, in their unpaid role of advising other citizens and magistrates about the content of the law, the proper forms for complaints and transactions, and the appropriate resolutions to cases. The reliance on jurists under the Republic represented a distinctive feature of Roman justice that continued under the Empire.

The reciprocal legal obligations of the patron-client relationship were supposed to be stable and long lasting. In many cases, these ties would endure over the generations by being passed down in the family. Ex-slaves, who automatically became clients for life of the masters who had granted them their freedom, often handed down to their children their relationship with the patrons' families. Romans with contacts abroad could acquire clients among foreigners. Especially wealthy and powerful Romans would sometimes even have entire foreign communities as their clients. The emphasis of the patron-client system on duty and permanence summed up the Roman idea that social stability and well-being were achieved by faithfully maintaining the web of ties that linked people to one another in public and private life. In the friction of conflicts that real life brings, the relationships were in truth often fluid, with patrons and clients shifting their allegiances and forming new relationships. But the ideal was that of enduring obligations.

THE FAMILY, WOMEN, AND EDUCATION

Roman law made the "power of a father" (*patria potestas*) the dominant force in all relationships within the household (*familia*), except for the wife's relationship with her husband. This granting of dominance to older men made Rome a patriarchal society. A father possessed legal power over his children, no matter how old, as well as over his slaves (who counted as members of his household). *Patria potestas* also made him the sole owner of all the property acquired by any of his children. So long as their father was alive, no son or daughter could legally own anything, accumulate money of his or her own, or indeed possess any independent legal standing—in theory, at least. In practice, however, adult children could hold personal property and acquire money, much as favored slaves might build up some savings of their own. The father also held a legal power of life and death over these members of the household. Nevertheless, fathers rarely exercised this power on anyone except newborn babies. Exposing unwanted infants, so that they would die or be found and adopted or raised as slaves by strangers, was an accepted practice to control the size of families and dispose of physically imperfect babies. Until a Roman father picked up a newborn, thereby signaling that he accepted the child as his own and committed to raising it, a child literally did not exist as a legal person. Baby girls probably suffered this fate more often than boys, as a family enhanced its status to a greater extent by spending its resources on sons more than on daughters.

No Roman father would have made the rare and drastic decision to execute an adult member of his household completely on his own. As in government, for which the Senate of Rome (see Chapter 3) acted as a body of advisers to the top officials, or in legal matters, for which jurists provided advice, Romans in their private lives regularly consulted others on important family issues, seeking consensus on what should be done. Each Roman man therefore relied on his own personal body of advisers (a circle of friends and relatives called his "council") that he consulted before making any big decision. In this way, decision-making in the Roman family and in Roman government closely resembled each other. A father's council of friends would strongly advise him to think twice if he proposed the irreversible step of killing his adult son for anything except a totally compelling reason. For instance, when Aulus Fulvius in 63 B.C. had his son put to death, he had been provoked by his son's treason in joining a conspiracy to overthrow the government. Either treason or dereliction of military duty was in fact practically the only reason for which a father would have executed his own offspring. Such a violent use of a

Figure 5. On a Greek vase, Aeneas, ancestor of the Romans and famed for his devotion to duty, flees Troy while carrying his father on his back. Romans saw such examples of heroic conduct by their ancestors in the distant past, commemorated in literature such as Vergil's *Aeneid*, as a crucial component of their traditional values. Réunion des Musées Nationaux/Art Resource, NY.

father's power against a family member was very rare. In fact, by far the most important aspect of the "power of a father" in everyday life was the moral obligation that it laid upon him to take faithful care of his family justly and compassionately.

For wives, the "power of the father" had only a limited effect on their lives. Early in the history of the Republic, a wife could fall under the power of her husband, but her marriage agreement could specifically prohibit this subordination and free her from any legal control by her husband. By the late Republic, this form of "free" marriage had become by far the most common. Under its provisions, the wife remained in the power of her father so long as he lived. In reality, there were relatively few instances of aged fathers still controlling the lives of their mature, married daughters because so many people died young in the ancient world; most fathers would not have lived long enough to oversee the lives of their adult daughters. By the time most Roman women married, in their late teens, half of them had already lost their fathers. This demographic pattern also meant that the "power of a father" had only a limited effect on most grown sons.

Since males generally did not marry until their late twenties, by the time they married and formed their own households only one man in five still had a surviving father. The other 80 percent were legally independent of any control. An adult woman without a living father was also her own person for all practical purposes. Legally she needed a male guardian to conduct business for her, but the guardianship of adult women had become an empty formality by the end of the Republic. A later jurist commented on the reality of women's freedom of action even under a guardian: "The common belief, that because of their instability of judgment women are often deceived and that it is only fair to have them controlled by the authority of guardians, seems more deceptive than true. For women of full age manage their affairs themselves" (Gaius, *Institutes* 190–191).

Roman society expected women to grow up fast and take on major responsibilities in the family. Tullia (79 B.C.–45 B.C.), the daughter of the famous politician and orator Cicero, was engaged at twelve, married at sixteen, and widowed by twenty-two. Women of wealth had duties managing their family's property, including the household slaves. Wives oversaw the nurturing of their young children by wet-nurses and accompanied their husbands to the dinner parties that were important for building relationships between families. Since both women and men could control property, prenuptial agreements were common to outline the rights of both partners in the marriage. Divorce was legally a simple matter, with fathers usually keeping the children after the dissolution of a marriage, a reflection of the traditional Roman "power of the father." Many wives maintained account books to track income and expenses for their own property separately from that of their husbands. Archaeological discoveries reveal that, by the end of the Republic, some women owned large businesses, such as brick-making companies.

The influence of mothers in shaping the moral outlook of their children was especially valued in Roman society and constituted a major component of female virtue. Cornelia, a wealthy member of the upper class in the second century B.C., won enormous respect for her accomplishments both in managing her family's property and in giving birth to and overseeing the education of her many children (Cicero, *Brutus* 104, 211). When her distinguished husband died, Cornelia refused an offer of marriage from the king of Egypt so that she could oversee the family estate and educate her daughter and two sons. Her other nine children had died, and the twelve children she gave birth to provide an example of the level of fertility required of Roman wives to ensure the survival of their husbands' family lines. Cornelia became well known for entertaining important people and writing stylish letters, which were widely distributed among the upper class and were still being read a century after her death. Her sons, Tiberius and Gaius Gracchus, grew up to be among the most influential—and controversial—political leaders and reformers of the late Republic.

Poor women had not only to raise their children but also to work hard for a living. Fewer occupations were open to them than to men. Usually they had to settle for jobs selling craft items or food in small shops or stands. Even if they were members of crafts-producing families, the predominant form of manufacturing in the Roman economy, women normally sold rather than made the goods the family produced. The men in a crafts-producing family worked the raw materials and finished the goods. Those women with the worst luck or the poorest families ended up as prostitutes. Prostitution was legal, but women and men who made their living by selling sex were regarded as lacking social status. Female prostitutes wore the outer garment of men, the *toga*, to signal their lack of the traditional chastity associated with legendary Roman heroines such as Lucretia.

Women were not allowed to vote in Roman elections or become government officials, but they could have indirect political influence by expressing their views to their male relatives holding public office. Marcus Porcius Cato the Elder, a famous senator and author (234 B.C.–149 B.C.), only half-jokingly described the influence that women could exert on their

male family members: "All mankind rule their wives, we rule all mankind, and our wives rule us" (Plutarch, *Life of Cato the Elder* 8). On rare occasions during the Republic, Roman women held public demonstrations
to influence government policy. The ones that we hear about in the historical record involved well-off women protesting limits imposed on their
riches and display of status. In 215 B.C., for instance, at the height of a
wartime financial crisis, a law was passed prohibiting women from possessing more than a half-ounce of gold, wearing multicolored clothing
in public, or riding in horse-drawn carriages within a mile of Rome or
other Roman towns, except to attend public religious events. This law was
meant to address men's discontent over resources controlled by wealthy
women at a time when the state faced an acute need for funds, even
though the Senate had required women to contribute to the war's expenses two years earlier. In 195 B.C., after the war, the women affected
by the law staged large-scale demonstrations against the restrictions. They
poured out into the streets to express their demands to all the men they
met, and they besieged the doors of the houses of the two political leaders who had been blocking repeal. The law was rescinded (Livy, *From the
Foundation of the City* 34.1–8). This dramatic exception to the ordinarily restricted public behavior of Roman women underlines the fact that women
mainly influenced Roman government through their effect on the male
citizens who controlled politics.

Roman education for children was private for the wealthy and the
poor alike; there were no public schools. If parents in the many poorer
families that worked as crafts-producers knew how to read, write, and do
arithmetic, then they could pass that knowledge on to their children by
informal home-schooling as their children worked alongside them;
Rome had no laws limiting child labor. Nevertheless, the large majority
of the population was probably barely literate at best. Roman children in
wealthier families also received their basic education at home. In the early
Republic, parents did the educating, at least until the children reached
the age of seven, when they might begin to be instructed by hired tutors,
or sent to classes offered for a fee by independent schoolmasters in their
lodgings. Fathers took special care to instruct their sons in the basics of
masculine virtue, especially physical training, fighting with weapons, and
courage. When Roman expansion brought wealthier people into closer
contact with Greek culture, they began to buy educated Greek slaves to educate their children, many of whom became bilingual in Greek and Latin.

Girls usually received less training than boys, but in upper-class households both girls and boys learned to read. Repetition was the ordinary
teaching technique, with corporal punishment frequently applied to keep

pupils attentive to their rote work. Richer families would have their daughters taught literature, perhaps some music, and conversational topics for dinner parties. A principal aim of the education of women was to prepare them for the important role Roman mothers were expected to play in teaching their children respect for Roman social and moral values.

The goal of an upper-class Roman boy's education was to become expert at rhetoric—skill in persuasive public speaking—because this was crucial to success in a public career. To win elections, a man had to be able to speak persuasively to voters, and he also had to learn to speak effectively in the courts, where lawsuits were the vehicle for protecting private property, building political coalitions, and fighting personal feuds. A boy would hear rhetorical techniques in action by going with his father, uncle, older brother, or family friends to public meetings, assemblies, and court sessions. By listening to the speeches given in debates on politics and cases at law, the boy would learn to imitate winning techniques. Rich parents would also hire special teachers to instruct their sons in the skills and the large amount of general knowledge of history, literature, geography, and finance that an effective speaker required. Roman rhetoric owed much to Greek rhetorical techniques, and many Roman orators studied with Greek teachers. When in the second century B.C. Romans began to produce textbooks on rhetoric in Latin, these new tools for success depended on material derived from Greek works.

The career of Marcus Tullius Cicero (106 B.C.–43 B.C.) provided the Republic's most famous example of the prominence to which rhetorical skill could carry a man. Cicero's father paid for his son to leave home to study rhetoric both in Rome and Greece. There Cicero developed a brilliant style of public speaking that allowed him to overcome his originally low social status as the child of a local family from a small Italian town instead of an elite family in Rome. Cicero began his career as a public speaker by defending men accused of crimes, a relatively safe start for an unknown orator because defendants were grateful for such support and prosecutors usually did not retaliate against the defendants' supporters. Speaking for the prosecution was far riskier because a man who accused a powerful public figure could expect his target to seek revenge by bringing a countercharge. Cicero therefore electrified the Roman social elite in 70 B.C. when he spoke to prosecute for corruption Gaius Verres, a high-ranking official of great status. Cicero's speech stunned the capital by frightening the prominent Verres into exile (Cicero, *Oration Against Verres* 1). In 63 B.C., Cicero achieved the pinnacle of success by being elected consul, the highest office of the government of the Republic.

Throughout his career, Cicero used his rhetorical skills to attempt to reconcile the warring factions in Rome's upper class during the violent struggles over political power at the end of the Republic. He gained lasting fame as the speaker whose verbal sting was the most feared by political leaders. Later speakers studied his speeches, many of which he prepared for written publication after delivery, to learn the techniques of their carefully structured arguments, clarity in expression, and powerful imagery. Cicero also wrote influential essays on rhetoric, in which he explained his rhetorical doctrines and his belief that to be a good speaker a man had to live by a code of moral excellence. A letter to Cicero once thought to be from his brother Quintus summarized the importance of rhetoric for Roman men: "Excel in public speaking. It is the tool for controlling men at Rome, winning them over to your side, and keeping them from harming you. You fully realize your own power when you are a man who can cause your rivals the greatest fears of meeting you in a trial" (*Handbook of Electioneering* 14).

RELIGION IN THE STATE AND THE FAMILY

Roman religion affected every aspect of life. Romans worshiped a wide range of supernatural beings, ranging from the great gods said to have palaces on Mount Olympus in Greece to spirits believed to inhabit practically every natural environment and phenomenon, from storms to trees and rocks. The Romans' chief divinity was Jupiter, whom they saw as a powerful and stern—but not always loving—father and king of the gods. Juno, queen of the gods as sister and wife of Jupiter, and Minerva, virgin goddess of wisdom and daughter of Jupiter (born, according to Greek mythology, directly out of her father's head), joined Jupiter to form a central triad in the official public cults of the state. ("Public cult" means a traditional set of sacrifices, prayers, and rituals that the state sanctioned and supported financially.) These three gods shared Rome's most famous temple, the Capitolium atop the Capitoline Hill at the center of the city. This rocky hill looming over the Roman Forum had originally served as a fortress and refuge for early Rome. Since the gods were closely connected with defense of the community, the Capitoline therefore over time became Rome's sacred center. A giant temple was built there already in the sixth century B.C., on an enormous platform extending 170 feet by 200 feet. The building was adorned with twenty-four stone columns more than 65 feet high. It had three long inner rooms, with the room in the center housing a statue of Jupiter the Best and Greatest, the one on the left a statue of Juno, and the one on the right a statue of Minerva. The division of the temple into three rooms resembled the temple architecture of the Etruscans. Sacrifices of animals were regularly offered to these three gods as protectors of the city because guarding the physical safety and prosperity of Rome was their major function in Roman religion. To honor Jupiter the Best and Greatest, the Romans also celebrated a festival of military drills and chariot racing in the Circus Maximus nearby between the Palatine and Aventine hills. By the time of the Empire, this race track and stadium could accommodate 250,000 people in concrete and stone seats to watch chariot races, gladiatorial combats, public executions, and staged hunts of wild animals imported from around the Roman world.

Constructing the temple on the Capitoline represented a tremendous financial expense for a Rome that was still relatively small in the sixth century B.C., but the cost was worth it to the Romans because they believed that winning the goodwill of the gods was a necessity for their national defense against hostile neighbors. At the same time, the Romans also believed that the gods required people to take responsibility for their own safety. Therefore, in addition to building the Capitoline temple, the Romans in the sixth century B.C. also constructed a massive defensive wall to encircle their city.

The cults of these and the numerous other major deities of public religion had only limited connections with human morality because the Romans did not see the gods as the originators of the society's moral code, in contrast to the Hebrew belief that their God handed down the Ten Commandments and other laws that they had to obey. The gods cared about human behavior toward themselves, but usually not about how people treated one another. So, though Romans believed that Jupiter would punish people who broke sworn agreements, punishment came because they offended the god by ignoring the pledges they had made with him as a witness to their swearing. Cicero summed up the meaning of Rome's official religion with this explanation of Jupiter's official titles: "Jupiter is called the Best (*Optimus*) and Greatest (*Maximus*) not because he makes us just or moderate or wise, but because he makes us safe and rich and well supplied" (*The Nature of the Gods* 3.87). Romans over the centuries retained this understanding of the nature of divinity.

Romans nevertheless regarded their most important values, such as faithfulness, as special divine beings or forces. So important was this aspect of Roman religious belief that a temple to Pietas, a personification of the central value of showing respect for gods and moral obligations, was dedicated in Rome in 181 B.C. The temple held a statue of Pietas represented in the form of a goddess. This kind of concrete representation of abstract moral qualities gave a focus for the rituals of their cults. This religious aspect of traditional social values emphasized their role as ideals that Romans were expected to cultivate in ways that were fitting for their family and individual social status.

Priesthoods and Festivals

Men and women from the top of the Republic's social hierarchy filled the priesthoods that directed official worship of the many gods important to the Romans. The people who served as priests and priestesses were usually not professionals devoting their lives purely to religious activity; rather, they were simply fulfilling one aspect of a successful Roman's public life. The principal duty of these directors of official religion was to serve the public interest by ensuring the gods' goodwill toward the state, a crucial relationship that the Romans called the "peace of the gods" (pax deorum). To maintain the gods' favor toward Rome, priests and priestesses had to conduct frequent festivals, sacrifices, and other rituals in strict conformity with ancestral tradition. Mispronouncing or mistaking even one word in the performance of the ancient formulas of official prayers required starting all over again. Because Rome came to house hundreds of shrines and temples, these sacred activities required much time, energy, and expense.

One particularly important state cult was that of Vesta, the goddess of the hearth and therefore a protector of the family. Her shrine housed the official eternal flame of Rome. Priestesses called Vestal Virgins maintained Vesta's cult; they were six unmarried women who swore not to have sex for thirty years during their terms serving the goddess. Their most important responsibility was to keep the eternal flame burning because, as Dionysius of Halicarnassus reports, "the Romans fear the flame going out above all other troubles, looking upon it as an omen predicting the destruction of the city" (Roman Antiquities 2.67). If a Vestal Virgin was convicted of a minor offense, she was publicly whipped. If the flame happened to go out, the Romans assumed that one of the Vestal Virgins had broken her sworn promise to remain a virgin. If a Vestal Virgin was then convicted of breaking her promise, she was carried on a funeral bed, as if a living corpse, to be entombed in an underground chamber, where she was walled up to die. In this way, female sexual purity was publicly acknowledged as a symbol of the safety and protection of the Roman family structure and thus of the preservation of the state itself.

Roman government and Roman state religion were closely connected. No official occasion could proceed without the completion of a preparatory religious ritual. The agenda of the Senate at every meeting began with the consideration of religious affairs relevant to the state. Military commanders performed rituals of divination to discover the will of the gods to help them decide the best time for launching attacks. The most important board of priests, which had fifteen members for most of the Republic's history, had the duty of advising magistrates on their religious responsibilities as agents of the Roman state. The head of this group, the "highest priest" (*pontifex maximus*), served as the top official in the public religion of Rome and the ultimate authority on religious matters affecting government. The political importance of the "highest priest" motivated Rome's most prominent men to seek the post, which by the third century B.C. was filled by a special election.

Many Roman religious festivals continued to center on the concerns of an agricultural community with an unstable future, the condition of early Rome. Roman religion traditionally sought to protect farming, which remained the basis of the community's survival. Roman prayers therefore commonly requested the gods' aid in securing good crops, warding off disease, and promoting healthy reproduction among domestic animals and people. Perhaps the best evidence for the importance of religion in bringing a sense of divine aid and refuge in times of trouble comes from the mammoth, multitiered sanctuary built to Fortuna Primigenia ("Firstborn Luck") in Praeneste (now Palestrina), a town some twenty miles southeast of Rome. Begun perhaps in the second century B.C. and then rebuilt and enlarged for centuries, this terraced site extended five levels up a hillside to make up what was one of the largest religious structures in all of ancient Italy.

Ancestral Roman religious rituals did not usually change over time because adding anything new to the customary honors paid to the gods might offend the divine beings and thus provoke their anger against the human community they were supposed to protect. The religion of the late Republic therefore preserved many ancient rituals, such as the Lupercalia festival. During this celebration, naked young men streaked around the Palatine Hill in the center of the city, whipping any women they met with strips of goatskin. Women who had been unable to become pregnant would run out to be hit, believing this would help them become fertile. At the Saturnalia festival at the time of the winter solstice in December (a date that Christians much later adopted for the celebration of Christmas), by ancestral tradition the social order was temporarily turned upside down on purpose. As the playwright and scholar Accius (170 B.C.–80 B.C.) described the Saturnalia, "people joyfully hold feasts all through the country and the towns, each owner acting as a waiter to his slaves" (*Annals* 2–7, preserved in Macrobius, *Saturnalia* 1.7.36). The social inversion of slave owners serving their servants simultaneously and paradoxically released tensions caused by the inequalities between owner and slave in ordinary life and reinforced the slaves' ties of obligation to their owners, by symbolizing the kindnesses of the owner that the slave was obligated to repay with faithful service.

As polytheists, Romans did recognize that there might be gods whom they needed to worship but had not yet accepted. In national emergencies, the state might seek divine protection from foreign gods who had no traditional cult at Rome. For example, the government imported the cult of the healing god Asclepius from Greece in 293 B.C. in the hope that he would save Rome from a plague. Private individuals imported other foreign cults to satisfy their personal religious feelings, such as the worship of the Greek god Dionysus (called Bacchus by the Romans). The cult of Bacchus stirred controversy because its worshipers held meetings at night that aroused others' fears of hidden scandalous sexual behavior and, more seriously, of potential political conspiracies. So long as foreign religious cults avoided any appearance of threatening the stability of the state, however, they were permitted to exist. The government took no interest in these cults' religious doctrines, only in their worshipers' loyalty to the state.

Religion in the Family

Reverence for the cult of Vesta was only one of the ways in which Roman religion was associated with the family as well as the state. Every Roman home had its sacred spaces. A statue of the two-faced god Janus was placed at the entrance door of the house, with one face looking to the street and the other facing inside. In this way the god was thought to protect the house by blocking enemies and protecting those inside. Every family also maintained a cabinet-like shrine in the house to hold its Penates (spirits of the pantry) and Lares (spirits of the ancestors). The open-shelved cabinet held statuettes representing these family spirits. Romans believed these divinities helped keep the family well and preserve its ancestral moral purity. They also hung up death masks of distinguished ancestors on the walls of their home's main room. These images reminded the current generation of their responsibility to live up to the ancient and virtuous ideals of their ancestors. The strong sense of family tradition instilled by these practices and by instruction from parents (especially mothers) represented the principal source of Roman morality. The strongest deterrent to immoral behavior against other people came from the fear of losing respect and status by outraging this tradition, not from any fear of punishment of individual behavior from the gods.

Romans believed that many divine spirits participated in crucial mo-

Figure 6. This painting stood atop a family shrine for worshiping the gods in a house in Pompeii. Romans with sufficient wealth furnished their houses with these shrines to pay the proper respect to the divinities they believed were protecting their households. Patricio Lorente/Wikimedia Commons.

ments in private life, above all at birth, marriage, and death. All members of the household, including slaves, had a place in the family's religious rituals at home. So frequent was religious activity in Roman private life that special rituals accompanied activities as diverse and commonplace as breast-feeding babies and spreading manure to fertilize crops. People performed these rituals to express respectful awe for the enormous power of the divine as displayed in the forces of nature, and in search of protection from harm in a world filled with dangers and uncertainties.

From the Roman perspective, their religious beliefs and practices made sense as a reflection of their conception of the precariousness of the human condition. They recognized the tremendously asymmetrical nature of the relationship between the human and the divine, in which gods clearly exercised an overwhelming power that humans could barely comprehend. Moreover, the gods were seen as willing to use their great power to help—or harm—human beings. This divine willingness to intervene in everyday life, in all aspects from international politics to individual illness, made relations with the gods especially problematic because the Romans did not believe that the gods had any necessary tendency to love human beings. If the gods became angry, they could punish such inferior creatures with no obligation to explain why. It made things even harder that the gods did not communicate with mortals directly or clearly, except in rare circumstances. Instead, it was the responsibility of human beings to do the difficult, sometimes impossible, work of discovering the divine will and then following it. Sins of omission therefore counted just as heavily as sins of commission. The constant obligation that people felt to do everything possible to recognize the will of the gods so as to be able to obey it motivated private religious activity in the family, just as it did the state cults of Rome.

3

From the Founding of Rome to the Republic

Romans believed that their community first took shape under the rule of kings in the eighth century B.C. The surviving sources are full of colorful stories whose accuracy is controversial and difficult to evaluate. Most historians today conclude there is little that we can know for certain about the events in this formative period of Roman history. It is clear nevertheless that the legends about the monarchy reveal important ideas that later Romans held about their origins. These ideas in turn help explain how Romans structured society and politics under the Republic, the system that emerged after the monarchy was overthrown at the end of the sixth century B.C.

Since the Romans for the rest of their history referred to their government as a Republic, even after monarchy had been restored under the Empire, it is crucial to understand the constituent parts of that system and their relationship to the values that characterized Roman ways of life. Those parts were above all the elected officials and voting assemblies that historians often call the "Roman constitution," even though ancient Rome had no written document like the U.S. Constitution to specify the political structure and powers of government. Under the "Roman constitution," powers and responsibilities overlapped among governmental institutions, or were divided among them in complex ways.

TIMELINE (ALL DATES B.C.)

Ninth/eighth centuries: Villanovans, Greeks, and Etruscans flourish in Italy.

753: Romulus founds Rome as its first king.

716: Romulus dies under mysterious circumstances.

715–673: Numa Pompilius is king, establishing public religious rituals and priesthoods.

578–535: Servius Tullius is king, organizing the citizens into political and military groups and establishing the practice of granting citizenship to freed slaves.

Mid-sixth century: Rome has expanded to control about 300 square miles of territory in central Italy and creates the Forum in the center of the city.

509: Following Lucretia's rape and suicide, Brutus and other members of the elite abolish the monarchy and establish the Republic.

479: The Fabius family assembles its own army to wage war for Rome against the Etruscan town of Veii.

458: Cincinnatus serves as dictator to save Rome in a military emergency and immediately returns to private life.

Fifth/fourth centuries: The Struggle of the Orders between patricians and plebeians creates political and economic turmoil.

451–449: The Twelve Tables, the first written code of Roman laws, emerges as a compromise between patricians and plebeians.

337: The plebeians force passage of a law opening all political offices to both orders.

287: Patricians agree that proposals passed in the Tribal Assembly will be official laws, ending the Struggle of the Orders.

The Romans' technical term for their political community as a whole was "the Roman People" (*populus Romanus*), but in reality it was not the democracy that this term implies. The upper class always dominated Roman government. Therefore, before describing the officials and assemblies of the Republic, it is necessary to sketch the two-part division of Roman society into legally defined classes, the patricians and the plebeians, and how an upper class of patricians and well-off plebeians gradually and violently emerged as the dominant force in Roman society and politics. This background on the formal structuring of social status is required in particular to understand the nature of the consuls and the Senate, the so-called "ladder of offices" that well-off Roman men aspired to climb as elected officials of government, and, finally, Rome's complicated voting assemblies.

THE FOUNDATION OF THE CITY AND THE MONARCHY

Modern archaeology, as we saw, shows that Villanovans, Greeks, and Etruscans influenced the Romans as they developed their own cultural identity as part of a wider Mediterranean world. Ancient Roman legend also linked the early Romans to others, in particular the Trojans, but it also emphasized the separateness of the tiny settlement in central Italy that was remembered as the origin of Rome as a state. As Livy's narrative (*From the Foundation of the City* 1.5–7) explained, Romulus and his brother Remus originally founded the city in 753 B.C. The story included the grim report that Romulus became the first and sole king after murdering his brother Remus during bitter arguments over the location for Rome and sharing its rule (see also Dionysius, *Roman Antiquities* 1.85–87). This tale taught Romans that monarchy led to murder by rivals for power. Therefore, the legend that Romans remembered about the origins of their city reminded them just how dangerous disputes over the best political system could become.

The legend also said that after ruling for thirty-seven years Romulus permanently disappeared in 716 B.C. in the blinding swirl of a violent thunderstorm. The mysterious loss of their monarch angered the majority of early Rome's population because they suspected that Romulus's circle of upper-class advisers had murdered the masses' beloved leader and hidden his corpse. To prevent a riot, a prominent citizen shouted out this explanation to the angry crowd: "Romulus, the father of our city, descended from the sky at dawn this morning and appeared to me. In awe and reverence I stood before him, praying that it would be right to look upon his face. 'Go,' Romulus said to me, 'and tell the Romans that, by the will of the gods, my Rome shall be capital of the world. Let them learn to be soldiers. Let them know, and teach their children, that no power on earth can stand against Roman arms.' When he had spoken these words to me, he returned to the sky" (Livy, *From the Foundation of the City* 1.16). The speech calmed the people because they now felt assured of their founder's immortality and their divinely favored destiny. Despite the reconciliation with which it ended, this story showed that conflict between the small number of elite Romans and the mass of ordinary Romans had been part of their history from the beginning.

This story brilliantly summed up the truth about the way in which later Romans viewed the lessons of their history: if the people were brave, maintained their traditions over the generations, and followed the guidance of the upper class, then the gods would favor Rome and ensure that Roman military might would rule the world. At the same time, it also made clear the distrust that ordinary citizens felt toward the upper class. Finally, it also showed that the masses were content to be ruled by a king and knew that the upper class hated the monarchy for the power that it held over even them, no matter how elite they might be. This legend, then, communicated an enduring truth about Roman society: although Romans agreed that they had a special destiny to rule others by conquest, the upper and lower classes held radically different attitudes about what sort of government they believed to be best, creating a fundamental and lasting disagreement about how to structure official power as it affected people's lives.

Rome at its foundation faced a great challenge to its survival because its population was small and poor compared to its stronger neighbors. The other peoples in the area in which Rome was located, called Latium, were mostly poor villagers themselves, but some of the neighboring settlements were much more populous and more prosperous. Most of the peoples in Latium spoke the same language as the Romans, an early form of Latin, but this linguistic kinship did not mean that these neighboring communities saw themselves as ethnically united. Likewise, the non–Latin-speaking peoples in the region had no inherited reason to respect the existence of the Romans. In this world, every community had to be ready to defend itself against attacks from neighbors.

Counting Romulus as the first king, seven monarchs ruled Rome one after the other for two and a half centuries after the foundation. Rome under the rule of the kings slowly became a larger settlement better able to protect itself by adopting a two-pronged strategy for population growth: absorbing others into its population, or making alliances with them to cooperate militarily. This strategy formed the basis of Rome's long-term expansion: make outsiders into Romans, or cooperate with them on mutual defense. Incorporating outsiders into the citizen body to become more powerful and prosperous was a necessity for survival for a community like early Rome that began so weak and small. It was also a tremendous innovation in the ancient world. Neither Greeks nor any other contemporary society had this policy of inclusion of foreigners. In fact, nonlocals could almost never become citizens in a Greek state. Greeks employed new citizenship as a way to honor rich foreigners who had benefited the community and had no need or intention of becoming an everyday citizen.

Rome's unique and innovative policy of taking in outsiders to increase the number of its citizens and thereby strengthen itself was the long-term secret to its eventually becoming the most powerful state the world had yet seen. The policy was so fundamental that Rome even offered slaves a chance for upward social mobility. Romans were slave owners, like every other ancient society. They regarded slaves as their owners' property, not as human beings with natural rights. Therefore, it is an extraordinary feature of Roman society that slaves who gained their freedom immediately became Roman citizens. People became slaves by being captured in war, being sold on the international slave market by raiders who had kidnapped them, or being born to slave mothers. Slaves could purchase their freedom with earnings that their masters let them accumulate to encourage hard work, or they could be granted freedom as a gift in their owners' wills. Freed slaves had legal obligations to their former owners as clients, but these freedmen and freedwomen, as they were officially designated, otherwise had full civic rights, such as legal marriage. They were barred from being elected to political office or serving in the army, but their children became citizens of Rome with full rights. In other Mediterranean states, the best that ex-slaves and their offspring could hope for was to become legal aliens with the right of residence, but without citizenship or any hope of obtaining that status and the protections and privileges it carried. Rome's policy was firmly different, to the state's great advantage.

As usual for any aspect of Rome's culture that called for justification, there was a legend to provide an ancient origin for this extremely unusual policy of inclusion of outsiders. Both Livy (From the Foundation of the City 1.9–13) and Dionysius (Roman Antiquities 1.30–32, 38–46) preserve stories that reminded Romans why they needed to take in others if their state was to survive and thrive in a threatening world. Romulus, the legend reported, realized that Rome after its foundation was not going to be able to grow or even preserve itself because it lacked enough women to bear the children needed to increase the population and therefore strengthen the community. So he sent representatives to Rome's neighbors to ask for the right for its men, regardless of their poverty, to marry women from these nearby communities. (In the ancient world this kind of intermarriage was usually available only to prosperous families.) He instructed Rome's messengers to say that, although their community was at that point tiny and poor, the gods had granted it a brilliant future and that its more prosperous neighbors, instead of looking down on their impoverished neighbor, should recognize the Romans' wondrous destiny and therefore make an alliance for their mutual benefit.

Every neighboring community refused Romulus's request for marriage alliances. Desperate for a solution, the Roman king came up with a risky plan to kidnap the women he knew his community needed if it was to have a future. He invited the neighboring Sabine people to a religious festival at Rome. At a prearranged moment, Rome's men dragged away the unmarried Sabine women. Unprepared for this assault, the Sabine men had to retreat home. The Roman men immediately married the kidnapped women, making them citizens. When a massive Sabine counterattack on Rome led to a bloody battle in which many Roman and Sabine men were being injured and killed, the Sabine brides suddenly rushed between the warring bands, shocking them into stopping the fight. The women then begged their new Roman husbands and their Sabine parents and brothers either to stop slaughtering each other and make peace, or kill them on the spot, their wives and daughters and sisters. Shamed by the women's plea, the men not only made peace but also merged their two populations into an expanded Roman state. The role of women in this legendary incident both explained how immigration and assimilation of others were a foundation of Rome's power and underlined the traditional Roman ideal of women as the mothers of Roman citizens, ready to sacrifice themselves for the survival of the community.

We do not have to decide how accurate this dramatic story is to see that it expressed the basic truth that early Roman history was a story of successful expansion and inclusion of others, through both war and negotiation. Moving out from their original settlement of a few thatched-roof huts on the hills of Rome, the Roman population grew over the next two centuries to such an extent that it occupied some three hundred square miles of Latium, enough agricultural land to support thirty to forty thousand people. Perhaps contracting with specialized Etruscan engineers to do the design work, the Romans in the mid-sixth century B.C. drained the formerly marshy open section at the foot of the Palatine Hill and Capitoline Hill to be the public center of their emerging city. Called the Roman Forum, this newly created central space remained the most historic and symbolic section in Rome for a thousand years. The creation of the Forum as a gathering place for political, legal, and business affairs, as well as public funerals and festivals, happened at about the same time that the Athenians in Greece created the *agora* to serve as the open, public center of their growing city. These roughly simultaneous rearrangements of urban space in Rome and Athens reveal the common cultural developments taking place around the Mediterranean region in this period. Over time, the Romans erected large buildings in and around the Forum to serve as meeting spaces for political gatherings, speeches, trials, and administrative functions of the government. Today the Forum

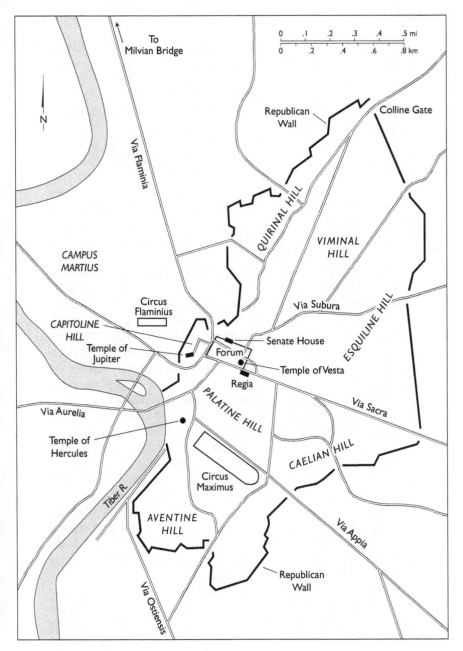

Map 2. The City of Rome During the Republic

presents a crowded array of ruins from centuries of Roman history. Walking through the Forum literally puts visitors into the footprints of the ancients, and standing there to read aloud a speech of Cicero, Rome's greatest orator, or a poem of Juvenal, Rome's most sharp-tongued satirist, can stir a visitor's historical imagination to behold the ghosts of Rome's glory and violence with a vividness attainable nowhere else on earth.

Romans remembered and valued most of the seven kings as famous founders of lasting traditions. They credited the second king Numa Pompilius (ruled 715 B.C.–673 B.C.), for example, with establishing the public religious rituals and priesthoods that worshiped the gods to ask for their support for Rome. Servius Tullius (ruled 578 B.C.–535 B.C.) was believed to have created basic institutions for organizing Rome's citizens into groups for political and military purposes, as well as the practice of giving citizenship to freed slaves. In the end, however, the monarchy failed as a result of opposition from the city's upper class. These rich families thought of themselves as the king's social equals and therefore resented the monarch's greater power and status. They also resented the ordinary people's support for the monarchy. The kings, in turn, feared that a powerful member of the upper class might use violence to take the throne for himself. To secure allies against such rivals, the kings cultivated support from citizens possessing enough wealth to furnish their own weapons but not enough money or social standing to count as members of the upper class. Around 509 B.C., some upper-class Romans deposed King Tarquin the Proud, an Etruscan who had become king, legend says, after Servius's daughter Tullia forced Tarquin to murder her husband. She had made Tarquin marry her, and then kill Servius to become king of Rome himself. Tarquin the Proud lost his throne as a consequence of the unbending will of another, very different Roman woman, Lucretia. Tarquin's son raped this virtuous upper-class wife at knifepoint. Even though her husband and father begged her not to blame herself for another's crime, Lucretia committed suicide after identifying her rapist and calling on her male relatives to avenge her. She became famous as the ideal Roman woman: chaste, courageous, and ready to die rather than run the risk of even a suspicion of immoral behavior (Livy, From the Foundation of the City 1.57–60).

Led by Lucius Junius Brutus and calling themselves liberators, an alliance of upper-class men drove Tarquin from power and abolished the monarchy. They then established the Roman Republic, justifying their revolution with the argument that government dominated by one man inevitably led to abuses of power such as the rape of Lucretia. A sole ruler amounted to tyranny, they proclaimed. As mentioned at the beginning, the term "Republic" comes from the Latin phrase res publica ("the people's

Figure 7. A statue of an upper-class Roman man shows him wearing formal clothing—a toga—and holding sculpted portraits of his ancestors. Standards of proper conduct called for Romans to demonstrate their respect for the "elders" of their family, living and dead. Alinari/Art Resource, NY

thing, people's business"; "commonwealth"). This name expressed the ideal of Roman government being of and for the entire community, with the people's consent and in their interest (Cicero, *The Republic* 1.39). This ideal never became a full reality: the upper class dominated Roman government and society under the Republic.

The upper class's hatred of monarchy remained a central feature of Roman history for hundreds of years, a tradition enshrined in the legend of Horatius (Livy, *From the Foundation of the City* 2.10). Along with two fellow soldiers, he held off an Etruscan attack on Rome aimed at reimposing a king on the Romans, not long after the expulsion of Tarquin the Proud. Horatius blocked the enemy's entry into Rome by driving their soldiers from a bridge over the Tiber River until his fellow Romans could destroy it, thereby blocking the foreign invasion. As the bridge collapsed into the water below, Horatius shouted out his mockery of the Etruscans as slaves who had lost their freedom because they were ruled by arrogant kings. He then jumped into the river still wearing his full metal armor and swam to safety and liberty. For the rest of their history, Romans of all social classes treasured the political liberty of their state that these legends described, but elite and ordinary citizens continued to disagree, sometimes violently, over how to share power in the government of the Republic that emerged from the struggles of their early history.

SOCIAL STATUS AND POLITICAL POWER

Romans, like other ancient peoples, believed that social inequality was a fact of nature. Consequently, they divided citizens by law into two groups called "orders," one with much higher social status—the patrician order—than the other—the plebeian order. This division lasted throughout Roman history. The patricians were Rome's original aristocrats, having inherited their status by being born in one of a tiny percentage of families—around 130 in total—ranked as patrician; no others could achieve this status. It is unknown how families originally gained patrician status, but it probably happened in a gradual process at the beginning of Rome's history in which the richest Romans designated themselves as an exclusive group with special privileges to conduct religious ceremonies for the safety and prosperity of the community. Eventually, patricians leveraged their originally self-created elite status into almost a monopoly on the secular and religious offices of the early government of the Republic. Patricians proudly advertised their superior status. In the early Republic, they wore red shoes to set themselves apart. Later, they changed to the black shoes worn by all senators but adorned them with small metal crescents to mark their own particular prestige.

Because they possessed both high birth and great property, patrician men became Rome's first social and political leaders, often controlling large bands of followers that they could command in battle. An inscription (the *Lapis Satricanus*) from about 500 B.C., for instance, says that "the comrades of Publius Valerius" erected a monument to honor Mars, the Roman war god. Valerius was a patrician, and it is significant that, when making this dedication to a national divinity, these men designated them-

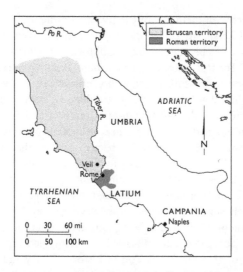

Map 3. Rome and Central Italy, Fifth Century B.C.

selves as his supporters, instead of referring to themselves as citizens of Rome. There is also the famous story of the patriotism of the Fabius family. These patricians had so many followers that, when the state had already committed its regular forces to war on other fronts and therefore could not raise any more troops to fight against the neighboring Etruscan town of Veii in 479 B.C., the Fabians could raise a private army by assembling 306 men from their own family and a crowd of clients to wage the war on Rome's behalf (Livy, *From the Foundation of the City* 2.48–49). That they were all wiped out by the army of Veii only makes the Fabians' influence over their followers all the more impressive.

Plebeians made up all the rest of the population. They therefore greatly outnumbered the patricians. Many plebeians were of course poor, as was the majority of the population in all ancient civilizations. Some plebeians, however, were rich property owners and held important roles in public life. It would therefore be a mistake to see the plebeians only as "Rome's poor and disrespected." In fact, the wealthiest plebeians felt that they should have just as much influence in Roman society and politics as patricians. The poorest plebeians, on the other hand, were necessarily concerned with mere survival in a world with no social safety net. The plebeians were therefore a highly diverse group of citizens, whose interests did not necessarily coincide, depending on their relative wealth and position in society.

Conflict between members of the patrician order and well-off members of the plebeian order filled the two centuries following the creation of the Republic, deeply influencing the ultimate structure of the "Roman constitution." For this reason, historians have usually referred to this period of turmoil in the fifth and fourth centuries B.C. as the Struggle of the Orders. This label implies that the trouble originated from plebeians demanding entry to the same high-level political and religious offices that the patricians had made into a near monopoly for themselves. Certainly, there was tension over the restrictive policies that the patricians imposed to wall themselves off socially from plebeians. Most strikingly, the patricians in the middle of the fourth century carried their exclusionary social policy to the limit: they banned intermarriage between themselves and plebeians. Recent research, however, shows that analyzing the unrest at Rome in this period as being only about political leadership and social status places too much emphasis on the struggle for political office, a mistake retrojected onto early Roman history by Livy and other historians of the first century B.C. By that time, the streets of Rome had been awash in bloodshed for decades from conflicts between plebeian and patrician leaders over access to privileged positions in the Roman state. It was therefore tempting to interpret the stories of unrest from early Roman history as previews of the conflicts of the time of the end of the Republic.

The sources of conflict between patricians and plebeians in the early Republic were as much economic as political. While well-off plebeians did want patricians to share with them access to the highest political offices and the social status that these positions brought, poor plebeians were the people most desperate for relief from the policies of the patricians in this period. In other words, the class conflict of the Struggle of the Orders was, for the majority of people, all about their literal survival because the poor, with their numbers increasing as Rome's population grew, needed more land to farm to feed their families. Rich patricians, however, dominated the ownership of land and were also the source of loans to the poor.

The shortage of land to farm and the high interest rates charged on debts eventually led large numbers of plebeians to resort to drastic measures to try to protect their interests. In the bitterest disputes, they even physically withdrew outside the sacred boundary of the city to a temporary settlement on a neighboring hill. The plebeian men then refused to serve in the citizen-militia army. This "secession," as it is called, worked because it devastated the national defense of the city, which had no professional standing army at this date. Instead, in times of war Rome's male citizens gathered in the open, grassy area near the Tiber River called the Campus Martius (the field dedicated to Mars) for military training and exercise. At other times, they stayed at home to farm and support their families. When plebeian male citizens refused to take part in training for war or to show up when called from their homes and fields to defend the city in battle, then Rome was in grave danger because the patricians were far too few to protect Rome by themselves. The need to have plebeians serve in the national defense force was the fundamental reason why the patricians ultimately had to compromise with them, even though the elite hated yielding to the demands of those whom they considered their social inferiors.

Roman tradition says that the compromise between patricians and plebeians led to Rome's first written laws. The new legal code was put in place following the mission of a Roman delegation to Athens, where they studied how that famous Greek city had created a written law code. Even with this research, it took a long time for the two Roman orders to reach final agreement on laws to protect the plebeians, while also maintaining the status of the patrician order. The earliest written code of Roman law, called the Twelve Tables, was enacted between 451 and 449 B.C. As a compromise between two powerful groups, it was inevitably less than a clear-cut victory for plebeian interests. In fact, patricians took advantage of this occasion to impose the infamous ban on intermarriage with plebeians. Importantly for plebeians, however, having a written code of laws prevented the patrician magistrates who judged most legal cases from arbitrarily and unjustly deciding disputes merely according to their own personal interests or those of their order. At the very least, the existence of the Twelve Tables as written and therefore publicly accessible laws made it harder for a magistrate to make up a law on the spot to use against a plebeian. The concise provisions of the Twelve Tables encapsulated the prevailing legal customs of the agricultural society of early Rome with simply worded laws such as, "If a plaintiff calls a defendant to court, he shall go," or "If a wind causes a tree from a neighbor's farm to be bent and lean over your farm, action may be taken to have that tree removed" (Warmington vol. 3, pp. 424–515).

In later times the Twelve Tables became a national symbol of the Roman commitment to legal justice. Children were still being required to memorize these ancient laws four hundred years later. Emphasizing legal matters such as disputes over property, the Twelve Tables demonstrated the overriding Roman interest in civil law. Roman criminal law, on the other hand, never became extensive. Courts therefore never had a full set of rules to guide their verdicts in all cases. Magistrates decided most cases without any juries. Trials before juries began to be common only in the late Republic of the second and first centuries B.C. Nevertheless, the Twelve Tables marked a beginning, if a flawed one, in establishing written law as a source of justice to reduce violent class conflict in Roman society.

ELECTED OFFICIALS AND VOTING ASSEMBLIES

The "Roman constitution" included a range of elected officials and one special body, the Senate. Only the most ambitious and most successful of Roman men could hope to win election as the highest officials in the government of the Republic, the consuls. The Republic had been created to prevent Rome from being ruled by a single leader inheriting his position and governing by himself for an indefinite term. The office of consul was therefore created so that each year two leaders of the state would be elected to serve together, with a single-year term limit and a ban on reelection to consecutive terms. They received the name "consuls," meaning something like "those who take care [of the community]," to make the point that these officials, despite the great status they derived from their positions, were supposed to act in the interests of all Romans, not just themselves or their supporters. The consuls' duties were to provide leadership on civil and political policy and command the army in times of war. The competition to reach this office was intense not only because it gave a man enormous individual status but also because it elevated his family's prestige forever. Families with even a single consul among their ancestors called themselves "the nobles." Upper-class Roman men without a consul in their family history strongly wanted to win election as a consul, to elevate themselves and their descendants into this self-identified status group.

The Senate was the most prestigious institution of the "Roman constitution" and lasted throughout all the centuries of Roman history. Its origins lay in the time of the Monarchy because the kings of Rome did not make important decisions by themselves, in accordance with the Roman tradition of always asking for advice from one's friends and elders. The kings therefore had assembled a select group of elite men to be their royal council; these senior advisers were called senators (from the Latin word for "old men"). The tradition that the leaders of Roman government should always seek advice from the Senate continued under the Republic even after the expulsion of the monarchy. For most of the Senate's history, it had 300 members. The general and politician Sulla increased the membership to 600 as part of his violent reforms of Roman government in 81 B.C., Julius Caesar raised it to 900 to gain supporters during the civil war of the 40s B.C., and finally Augustus brought it back to 600 by 13 B.C. So far as we can tell, the Senate had always included both patricians and elite plebeians. Eventually, men had to own a set (and high) amount of property to be eligible to serve as senators.

During the Republic, senators were at first selected by the consuls from the pool of men who had previously been elected as lesser magistrates. Later, the choice was made from that same population pool by two special magistrates of high prestige called censors. In time, the Senate achieved a tremendous influence over Republican domestic and foreign policy, state finances, official religion, and all types of legislation. Senatorial influence was especially prominent in decisions about declaring and conducting wars. Because Rome in this period fought wars almost continually, this function of the Senate was critically important. The Senate endured as a high-prestige institution throughout Roman history, even under the emperors, when the political influence that it had possessed in the government of the Republic was reduced to cooperating with the emperor as a much inferior partner in governing. The Senate House that today stands in the Roman Forum was built in the late Empire, showing that the position of senator still enjoyed great status even more than a thousand years after the foundation of Rome.

The basis of the Senate's power provides one of the most revealing clues to the nature of Roman society, in which social status brought influence and authority that could equal or even exceed the power of statute law. The power of the Senate legally consisted only in the right to give advice to the leading officers of the state, by voting to express its approval or disapproval of policies or courses of action. It did not have the right to pass laws. Moreover, the Senate had no official power to force officials to carry out its wishes. In other words, the senators' ability to affect, even to direct, Roman law and society came not from any official right to impose policy or legislation, but solely from their status as Rome's most respected male citizens. Therefore, the Senate's power depended entirely on the influence over officials and citizens that it derived from the social importance of its members. To understand the inner workings of Roman society and politics, it is necessary to recognize that it was simply the high status that senators enjoyed that endowed their opinions with the force—although not the form—of law. For this reason, no government official could afford to ignore the advice of the Senate. Any official who defied its wishes knew that he would likely face serious opposition from many of his peers. The extraordinary status of the senators was made visible for all to see, as usual in Roman society. To broadcast their identity, Senators wore black, high-top shoes and a broad purple stripe embroidered on the outer edge of their togas.

The Senate used an apparently democratic procedure, majority vote of its members, to decide what advice to offer the officials of government. In reality, however, considerations of relative status among the senators themselves had a major impact on decisions. The most distinguished senator had the right to express his opinion first when a vote was taken. The other senators then spoke and voted in descending order of prestige. The opinions of the most distinguished, usually older senators carried by far the most weight. Only foolish junior senators with no eye on their political futures would dare give an opinion or cast a vote different from those already expressed by their elders.

As in ancient Greece, at Rome the only honorable and desirable career for a man of high social standing was holding public office, or, as we might label it, a career in government. The office of consul, of course, was the most prestigious of the annually elective public offices under the Roman Republic. The other elective civil offices were ranked in order of prestige below consul in what is often called the "ladder (or course) of offices" (cursus honorum). There were also elective priesthoods laddered according to the status that they brought to their holders. At the beginning of the Republic, the patricians dominated election to the highest positions in the ladders of offices, especially that of consul, even passing laws that restricted a certain number of these coveted posts to members of their own order.

An ambitious Roman man with the resources to win over voters with financial favors and entertainments would climb this ladder of success by winning election to one post after another in ascending order. He would begin his career at perhaps twenty years old by serving on military campaigns for as much as ten years, usually as an assistant officer appointed to the staff of an older relative or friend. He would next begin his climb up the ladder of offices by seeking election to the lowest of the important annual positions, that of quaestor. Candidates to be elected quaestor would usually be in their late twenties or early thirties. During their year in office, quaestors performed a variety of duties in financial administration, usually concerning the oversight of state revenues and payments, whether for the treasury in the capital, for commanders on campaign, or for the governing staffs of the overseas provinces that Rome established beginning in the third century B.C. Eventually, minimum age requirements for the various positions in the ladder of offices were set by law. After Sulla in 81 B.C. prescribed strict regulations for progress up the ladder, a

ROMAN CURSUS HONORUM

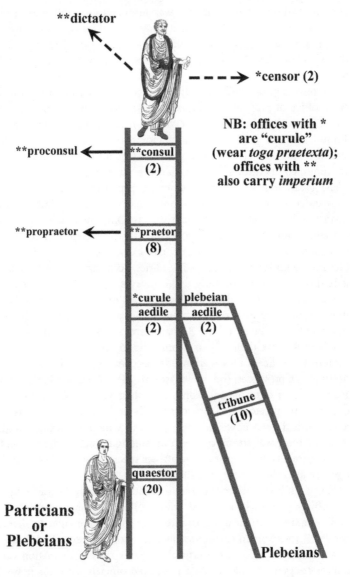

**dictator

*censor (2)

NB: offices with *
are "curule"
(wear *toga praetexta*);
offices with **
also carry *imperium*

**proconsul ⟵ **consul
(2)

**propraetor ⟵ **praetor
(8)

*curule | plebeian
aedile | aedile
(2) | (2)

tribune
(10)

quaestor
(20)

Patricians
or
Plebeians

Plebeians

Figure 8. This diagram plots the highly competitive career path—the ladder of offices—in government and politics that upper-class Roman men aimed to climb. The competition became more heated the higher a man climbed, and comparatively few made it to the small number of offices at the top. Diagram created by Barbara F. McManus, used courtesy of the VRoma Project, www.vroma.org.

man who had served as a quaestor was automatically eligible to be chosen as a senator when a place in that body opened up. After quaestor, the next rung up the ladder was the office of aedile. Aediles had the difficult duty of maintaining Rome's streets, sewers, temples, markets, and other public works.

The next step up the hierarchy of offices was to win election to the annual office of praetor, a prestigious magistracy second only to being a consul. Praetors had a variety of civil and military duties, including the administration of justice and commanding troops in war. Since there were fewer praetors elected than quaestors (the number of both changed over time), competition for this high office was fierce.

The great prestige of praetors sprang primarily from their role as commanders of military forces, because success as military leader earned a man the highest status in Roman society. Only those who succeeded as praetors and had strong support from a broad section of the voting population could hope to become consuls. Consuls were supposed to be older men with long experience in politics; according to the regulations established by Sulla in the early first century B.C., candidates for election as consuls had to be at least forty-two years old. The two consuls had influence on every important matter of state and commanded the most important detachments of the Roman army in the field. Like praetors, consuls could have their military command extended beyond their one-year terms of office if they were needed as commanders abroad or as the governors of provinces (on which see p. 73). When serving on these special tours of duty outside Rome after their year in office, they were designated propraetors and proconsuls. These "promagistrates," as they are called, had great power in the regions to which the Senate assigned them, and there was strong competition among Roman leaders to get the best assignments. Promagistrates lost their special power to command or to govern after they returned to Rome.

Consuls and praetors could exercise military command because by law their offices gave them a special power called imperium (the root of the word "empire"). Imperium guaranteed an official the right to demand obedience from Roman citizens to any and all of his orders. It also carried the authority to perform the crucial religious rites of divination called auspices (auspicia). Roman tradition required officials with this power to take the auspices to discern the will of the gods before conducting significant public events, such as elections, inaugurations into offices, officials' entrance into provinces, and, especially, military operations. The power and the prestige of these positions made them the center of the dispute between patricians and plebeians over political offices. The conflict over these valued capstones to a man's career finally came to an end in 337 B.C., when pressure from the plebeians forced the passage of a law that opened all offices equally to both orders.

The "Roman constitution" also included two special, nonannual posts that were not part of the regular ladder of offices. These were the offices of censor and dictator. Every five years, two censors were elected to serve for eighteen months. They had to be ex-consuls, elder statesmen believed to possess the exceptional prestige and wisdom necessary to carry out the office's most crucial duty: conducting a census listing all male Roman citizens and the amount of their property, so that taxes could be levied fairly and male citizens could be classified for military service in war. The censors also controlled the membership of the Senate, filling any empty seats with worthy candidates and removing from its rolls any man they decided had behaved improperly. Censors also supervised state contracts and oversaw the renewal of official prayers for the goodwill of the gods toward the Roman People.

The office of dictator was the only kind of one-man rule allowed under the "Roman constitution." It was filled only in dire national emergencies when quick decisions needed to be made to save the state. This usually meant that Rome had suffered a military catastrophe and needed swift action to prevent further disaster. The Senate chose the dictator, who had absolute power to make decisions that could not be questioned. This extraordinary office was meant to be strictly temporary, and dictators were allowed to stay in office for a maximum of six months. The most famous dictator under the Republic was Cincinnatus, who because of his selfless conduct in this office in 458 B.C.—he refused to remain in office even though many wanted him to continue as sole ruler—summed up the Roman ideal of community-minded public service being more important than individual success.

It is important to stress how much the holding of an elective position or a special office in Roman government meant to patricians and upper-class plebeians from the status that such posts brought them. Since status by definition was meaningless unless others recognized it, the prestige attached to top-ranking offices was expressed in highly visible ways. Each consul, for example, was preceded wherever he went by twelve attendants. These attendants, called lictors, carried the *fasces*. The fasces were the symbol of the consul's imperium. Inside the city limits, the fasces consisted of a bundle of sticks to symbolize the consul's right to beat citizens who disobeyed his orders; outside the city, an axe was added to the sticks to symbolize his right to execute disobedient soldiers in the field without a trial. Lictors also accompanied praetors because they, too, were

Figure 9. The Via Appia was the main route from Rome to south Italy, named after Appius Claudius Caecus, the upper-class man who paid for its first 132 miles of paving. These hard-surfaced highways allowed travel in all weather, making the deployment of military forces and the transportation of passengers and goods more reliable. MM/Wikimedia Commons.

magistrates with imperium, but praetors had only six lictors apiece to show that their status was less than that of the consuls.

The value of a public career had nothing to do with earning a salary, which Roman officials did not receive, or with gaining money by exploiting the power of one's official position, at least not in the earlier centuries of the Republic. On the contrary, officials were expected to spend their own money on their careers and public service. Therefore, the only men who could afford to serve in government were those with income from family property or friends who would support them financially. The expenses required to win an electoral campaign and secure a reputation for community-minded service in office could be crushing. To win the support of voters, candidates often had to go deeply into debt to finance hugely expensive public festivals featuring fights among gladiators and staged killings of exotic wild animals imported from Africa. Once he was elected, an official was expected to pay personally for public works such as roads, aqueducts, and temples that benefited the whole populace. In this way, successful candidates were expected to serve the common good by spending their own money—or money they borrowed from their friends and clients.

Roman officials originally found personal rewards for their service only in the status that their positions brought while in office and in the high esteem that they could enjoy afterwards if they were seen as having been morally upright and generous public servants. But as the Romans later in the Republic came to dominate more and more overseas territory won as the spoils of war, the opportunity to make money from conquering and governing foreigners became an increasingly important component of a man's successful public career. Officials could legally enrich themselves by winning booty while serving as commanders in successful wars of conquest against foreigners. Corrupt officials could also profit by taking gifts and bribes from local people while administering the provinces created from Rome's conquered territories. In this way, Rome's former enemies financed their conquerors' public careers and private riches.

Romans voted in assemblies to decide elections, set national policy, and pass laws. The complexity of the Republic's voting assemblies almost defies description. Rome's free, adult male citizens met regularly in these open-air gatherings to vote on legislation, hold certain trials, and elect officials. Roman tradition specified that an assembly had to be summoned by an official, held only on days seen as proper under religious law, and sanctioned by favorable auspices. Assemblies were for voting, not for discussing candidates for office or possible policies for the government to adopt. Discussion and debate took place before the assemblies, in a large public meeting that anyone, including women and noncitizens, could attend but at which only male citizens could speak. Since a presiding official decided which men could speak, he could control the course of the debate, but nevertheless there was a considerable opportunity for expressing different opinions and proposals. Everyone listening to the speakers could express their views at least indirectly by cheering or booing what was said. An unpopular proposal could expect to be greeted with loud jeers and shouts of ridicule at these meetings. Once the assembly itself began, votes could be taken only on matters proposed by the officials, and amendments to the official proposals were not permitted at that point.

Rome had three main voting assemblies: the Centuriate Assembly, the Tribal Assembly of the Plebeians, and the Tribal Assembly of the People. It is crucial to recognize that there was no "one man, one vote" rule. Instead, the men in the assemblies were divided into a large number of groups according to specific rules that were different for each type of assembly. The groups were not equal in size. The members of each group would first cast their individual votes to determine what the single vote of their group would be in the assembly. Each group's single vote, regardless of the number of members of that group, then counted the same in determining the decision of the assembly by majority vote of the groups.

This procedure of voting by groups placed severe limits on the apparent democracy of the assemblies. The Centuriate Assembly offers us the clearest example of the effects of the Roman principle of group voting. This important assembly elected censors, consuls, and praetors; enacted laws; declared war and peace; and could inflict the death penalty in trials. The groups in this assembly, called centuries (hence the assembly's name), were organized to correspond to the divisions of the male citizens when they were drawn up as an army. Since early Rome relied not on a standing army financed by taxes but on a citizen militia, every citizen had to arm himself at his own expense as best he could. The richer he was, the more a man contributed by spending more on his weapons and armor. This principle of national defense through individual contributions meant that the richer citizens had more and better military equipment than did the poorer, much more numerous citizens.

Consequently, the rich were seen as deserving more power in the assembly to correspond to their greater personal expenses in military service defending the community. In line with this principle, the cavalrymen, who had the highest military expenses because they had to maintain a warhorse year round, made up the first eighteen groups of the total of 193 voting groups in the Centuriate Assembly. The next 170 groups in this assembly consisted of foot soldiers ranked according to how much property they owned, from highest to lowest. The next four groups consisted of noncombatants providing services to the army, including carpenters and musicians. The final group, the proletarians, was made up of those who were too poor to afford military weapons and armor and therefore did not serve in the army. All they contributed to the state were their children (their *proles*, hence the term proletarian).

The grouping of voters in the Centuriate Assembly therefore corresponded to the distribution of wealth in Roman society. Far more men belonged to the groups at the bottom of the social hierarchy than to those at the top, and the proletarians formed the most numerous group of all. But these larger groups still had only one vote each. Moreover, the groups voted in order from richest to poorest. As a result, the rich could vote as a bloc in the assembly and reach a majority of the group votes well before the voting even reached the groups of the poor. When the elite groups voted the same way, then, the Centuriate Assembly could make a decision in an election or on legislation without the wishes of the lower classes ever being expressed at all through their votes.

The voting groups in the Tribal Assembly of the Plebeians were determined on a geographical basis, according to where the voters lived. The assembly got its name from the Roman institution of tribes, which were not kinship associations or ethnic groups but rather a set of area subdivisions of the population for administrative purposes. By the later Republic, the number of tribes had been fixed at thirty-five, four in regions of the capital city and thirty-one in the Italian countryside. The tribes were structured geographically so as to give an advantage to wealthy landowners from the countryside. This Tribal Assembly excluded patricians. Consisting therefore only of plebeian voters, it conducted nearly every form of public business imaginable, including holding trials.

In the first centuries of the Republic, the proposals passed by the plebeians in this assembly, called plebiscites, were regarded only as recommendations, not laws, and the aristocrats who dominated Roman government at the time often ignored the plebiscites. Plebeians became angrier and angrier at the elite's arrogant disregard for their wishes as the majority of the population. By repeatedly employing their tactic of secession from the state, the plebeians eventually forced the patricians to give in. The plebeians' final withdrawal in 287 B.C. led to an official agreement to make plebiscites the source of official laws. This reform transformed the results of votes taken in the Tribal Assembly of the Plebeians from mere recommendations into a principal source of legislation binding on all Roman citizens, including patricians. The recognition of plebiscites as official law finally ended the Struggle of the Orders between plebeians and patricians because it formalized the electoral, legislative, and judicial power of the majority of the population.

The Tribal Assembly of the Plebeians elected the plebeian aediles and, most importantly, the ten tribunes, special and powerful officials devoted to protecting the interests of the plebeians. As plebeians themselves, tribunes derived their power not from official statutes or rules but rather from the sworn oath of the plebeians to protect them against all attacks. This sacred inviolability of the tribunes, called sacrosanctity, allowed them to exercise the right of veto (a Latin word meaning "I forbid") to block the action of any official, even a consul, and to prevent the passage of laws, to suspend elections, and to reject the advice of the Senate. Tribunes' power to obstruct the actions of officials and assemblies gave them an extraordinary potential to influence Roman government. Tribunes who exercised their full powers in controversial situations could become the catalysts for bitter political disputes, and the office of tribune itself became one hated by many of the most elite Romans, who resented its ability to obstruct their wishes.

In a later development, the Tribal Assembly also met in an expanded form that included patricians as well as plebeians. When meeting in this form, it became Rome's third type of political assembly. Called the Tribal Assembly of the People, it elected the quaestors; the two curule aediles (whose higher status was indicated by their special portable chairs, the *sella curulis* also used by consuls and praetors; originally, only patricians could hold these positions); and the six senior officers (military tribunes) of the largest units in the army. The Tribal Assembly of the People also enacted laws and held minor trials.

In sum, then, the "Roman constitution" included a network of government offices and voting assemblies whose powers often overlapped and conflicted. Very little was clear or unambiguous about the distribution of power in the government of the Republic, which opened the door to frequent political conflicts. Perhaps the most serious source of conflict was the fact that multiple political institutions could make laws or their equivalent (meaning the advice given by the Senate), but Rome had no central authority or judicial body, such as the United States Supreme Court, to resolve disputes about the validity of overlapping or conflicting laws. Rather than depend on institutions of government with clearly defined and limited competencies, the Romans entrusted the political health and stability of their Republic to a generalized respect for tradition, the famous "way of the elders." This characteristic in turn ensured that the socially most prominent and richest Romans dominated government because their status enabled them to control what that "way" should be in the context of politics.

4

War and Expansion During the Republic

The major wars fought by the Romans in Italy and throughout the Mediterranean region during the time of the Republic resulted in a tremendous expansion of Roman territory. This creation of a territorial empire—control over lands previously ruled by others—had enormous consequences for Roman society. Many historians use the label "imperialism" to characterize Rome's expansion of its power through war. That word comes from the Latin term *imperium*, the power to compel obedience, to command and to punish. The negative meaning attached to imperialism today comes primarily from criticism of the history of modern European states in establishing colonial empires in Africa and Asia. To decide how—or whether—this term is a fair description of Rome's expansion requires us to try to understand what motivated the Romans in this process. As we will see, it is a controversial question to what extent Rome's wars and conquest during the Republic were the result of a desire to profit from dominating others, or of the belief that preemptive wars to weaken or absorb perceived enemies were the best defense against attacks by others. Therefore, the most debated question about Roman expansion through war under the Republic concerns the intentions motivating it.

What is clear is that the great expansion of Rome's

TIMELINE (ALL DATES B.C.)

499: The Romans defeat their neighbors in Latium.

396: The Romans achieve final victory over the Etruscan town of Veii, doubling their territory through the conquest.

387: Invading Gauls (Celts) attack and sack Rome.

300: As many as 150,000 people now live in the city of Rome.

280–275: The Romans fight and defeat the mercenary general Pyrrhus commanding the forces of the Greek cities in south Italy.

264–241: The Romans defeat the Carthaginians in the First Punic War, with great losses on both sides.

Late third century: Livius Andronicus composes the first Roman literature in Latin, an adaptation of Homer's *Odyssey*.

227: The Romans make provinces out of Sicily, Corsica, and Sardinia, beginning their territorial empire.

220: After centuries of war, the Romans now control the entire Italian peninsula south of the Po River.

218–201: The Romans defeat the Carthaginians in the Second Punic War despite Hannibal's invasion of Italy.

196: The Roman general Flamininus proclaims the freedom of the Greeks at Corinth.

149–146: The Romans defeat the Carthaginians in the Third Punic War, converting Carthage and its territory into a province.

146: The Roman general Mummius destroys Corinth; Greece and Macedonia are made into a Roman province.

133: Attalus III, King of Pergamum, leaves his kingdom to the Romans in his will.

Late 130s and late 120s: Tiberius Gracchus and Gaius Gracchus as consuls stir up violent political conflict and are murdered by their opponents from the Senate.

territory and international power brought major changes to Roman society and culture. Rome's overseas wars meant long-term contacts with new peoples that produced unexpected and often controversial influences on Roman life. To give one major example, increased interaction with Greeks led to the creation of the first Roman literature written in Latin. A different kind of change came from the effects on Roman values of the stupendous wealth and personal power that Rome's upper-class leaders acquired as their rewards in the wars of conquest under the Republic. On the other hand, Rome's expansion also meant that many of Italy's small farmers, the main source of manpower for the army, fell into poverty that contributed to social instability. Rome's political leaders disagreed fiercely about how, or even whether, to help their impoverished fellow citizens. The disagreements became so bitter that in the end they created a violent divide in the upper class, destroying any hope for preserving the Republic.

ROMAN IMPERIALISM

Rome's first wars were fought near its own borders, in central Italy. Soon after the establishment of the Republic, the Romans won a victory over their Latin neighbors in 499 B.C. They then spent the next hundred years fighting the Etruscan town of Veii situated a few miles north of the Tiber River. As a consequence of their eventual victory in 396 B.C., the Romans doubled their territory. The ancient sources present this first stage of expansion as a justified extension of Rome's defensive perimeter rather than as the result of premeditated wars of conquest. However, these accounts were written in a much later period and may be offering a justification for early Rome's expansion that created a historical precedent for what their authors thought should be the moral basis for Roman foreign policy in their own time.

Whatever the truth is about the Romans' motives for fighting their neighbors in the fifth century B.C., by the fourth century B.C. the Roman army had surpassed all other Mediterranean-area forces as an effective weapon of war. The success of the Roman army stemmed from the organization of its fighting units, which was designed to provide tactical flexibility and maneuverability in the field. The largest unit was the legion, which by later in the Republic numbered five thousand infantry soldiers. Each legion was supplemented with three hundred cavalry troops and various engineers to do construction and other support duties. Roman legions were also customarily accompanied by significant numbers of allied troops, and sometimes even mercenaries, especially to serve as archers. The legion's internal subdivision into many smaller units under experienced leaders, called centurions, gave it greater mobility to react swiftly to new situations in the heat of battle. Since the foot soldiers were drawn up in battle formation with space left between them, they could stand behind their large shields to make effective use of their throwing spears to disrupt the enemy line, and then move in with their swords drawn for hand-to-hand combat. Roman infantrymen's swords were specially designed for cutting and thrusting from close range, and men underwent harsh training to be able to withstand the shock and fear that this emphasis on close combat generated not only in the enemy but also in the Roman troops who had to carry it out. Above all, Romans never stopped fighting. Even a devastating sack of Rome in 387 B.C. by marauding Gauls (a Celtic group) from the distant north failed to end the state's military success in the long run. By around 220 B.C., the Romans had brought all of Italy south of the Po River under their control.

The conduct of these wars in Italy was often brutal. The Romans sometimes enslaved large numbers of the defeated. Even if they left their conquered enemies free, they forced them to give up large parcels of their land. Equally significant for evaluating Roman imperialism, however, is that the Romans also regularly extended peace terms to former enemies. To some defeated Italians they immediately gave Roman citizenship; to others they gave the protections of citizenship, though without the right to vote in Rome's assemblies; still other communities received treaties of alliance and protection. No conquered Italian peoples had to pay taxes to Rome. They did, however, have to render military aid to the Romans in subsequent wars. These new allies then received a share of the booty, chiefly slaves and land, that Rome and its allied armies won on successful campaigns against a new crop of enemies. In other words, the Romans co-opted their former opponents by making them partners in the spoils of conquest, an arrangement that in turn enhanced Rome's wealth and authority. All these arrangements corresponded to the Romans' original policy of incorporating others into their community to make it larger and stronger. Roman imperialism, in short, was inclusive, not exclusive.

To increase the security of Italy, the Romans planted colonies of citizens and constructed a network of roads up and down the peninsula. These roads aided the gradual merging of the diverse cultures of Italy into a more unified whole dominated by Rome, in which Latin came to be the common language. But the Romans, too, were deeply influenced by the cross-cultural contacts that expansion brought. In southern Italy, the Romans found a second home, as it were, in long-established Greek cities such as Naples. These Greek communities, too weak to resist Roman armies, nevertheless introduced their conquerors to Greek traditions in art, music, theater, literature, and philosophy, thereby providing models for later Roman cultural developments. When in the late third century B.C. Roman authors began to write history for the first time, for example, they imitated Greek forms and aimed at Greek readers with their accounts of early Rome, even to the point of writing in Greek.

Rome's urban population grew tremendously during the period of expansion in Italy. By around 300 B.C., as many as 150,000 people lived

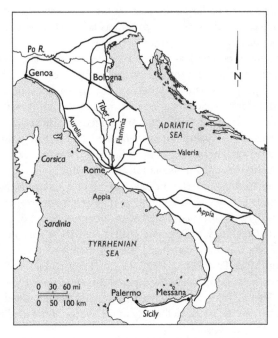

Map 4. Major Roman Roads under the Republic

within the city's fortification wall. Long aqueducts were built to bring fresh water to this growing population, and the plunder from the successful wars financed a massive building program inside the city. Outside the city, 750,000 free Roman citizens inhabited various parts of Italy on land taken from the local peoples. For reasons that are uncertain, this rural population encountered increasing economic difficulties over time, whether from a rise in the birth rate leading to an inability to support larger families, or from the difficulties of keeping a farm productive when many men were away on long military campaigns, or perhaps from some combination of these factors. It is clear that a large amount of conquered territory was declared public land, supposedly open to any Roman to use for grazing flocks. Many rich landowners, however, managed to secure control of huge parcels of this public land for their own, private use. This illegal monopolization of public land contributed to bitter feelings between rich and poor Romans.

The ranks of the rich by now included both patricians and plebeians; both these orders included "nobles." In fact, the tensions of the Struggle of the Orders were so far in the past by the third century B.C. that the wealthy and politically successful patricians and plebeians saw their interests as similar rather than as conflicting and competing. Their agreement on issues of politics and state finance amounted to a new definition of the upper class, making the old division of the "orders" obsolete for all practical purposes. The members of the upper class derived their wealth mainly from agricultural land, as in the past, but now they could also increase their riches from plunder gained as officers in successful military expeditions against foreign enemies. The Roman state had no regular income or inheritance taxes, so financially prudent families could pass this wealth down from generation to generation.

After their military success in Italy, the most pressing issues for Romans continued to be decisions about war. When the mercenary general Pyrrhus brought an army equipped with war elephants from Greece to fight for the Greek city of Tarentum against Roman expansion in southern Italy, Rome's leaders convinced the assemblies to vote to face this frightening threat. From 280 to 275 B.C. the Romans battled Pyrrhus in a seesaw struggle, until finally they forced him to abandon the war and return to Greece. With this hard-earned victory, Rome gained effective control of Italy in the south all the way to the shores of the Mediterranean at the end of the peninsula.

This expansion southward brought the Romans to the edge of the region dominated by Carthage, a prosperous state located across the Mediterranean Sea in western North Africa (today Tunisia). Phoenicians, Semitic explorers from the eastern coast of the Mediterranean Sea, had colonized Carthage around 800 B.C. on a favorable location for conducting trade by sea and controlling fertile agricultural areas inland. The Carthaginians had expanded their commercial interests all over the western Mediterranean, including the large island of Sicily, located across a narrow strip of sea from the toe of the Italian peninsula. Their centuries of experience at sea meant that the Carthaginians completely outstripped the Romans in naval capability; the Romans in the third century B.C. had almost no knowledge of the technology needed to build warships or the organization required to field a powerful navy. The two states were alike politically, however, because Carthage, like Rome, was governed as a republic dominated by a social elite.

Since the Romans were no rivals for the Carthaginians in overseas trade and had never conducted a military campaign at sea or even on land outside of Italy, the two states could have gone on indefinitely without becoming enemies. As it happened, however, a seemingly insignificant episode created by third parties under the control of neither Rome nor

Figure 10. On a painted plate, a war elephant carries warriors in a tower on its back, followed by its calf. The Romans first faced these beasts on the battlefield in the third century B.C., but, like the Greeks, they learned to disrupt their attacks by placing spiked traps in their way to injure the behemoths' soft feet. Scala/ArtResource, NY.

Carthage drew these two powers into what became a century of destructive wars that changed the power structure of the Mediterranean world—the Punic Wars, so called from *Punici* ("Phoenicians"), the Roman name for the Carthaginians. In 264 B.C., a band of mercenaries in the city of Messana at Sicily's northeastern tip close to Italy found themselves in great danger of their lives, after the military service for which they had been hired ended in failure. In desperation, the mercenaries appealed for help to Rome and Carthage simultaneously. There was no obvious reason for either to respond, except geography: Sicily was located precisely on the edge between the two powers' spheres of control in the region. In short, Messana was perfectly positioned to become a flashpoint for conflict between Roman and Carthaginian ambitions and fears.

The Senate could not agree about what to do about the mercenaries' request to be rescued, but a patrician consul, Appius Claudius Caudex, persuaded the people to vote to send an army to Sicily by promising them rich plunder. In this way, sending troops to Messana became Rome's first military expedition outside Italy. When Carthage also sent soldiers to Messana, a battle erupted between the forces of the two competing powers. The result was the First Punic War, which lasted a generation (264 B.C.–241 B.C.). This decades-long conflict revealed why the Romans were so consistently successful in conquest: they were prepared to sacrifice as many lives, to spend as much money, and to keep fighting as long as necessary. Staying loyal to their traditional values, they never gave up, whatever the cost. The Romans and their allies persevered in the First Punic War despite losing 250,000 men and more than 500 warships from their newly built navy. The Greek historian Polybius, writing a century later, regarded the First Punic War as "the greatest war in history in its length, intensity, and scale of operations" (*Histories* 1.13.10–13).

The need to fight at sea against an experienced naval power spurred the Romans to develop a navy from scratch. They overcame their inferiority in naval warfare with an ingenious technical innovation, outfitting the prows of their newly built warships with a beam fitted with a long spike at its outer end. In battle, they snared enemy ships by dropping these spiked beams, called ravens because of their resemblance to the sharp-beaked bird, onto the enemy's deck. Roman troops then boarded the enemy ship to fight hand-to-hand, their specialty. So successful were the Romans in learning and applying naval technology that they lost very few major battles at sea in the First Punic War. One famous loss in 249 B.C. they explained as divine punishment for the consul Claudius Pulcher's sacrilege before the battle. To meet the religious requirement that a commander take the auspices before beginning battle, he had sacred chickens on board ship. Before sending his force into action, a commander had to see the birds feeding energetically as a sign of good fortune. When his chickens, probably seasick, refused to eat, Claudius hurled them overboard in a rage, sputtering, "Well, then, let them drink!" (Cicero, *The Nature of the Gods* 2.7). He began battle anyway and lost 93 of his 123 ships in a spectacular naval defeat. The Romans later punished him for his arrogant defiance of tradition.

The Romans' victory in the First Punic War made them the masters of Sicily, whose ports and fields had brought prosperity to the island's diverse settlements of Greeks, Carthaginians, and indigenous peoples. The income from taxes that the Romans received from Sicily proved so profitable that in 238 B.C. the Romans also seized the nearby islands of Sardinia and Corsica from the Carthaginians. In 227 B.C., the Romans officially converted Sicily into one overseas province and Sardinia and Corsica into a second. These actions created the Roman provincial system, in which Romans served as the governors of conquered territories ("provinces") to oversee taxation, the administration of justice, and the protection of Roman interests. Unlike many of the peoples defeated and absorbed by Rome in Italy, the inhabitants of the new provinces did not become Roman citizens. They were designated "provincials," who retained their local political organization but also paid direct taxes, which Roman citizens did not.

The number of praetors was increased to fill the need for Roman officials to serve as governors, whose duties were to keep the provinces paying taxes, free of rebels, and out of enemy hands. Whenever possible, Roman provincial administration made use of local administrative arrangements already in place. In Sicily, for instance, the Romans collected the same taxes that the earlier Greek states there had collected. Over time, the taxes paid by provincials provided income for subsidies to the Roman poor, as well as opportunities for personal enrichment to the upper-class Romans who served in high offices in the provincial administration of the Republic.

Following the First Punic War, the Romans made alliances with communities in eastern Spain to block Carthaginian power there. Despite a Roman pledge in 226 B.C. not to interfere south of the Ebro River, the region where Carthage dominated, the Carthaginians were alarmed by this move by their enemy. They feared for their important commercial interests in Spain's mineral and agricultural resources. When Saguntum, a city located south of the river in the Carthaginian-dominated part of the Spanish peninsula, appealed to Rome for help against Carthage, the Senate responded favorably, ignoring their previous pledge. Worries about the injustice of breaking their word were perhaps offset by the Roman view that the Carthaginians were barbarians of lesser moral status. The Romans condemned the Carthaginians for what they (correctly) believed was the Punic practice of sacrificing infants and children in national emergencies to try to regain the favor of the gods.

When Saguntum fell to a Carthaginian siege, the Romans launched the Second Punic War (218 B.C.–201 B.C.). This second long war put even greater stress on Rome than the first because the innovative Carthaginian general Hannibal, hardened by years of warfare in Spain, shocked the Romans by marching a force of troops and elephants through the snow-covered passes in the Alps to invade Italy. The shock turned to terror when Hannibal killed more than thirty thousand Romans in a single day at the

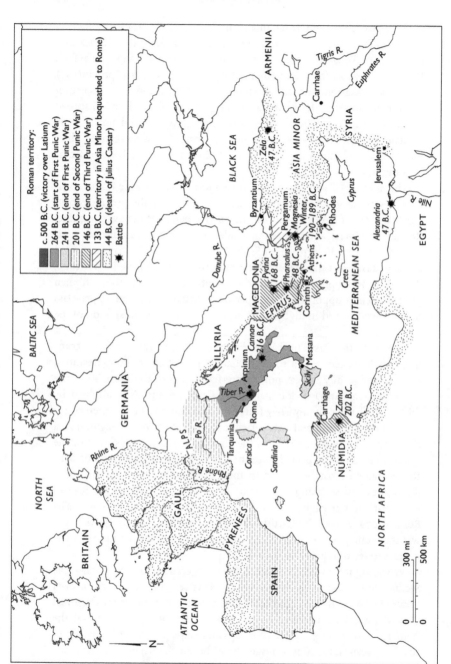

Map 5. Roman Expansion During the Republic

Roman territory:
- c. 500 B.C. (victory over Latium)
- 264 B.C. (start of First Punic War)
- 241 B.C. (end of First Punic War)
- 201 B.C. (end of Second Punic War)
- 146 B.C. (end of Third Punic War)
- 133 B.C. (territory in Asia Minor bequeathed to Rome)
- 44 B.C. (death of Julius Caesar)
- Battle

battle of Cannae in 216 B.C. The Carthaginian general's strategy was to try to provoke widespread revolts in the Italian cities allied to Rome. His alliance with King Philip V of Macedonia in 215 B.C. forced the Romans to fight in Greece as well to protect their eastern flank, but they refused to crack under the pressure. Hannibal made their lives miserable by marching up and down Italy for fifteen more years, ravaging Roman territory and even threatening to capture the capital itself. The best the Romans could do militarily was to engage in stalling tactics, made famous by the general Fabius Maximus, called "the Delayer." Disastrously for Hannibal, however, most of the Italians remained loyal to Rome. In the end Hannibal had to abandon his guerrilla campaign in Italy to rush back to North Africa with his army in 203 B.C., when the Romans, under their general Scipio, daringly launched an attack on Carthage itself.

Home at last after thirty-four years in the field in Spain and Italy, Hannibal was defeated at the battle of Zama in 202 B.C. by Scipio. He received the title *Africanus* to celebrate his outstanding victory over such a formidable enemy. The Romans imposed a punishing peace settlement on the Carthaginians, forcing them to scuttle their navy, pay huge war indemnities scheduled to last for fifty years, and relinquish their territories in Spain. The Romans subsequently had to fight a long series of wars with the indigenous Spanish peoples for control of the area, but the enormous profits to be made there, especially from Spain's mineral resources, made the effort worthwhile. The revenues from Spain's silver mines were so great that they financed expensive public building projects in Rome.

The Romans' success against Carthage allowed them to continue efforts to defeat the Gauls in northern Italy, who inhabited the rich plain north of the Po River. Remembering the sack of Rome by marauding Gauls in 387 B.C., a success that not even Hannibal had achieved, the Romans feared another invasion. The Romans therefore believed their wars against these Celtic peoples were just because they were, in Roman eyes, a preemptive defense. By the end of the third century B.C., Rome controlled the Po valley and thus all of Italy up to the Alps.

Expansion eastward followed Rome's military successes in the western Mediterranean. In the aftermath of the Second Punic War, the Senate in 200 B.C. advised that Roman forces should be sent abroad across the Adriatic Sea to attack Philip V, king of Macedonia in the Balkans. Philip's alliance with Hannibal had forced the Romans to open a second front in that difficult war, but the Macedonians then made peace with Rome on favorable terms in 205 B.C., when the Romans had their hands full dealing with Carthage. Now, the senators responded to a call from the Greek

Figure 11. This Greek-style theater seated thousands of spectators in Pergamum, the capital of the Attalid kingdom in Asia Minor (today Turkey). Used for theatrical performances and festival shows, its size testifies to the popularity of large-scale entertainments in the Greco-Roman world. Erika Praefcke/Wikimedia Commons.

states of Pergamum and Rhodes to prevent an alliance between the kingdom of Macedonia and that of the Seleucids, the family of a general of Alexander the Great who had founded a new monarchy in southwestern Asia in the tumultuous aftermath of Alexander's conquests. These smaller powers feared they would be overcome, and the senators took the invitation to help these faraway places as a reason to extend Roman power into a new area. Their motives were probably mixed. Most likely they both wanted to punish Philip for his treachery and also demonstrate that Rome could protect itself from any threat to Italy from that direction.

After defeating Philip, the Roman commander Flamininus in 196 B.C. traveled to a popular and well-attended international athletic festival near Corinth in southern Greece to proclaim the freedom of the Greeks. The locals were surprised and confused by this announcement. It certainly was not obvious to them why, or with what right, this foreigner was telling them that they were free. They assumed that freedom was their natural condition. Despite their puzzlement at the circumstances, the long-established cities and federal leagues of Greece certainly believed that the proclamation meant that they, the Greeks, were free to direct their own affairs just as they liked, so far as the Romans were concerned. After all, the Greeks thought, the Romans have now said we are their friends.

Unfortunately for them, the Greeks had misunderstood the message. The Romans meant that they had fulfilled the role of a patron by doing the Greeks the kindness of fighting a war on their behalf and then proclaiming their freedom, instead of asking for any kind of submission or even compensation for their losses in war. Therefore, in Roman eyes, their actions had made them the patrons of the liberated Greeks, who should then behave as respectful Roman clients, not as equals. The Greeks were their friends only in the special sense that patrons and clients were friends. They were politically and legally free, certainly, but that status did not liberate them from their moral obligation to behave as clients and therefore respect their patrons' wishes.

Since the Greeks' customs included nothing comparable, they failed to understand the seriousness of the obligations, and the differences in the kinds of obligations, between superiors and inferiors that Romans attributed to the patron-client relationship. As can happen in international diplomacy, trouble developed because the two sides failed to realize that common and familiar terms such as "freedom" and "friendship" could carry significantly different meanings and implications in different societies. The Greeks, taking the Roman proclamation of freedom literally and therefore thinking that they were free to manage their political affairs as they wished, resisted subsequent Roman efforts to intervene in the local disputes that continued to disrupt the peace in Greece and Macedonia after the proclamation of 196 B.C. The Romans, by contrast, regarded this refusal to follow their recommendations as a betrayal of the client's duty to respect the patron's wishes.

The Romans were especially upset by the military support that certain Greeks requested from King Antiochus III, the ruler of the Seleucid Kingdom, who invaded Greece after the Roman forces returned to Italy in 194 B.C. The Romans therefore fought against Antiochus and his allies from 192 to 188 B.C. in what is called the Syrian War. Again victorious, they parceled out Antiochus's territories in Asia Minor (today Turkey) to friendly states in the region and once more withdrew to Italy. When the expansionist activities of the Macedonian king Perseus led King Eumenes of Pergamum to appeal to Rome to return to Greece to stop Macedonian aggression, the Romans responded by sending an army that defeated Perseus over the course of 171 to 168 B.C. Not even this victory settled matters in Greece, and it took yet another twenty years before Rome could decisively restore peace there for the benefit of its friends and supporters in Greece and Macedonia. Finally, after winning yet another Macedonian war in 148 B.C.–146 B.C., the Romans ended Greek freedom by beginning to bring Macedonia and Greece into the system of Rome's provinces. In 146 B.C., the Roman commander Mummius destroyed the historic and wealthy city of Corinth as a calculated act of terror to show what continued resistance to Roman domination would mean for the other Greeks.

The year 146 B.C. also saw the annihilation of Carthage at the end of the Third Punic War (149 B.C.–146 B.C.). This war had begun when the Carthaginians, who had once again revived economically after paying the indemnities imposed by Rome following the Second Punic War, retaliated against their neighbor the Numidian king Masinissa, a Roman ally who had been aggressively provoking them for some time. Carthage finally fell before the blockade of Scipio Aemilianus, the adopted grandson of Scipio Africanus. The city was then destroyed and its territory converted into a Roman province. This disaster did not obliterate Punic social and cultural ways, however, and later under the Roman Empire this part of North Africa was distinguished for its economic and intellectual vitality, which emerged from a synthesis of Roman and Punic traditions.

The destruction of Carthage as an independent state corresponded to the wish of the famously plainspoken Roman senator Marcus Porcius Cato the Elder. For several years before 146 B.C., Cato had taken every opportunity in debates in the Senate to demand: "Carthage must be destroyed!" (Plutarch, *Life of Cato the Elder* 27). Cato presumably had two reasons for his order. One was the fear that a newly strong Carthage would once again threaten Rome. Another was a desire to eliminate Carthage as a rival for the riches and glory that Cato and his fellow nobles hoped to accumulate as a result of the expansion of Roman power throughout the Mediterranean region.

The Romans won every war they fought in the first four hundred years of the Republic, although usually only after years of fierce battles, terrible losses of life, and enormous expense. These hard-won victories had both intended and unintended consequences for Rome and the values of Roman society. By 100 B.C., the Romans had intentionally established their control of an amount of territory more vast than any one nation had conquered since the time of the Persian Empire in the sixth century B.C. But as said at the start of this section, even experts disagree concerning to what extent the Romans originally intended to fight wars of conquest, as opposed to attacking enemies for self-defense in a hostile and aggressive world.

Roman expansion was never a constant or uniform process, and Roman imperialism under the Republic cannot be explained as the result of any single principle or motivation. The Romans exercised considerable flexibility in dealing with different peoples in different locations. In Italy, the Romans initially fought to protect themselves against neighbors they found threatening. In the western Mediterranean and western North Africa, the Romans followed their conquests by imposing direct rule and maintaining a permanent military presence. In Greece and Macedonia, they for a long time preferred to rule indirectly, through alliances and compliant local governments. Roman leaders befriended their counterparts in the social elite in Greece to promote their common interests in keeping the peace. Following the destruction of Carthage and Corinth in 146 B.C., Rome's direct rule now extended across two-thirds the length of the Mediterranean, from Spain to Greece. And then in 133 B.C. the king of Pergamum, Attalus III, increased Roman power yet further with an astonishing gift: in his will he left his kingdom in Asia Minor as a bequest to the Romans. They were now the unrivaled masters of their world.

In sum, it seems fair to explain Roman imperialism as the combined result of (1) a concern for the security of Rome and its territory leading the Senate and the Assemblies to agree on preemptive strikes against those states perceived as enemies; (2) the desire of both the Roman upper class and of the Roman people in general to benefit financially from the rewards of wars of conquest, including booty, land in Italy, and tax revenue from provinces; and (3) the traditional drive to achieve glory, both among men of the upper class for personal gratification but also among Romans in general for the reputation of their state. Power was respected and honored in the world in which the Romans lived, and conquest was therefore not automatically regarded as a dirty word. At the same time, the Romans were always careful to insist—and sincere in believing—that they were not the aggressors but were fighting in defense of their safety or to preserve and enhance their honor. Whether we today should criticize them as more insincere or mistaken than modern imperialists is a question that readers must answer for themselves, while being careful to avoid the arrogance in judgment that modernity sometimes ignorantly assumes in comparing the contemporary world's moral scorecard of good and evil to that of the ancient world.

CONSEQUENCES OF EXPANSION

The Romans' military and diplomatic activity in southern Italy, Sicily, Greece, and Asia Minor intensified their contact with Greek culture, which deeply influenced the development of art, architecture, and literature in Roman culture. When Roman artists began creating paintings, they found inspiration in Greek art, whose models they adapted to their own taste and needs, and the same was true of sculpture. Painting was perhaps the most popular art, but very little has survived, except for frescoes (paintings on plaster) decorating the walls of buildings. Similarly, relatively few Roman statues are preserved from the period of the Republic. The first temple to be built of marble in Rome, erected in honor of Jupiter in 146 B.C., echoed the Greek tradition of using that shining stone for magnificent public architecture. A victorious general, Caecilius Metellus, paid for it to display his success and piety in the service of the Roman people. This temple became famous for starting a trend of expensive magnificence in the architecture and construction of Roman public buildings.

Roman literature also grew from Greek models. In fact, when the first Roman history was written about 200 B.C., it was written in Greek. The earliest literature written in Latin was a long poem, written sometime after the First Punic War (264 B.C.–241 B.C.), that was an adaptation of Homer's *Odyssey*. The diversity that was driving Roman cultural development is shown by the fact this first author to write in Latin was not a Roman at all, but rather a Greek from Tarentum in southern Italy, Livius Andronicus. Taken captive and enslaved, he lived in Rome after being freed and taking his master's name. Indeed, many of the most famous early Latin authors were not native Romans. They came from a wide geographic range: the poet Naevius (d. 201 B.C.) from Campania, south of Rome; the poet Ennius (d. 169 B.C.) from even farther south in Calabria; the comic playwright Plautus (d. 184 B.C.) from north of Rome, in Umbria; his fellow comedy writer Terence (190 B.C.–159 B.C.) from North Africa.

Early Roman literature therefore shows clearly that Roman culture found strength and vitality by combining the foreign and the familiar, just as the population had grown by bringing together Romans and immigrants. Plautus and Terence, for example, wrote their famous comedies in Latin for Roman audiences, but they adapted their plots from Greek comedies. They displayed their particular genius by keeping the settings of their comedies Greek, while creating unforgettable characters that were unmistakably Roman in their outlook and behavior. The comic figure of the braggart warrior, for one, mocked the pretensions of Romans who claimed elevated social status on the basis of the number of enemies they had slaughtered. These plays have proved enduring in their appeal. Shakespeare based *The Comedy of Errors* (A.D. c. 1594) on a comedy of Plautus; so, too, the hit Broadway musical and later film (A.D. 1966), *A Funny*

Figure 12. An actor or author of the kind of Greek comedies that inspired Roman ones inspects the masks that comic actors wore on stage. The masks' broad features helped spectators tell one character from another when viewing shows in giant theaters such as the one pictured in Figure 11. David C. Hill/ Wikimedia Commons.

Thing Happened on the Way to the Forum, took its inspiration from the bawdy humor of Plautus's *The Braggart Warrior*.

Not all Romans found Greek influence a good thing. Cato, although he studied Greek himself, repeatedly thundered against the corrupting effect that he believed the weakling Greeks were having on the sturdy Romans. He established Latin as a proper language for writing prose with the publication of his treatise on running a large farm, *On Agriculture* (published about 160 B.C.), and his history of Rome, *The Origins* (which he began writing in 168 B.C. and was still working on at his death in 149 B.C.). Cato glumly predicted that if the Romans became thoroughly infected with Greek literature, they would lose their power. In fact, early Latin literature reflected traditional Roman values despite its debt to Greek literature. Ennius, for example, was inspired by Greek epic poetry to compose his path-breaking epic, *Annals*, in Latin. Its subject, however, was a poetic version of Roman history from the beginnings to Ennius's time. Its contents were anything but subversive of ancestral tradition, as a famous line demonstrates: "On the ways and the men of old rests the Roman commonwealth" (preserved in Augustine, *City of God* 2.21; Warmington vol. 1, pp. 174–175, frag. 467). This was Ennius's poetic restatement of the traditional guide to proper conduct for Romans, the "way of the elders."

The unanticipated social and economic changes brought about by Roman imperialism were far more destabilizing to Roman society than was Greek influence on literature. Rome's upper class gained extraordinary financial rewards from Roman imperialism in the third and second centuries B.C. The increased need for commanders to lead military campaigns abroad meant more opportunities for successful men to enrich themselves from booty. By using their gains to finance public buildings, they could then enhance their social status by benefiting the general population. Building new temples, for instance, was thought to increase everyone's security because the Romans believed their gods to be pleased by having more shrines in their honor. Moreover, some festivals associated with temples provided benefits to the general population because their animal sacrifices meant that meat could be distributed to people who could not afford it otherwise.

The creation of the provinces created a need for an increased number of military and political leaders that could not be provided by the traditional number of elected officials. More and more officials therefore had their powers prolonged to command armies and administer provinces. Because a provincial governor ruled by martial law, no one in the province could curb a greedy governor's appetite for graft, extortion, and plunder. Not all Roman provincial officials were corrupt, of course, but some did use their unsupervised power to exploit the provincials to the maximum. Dishonest provincial officials only rarely faced punishment; the notorious Verres, prosecuted by Cicero in 70 B.C. for his crimes as an administrator in Sicily, was a rare exception. Enormous and luxurious country villas became a favorite symbol of wealth for men who had grown rich as provincial administrators. The new taste for a lavish lifestyle stirred up controversy because it contradicted Roman ideals, which emphasized moderation and frugality in one's private life. Cato, for instance, made his ideal Roman the military hero Manius Curius (d. 270 B.C.), legendary for his simple meals of turnips boiled in his humble hut. The new opportunities for extravagance financed by the financial rewards of expansion abroad fatally undermined this tradition among the Roman elite of valuing a modest, even austere life.

The economic basis of the Republic remained farming. For hundreds of years, farmers working modest-sized plots in the Italian countryside had been the backbone of Roman agricultural production. These property owners also constituted the principal source of soldiers for the Roman army; only men who owned property could serve. As a result, the Republic encountered grave economic, social, and military difficulties when the successful wars of the third and second centuries B.C. turned out to be disastrous for many family farms throughout Italy.

Before the First Punic War, Roman warfare had followed the normal Mediterranean pattern of short military campaigns timed not to interfere with the fluctuating labor needs of agriculture. This seasonal warfare allowed men to remain at home during the times of the year when they needed to sow and harvest their crops and oversee mating and culling of their flocks of animals. The long campaigns of the First Punic War, prolonged year after year, disrupted this pattern by keeping soldiers away from their land for long periods. The women in farming families, like those in urban families, had previously worked in and around the house, not in the fields. A farmer absent on military campaigns therefore either had to rely on hired hands or slaves to raise his crops and animals, or have his wife try to take on what was traditionally men's work. This heavy labor came on top of her already full day's work of bringing water, weaving cloth, storing and preparing food, and caring for the family's children and slaves. The load was crushing.

The story of the consul Marcus Atilius Regulus, who commanded a victorious Roman army in Africa in 256 B.C., reveals the severe problems a man's absence could cause. When the man who was managing Regulus's four-acre farm died while the consul was away fighting Carthage, a hired hand ran off with all the farm's livestock and tools. Regulus therefore begged the Senate to send another general to replace him, so he could return home to prevent his wife and children from starving on his derelict farm. The senators provided support to save Regulus's family and property from ruin because they wanted to keep Regulus as a commander on the battlefield (Valerius Maximus, *Memorable Deeds and Sayings* 4.4.6). Ordinary rank-and-file soldiers could expect no such special aid. Women and children in the same sorry plight as Regulus's family faced disaster because they had no marketable skills if they moved to a city in search of work. Even unskilled jobs were largely unavailable because slaves were used for domestic service, while manufacturing took place in small-scale businesses run by families through the labor of their own members. Many rural women, displaced from their farms and reduced to desperate poverty by their husbands' absence or death in war, could earn money only by becoming prostitutes in the cities of Italy. The new pattern of warfare thus had the unintended consequence of disrupting the traditional forms of life of ordinary people in the Roman countryside, the base of Rome's agricultural economy. At the same time, women in the propertied classes gained further wealth through dowry and inheritance, as the men in their families, who filled the elite positions in the army, brought home the greater share of booty to which their high rank entitled them under the Roman system of distributing the spoils of war.

The farmers' troubles continued with Hannibal's decade-long stay in Italy at the end of the third century B.C. during the Second Punic War. The constant presence of a Carthaginian army made it impossible for farmers to keep up a regular schedule of planting and harvesting in the regions that he terrorized, and the Roman general Fabius's tactics of delay and attrition made their losses worse. Farm families' troubles were compounded in the second century B.C. when many men had to spend year after year away from their fields while serving in Rome's nearly constant military expeditions abroad. More than 50 percent of Roman adult males spent at least seven years in military service during this period, leaving their wives and children to cope as best they could for long periods. Many farm families fell into debt and had to sell their land. Rich landowners could then buy up these plots to create large estates. Landowners further increased their holdings by illegally occupying public land that Rome had originally confiscated from defeated peoples in Italy. In this way, the rich gained vast estates, called latifundia, worked by slaves as well as free laborers. The rich had a ready supply of slaves to work on their mega-farms because of the great numbers of captives taken in the same wars that had promoted the displacement of Italy's small farmers.

Not all regions of Italy suffered as severely as others, and some impoverished farmers and their families in the badly affected areas managed to remain in their native countrysides by working as day laborers. Many displaced people, however, immigrated to Rome, where the men would look for work as menial laborers and women might hope for some piecework making cloth. It has recently been suggested that part of the reason that there were so many people on the move is that, for unknown reasons, there had been a surge in the birth rate that led to pockets of overpopulation in the countryside, with too many people to be supported by local resources. Whatever the reasons, the traditional stability of rural life had been terribly disrupted.

The influx of desperate people to Rome swelled the poverty-level population in the capital. The ongoing difficulty that these now landless urban poor experienced in supporting themselves from day to day in the closely packed city made them a potentially explosive element in Roman politics. They were willing to support with their votes any politician promising to address their needs. They had to be fed somehow if food riots in the city were to be averted. Like Athens before it in the fifth century B.C., Rome by the late second century B.C. needed to import grain to feed its swollen urban population. The Senate supervised the market in grain to prevent speculation in the provision of the basic food supply of Rome and to ensure wide distribution in times of shortage. Some of Rome's leaders believed that the only possible solution to the problem of the starving poor was for the state to supply low-priced and, eventually, free grain to the masses at public expense. Others vehemently disagreed, though without an alternative solution to propose. So, distributions of subsidized food became standard government policy. Over time, the list of the poor entitled to these subsidies grew to tens and tens of thousands of people. Whether to continue this massive expenditure of state revenue became one of the most contentious issues in the politics of the late Republic.

The damaging effect of Roman expansion on poor farm families became an issue heightening the conflict for status that had always existed among Rome's elite political leaders. The situation exploded into murderous violence in the careers of the brothers Tiberius Gracchus (d. 133 B.C.) and Gaius Gracchus (d. 121 B.C.). They came from one of Rome's most distinguished upper-class families: their prominent mother Cornelia was the daughter of the famed general Scipio Africanus. Tiberius won election to the office of plebeian tribune in 133 B.C. He promptly outraged the Senate by having the Tribal Assembly of the Plebeians adopt reform laws designed to redistribute public land to landless Romans without the senators' approval, a formally legal but highly nontraditional maneuver in Roman politics. Tiberius further outraged tradition by ignoring the will of the Senate on the question of financing this agrarian reform. Before the Senate could render an opinion on whether to accept the bequest of his kingdom made to Rome by the recently deceased Attalus III of Pergamum, Tiberius moved that the gift be used to equip the new farms that were supposed to be established on the redistributed land.

Tiberius's reforms to help dispossessed farmers certainly had a political motive, as he had a score to settle with political rivals and expected to become popular with the people by serving as their champion. It would be overly cynical, however, to deny that he sympathized with his homeless fellow citizens. He famously said, "The wild beasts that roam over Italy have their dens. . . . But the men who fight and die for Italy enjoy nothing but the air and light; without house or home they wander about with their wives and children. . . . They fight and die to protect the wealth and luxury of others; they are styled masters of the world, and have not a clod of earth they can call their own" (Plutarch, *Life of Tiberius Gracchus* 9).

Just as unprecedented as his agrarian reforms was Tiberius's persuasion of the Assembly to throw another tribune out of office: he had been vetoing Tiberius's proposals for new laws. He then violated another longstanding prohibition of the "Roman constitution" when he announced his intention to stand for reelection as tribune for the following year; consecutive terms in office were regarded as "unconstitutional." Even some of his supporters now abandoned him for disregarding the "way of the elders."

What happened next signaled the beginning of the end for the political health of the Republic. An ex-consul named Scipio Nasica instigated a surprise attack on his cousin, Tiberius, by a group of senators and their clients. This upper-class mob clubbed Tiberius and some of his companions to death on the Capitoline Hill in late 133 B.C. In this bloody way began the sad history of violence and murder as a political tactic in the late Republic.

Gaius Gracchus, elected tribune in 123 B.C., and then again in 122 B.C. despite the traditional term limit, also initiated reforms that threatened the Roman elite. Gaius kept alive his brother's agrarian reforms and introduced laws to assure grain to Rome's citizens at subsidized prices. He also pushed through public works projects throughout Italy to provide employment for the poor and the foundation of colonies abroad to give citizens new opportunities for farming and trade. Most revolutionary of all were his proposals to give Roman citizenship to some Italians and to establish jury trials for senators accused of corruption as provincial governors. The citizenship proposal failed, but the creation of a new court system to prosecute senators became an intensely controversial issue because it threatened the power of the Senate to protect its own members and their families from punishment for their crimes.

The new juries were to be manned not by senators, but instead by members of the social class called *equites*, meaning "equestrians" or "knights." These were wealthy men who mainly came from the landed upper class with family origins and connections outside Rome proper. In the earliest Republic, the equestrians had been what the word suggests— men rich enough to provide their own horses for cavalry service. By this time, however, they had become a kind of second level of the upper class tending to concentrate more on business than on politics. Equestrians with ambitions for political office were often blocked by the dominant members of the Senate. Senators drew a status distinction between themselves and equestrians by insisting that it was improper for a senator to dirty his hands with commerce. A law passed by the tribune Claudius in 218 B.C., for instance, made it illegal for senators and their sons to own large-capacity cargo ships. Despite their public condemnation of profit-seeking activities, senators often did involve themselves in business in private. They masked their income from commerce by secretly employing intermediaries or favored slaves to do the work while passing on the profits.

Gaius's proposal to have equestrians serve on juries trying senators accused of extortion in the provinces marked the emergence of the equestrians as a political force in Roman politics. This threat to its power infuriated the Senate. Gaius then assembled a bodyguard to try to protect himself against the violence he feared from his senatorial enemies. The senators in 121 B.C. responded by issuing for the first time what is called an Ultimate Decree: a vote of the Senate advising the consuls to "take care that the Republic suffer no damage" (Julius Caesar, *Civil War* 1.5.7; Cicero, *Oration Against Catiline* 1.2). This extraordinary measure authorized the consul Opimius to use military force inside the city of Rome, where even officials possessing imperium traditionally had no such power. To escape arrest and execution, Gaius ordered one of his slaves to cut his throat for him.

The murder of Tiberius Gracchus and the forced suicide of Gaius Gracchus set in motion the final disintegration of the political solidarity of the Roman upper class. That both the brothers and their enemies came from that class revealed its inability to continue to govern through a consensus protecting its own unified interests as a group. From now on, members of the upper class increasingly saw themselves divided into either supporters of the *populares*, who sought political power by promoting the interests of the common people (*populus*), or as members of the *optimates*, the so-called "best people," meaning the traditional upper class, especially the nobles. Some political leaders identified with one side or the other out of genuine allegiance to the policies that it proclaimed. Others simply found it convenient to promote their personal political careers by pretending to be sincere proponents of the interests of one side or the other. In any case, this division within the Roman upper class persisted as a source of political unrest and murderous violence in the late Republic.

5

The Destruction of the Republic

The violent conflict that turned Rome's ruling elite against itself eventually destroyed the Republic. The process of destruction took a century, from the time of the Gracchus brothers' terms as tribunes to the civil wars of the second half of the first century B.C. The process was also an outgrowth of a perversion of the ancient Roman tradition of the mutual obligations of patrons and clients. This corruption of the "way of the elders" began in the late second century B.C., when the Roman state faced dangerous new threats that demanded immediate military responses under competent commanders. For one, seventy thousand slaves escaped from large estates in Sicily and banded together to launch a revolt that lasted from 134 to 131 B.C. In 112 B.C., an overseas war broke out with Jugurtha, a rebellious client king in North Africa. Another threat closer to home arose soon thereafter, when bands of invading Gallic warriors launched raid after raid in the northern regions of Italy.

The intensity of these dangers gave an opening for the emergence of a new kind of leader—the man not born into the privileged circle of the highest nobility at Rome, but who had the abilities and military skill to propel him to election as a consul and the great status and influence that this office brought with it. Men who

TIMELINE (ALL DATES B.C.)

107: Marius becomes a "new man" by winning election as consul; he is re-elected for a total of six consecutive terms.

91-87: The Romans and their allies in Italy fight each other in the Social War.

88: Sulla commands his Roman army to capture Rome.

88-85: The Romans fight the First Mithradatic War against King Mithradates VI of Pontus in Asia Minor.

63: Pompey captures Jerusalem; Catiline attempts to seize control of Roman government in a violent conspiracy.

60: Pompey, Crassus, and Julius Caesar form the First Triumvirate to dominate Roman government.

59: Julia, daughter of Julius Caesar, marries Pompey in a political alliance between the two rival leaders.

58–50: Julius Caesar fights the Gallic War to conquer Gaul (today France).

53: Political violence in Rome's streets prevents the election of consuls for the year.

50s: Lucretius composes his epic poem *On the Nature of Things*, which explains atomic theory to dispel the fear of death.

49: Julius Caesar crosses the Rubicon River into Italy, and civil war begins.

45: Julius Caesar has defeated all his opponents in the Civil War and gained control of Rome; in his will he adopts Octavian (the future Augustus).

44: Julius Caesar declares himself "Dictator Always" and is murdered on the Ides of March.

became consuls despite lacking a distinguished family history were called "new men." To gain the support that they needed to overcome the social prejudice against them, as military commanders these "new men" were especially generous to their soldiers in distributing booty and looking after their needs. Ordinary Roman soldiers, many of whom were poor, became more and more willing to follow such a commander as their patron, operating as his clients and more obedient to him personally than to the Senate or Assemblies. In this way, the patron-client system became more a way for leaders to gain great individual power than a support for the interests of the community as a whole.

This undermining of Roman tradition came at a time of national crises, with wars to fight both against Rome's Italian allies and the charismatic and clever King Mithradates in Asia Minor. A crushing blow to the

stability of the Republic came with the commander Sulla's violent dem-
onstration of his contempt for the ancient Roman value of placing one's
loyalty to the community above one's own desire for power and glory.
The ideal that the poet Lucilius had long ago expressed—put your own
interests last, after your country's and your family's—had lost its power
to inspire Rome's most ambitious leaders.

THE RISE OF THE "NEW MAN"

"New men" departed from the traditional Roman path to leadership,
by which men from famous old families expected to inherit their positions at the top of society and politics. The man who more than anyone
else put this new political force into motion was Gaius Marius (157 B.C.–
86 B.C.). From a family of the equestrian order in the town of Arpinum
in central Italy, in the earlier Republic Marius would have had little
chance of cracking the ranks of Rome's elite leadership, which had almost monopolized the office of consul. The best that a man of Marius's
origins could usually hope for in a public career was to advance to the
junior ranks of the Senate, as the dutiful client of a powerful noble. For-
tunately for Marius, however, Rome at the end of the second century B.C.
had a pressing need for men with his ability to lead an army to victory.
Marius made his reputation by serving with great distinction in the North
African war. He first made his way up the political ladder of elective offices by supporting the interests of noble patrons, and he also helped his
career by marrying above his social rank into a famous patrician family.
Finally, capitalizing both on his outstanding military record and also on
the ordinary people's dissatisfaction with the nobles' conduct of the war
against Jugurtha, Marius stunned the upper class by winning election as
one of the consuls for 107 B.C., thereby becoming a "new man." Marius
reached this pinnacle because his exceptional accomplishments as a general came at a time when Rome desperately needed military success. The
African war had dragged on through the incompetence of its generals
until Marius took over, but the most significant reason for Marius's reputation and popularity with the voters were his victories over the Celtic
peoples from the north called Teutones and Cimbri, who repeatedly tried
to invade Italy in the last years of the second century B.C. Remembering
with horror the sack of Rome by other northern "barbarians" in 387 B.C.,
Rome's voters by 100 B.C. had elected Marius as consul for an unprecedented six terms. His tenure in Rome's highest office included service in
consecutive terms, a practice previously considered "unconstitutional."
So famous was Marius that the Senate voted him a triumph, Rome's

Figure 13. These Roman soldiers shown standing in a religious procession have armor of the type used in the Republic; rectangular shields later became more common. Soldiers had to train energetically to maintain the strength needed to wield their heavy weapons effectively in their ordered ranks in battle. Marie-Lan Nguyen/Wikimedia Commons.

ultimate military honor, a rare recognition granted only to generals who had won stupendous victories. On the day of a triumph, the general rode through the streets of Rome in a military chariot. His face (or perhaps his entire body) was painted red for reasons that the Romans could no longer remember. Huge crowds cheered him on. His army traditionally shouted off-color jokes about him, perhaps to ward off the evil eye or remind him not to be overcome by a more than human pride at this moment of supreme glory. For the same reason, someone (perhaps a slave) stood behind him in the chariot and kept whispering in his ear a warning to avoid being corrupted by hubristic pride: "Look behind you, and remember that you are a mortal man" (Tertullian, *Apology* 33; Jerome, *Letters* 39.2.8). For someone with Marius's relatively humble background to be granted a triumph was a social coup of mammoth proportions.

Despite his triumph, Marius never achieved full acceptance by Rome's highest social elite. They saw him as an upstart and a threat to their preeminence. Marius's genuine support came from both wealthy equestrians and ordinary people. Equestrians probably supported his attempt to break into the nobility as a proof of the worth of men of their social class, but most of all they were concerned that the demonstrated incompetence of contemporary leaders from the senatorial class was having a disastrous effect on their economic interests abroad.

Marius's reform of entrance requirements for the army was the key factor in his popularity with the poorer ranks of Roman society. Previously, only citizens who owned property could enroll as soldiers—and therefore hope to win the rewards of status and plunder that soldiers could gain in victorious military campaigns. Proletarians, who by definition had no property, had been barred from becoming soldiers. Marius, completing a process that others had started earlier, had this bar removed so that even proletarians could enroll in the army. For these people who owned virtually nothing, the opportunity to better their lot by acquiring booty under a successful general more than outweighed the risk of the danger of being injured or killed in war.

The Roman state at this time provided no regular compensation or pensions to ex-soldiers. Their livelihood depended entirely on the success and the generosity of their general. By this time, there was no more conquered land in Italy to distribute to veterans, and taking land from provincials outside Italy was generally avoided as a way to avoid provoking open hostility to Roman control. Therefore, ordinary troops depended on a share of the booty seized in battle if they were to benefit financially from war. Since, if the general wished, he was entitled to keep the lion's share of booty for himself and his high-ranking officers, his common soldiers could end up with little. Impoverished as they were, proletarian troops naturally felt extraordinary gratitude to a commander who led them to victory and then made a generous division of the spoils with them. As a result, the legions' loyalty came more and more to be directed at their commander, not to the state. In other words, poor Roman soldiers began to behave as an army of clients following their general as a personal patron, whose commands they obeyed regardless of what the Senate wanted.

The Roman army was most likely also reorganized to fight with new tactics and improved weapons at this time. Legions were now composed of ten units of 480 men each, called "cohorts." Each cohort had six "centuries" of 80 men, commanded by a centurion. On the battlefield the soldiers faced the enemy in an arrangement of four cohorts in the front line, with two lines of three cohorts behind. Each cohort was separated by a gap from the others, and the two lines in the back were lined up in the gaps among the cohorts in the front line. This spacing gave the cohorts room for flexible movement in response to changing conditions during battle. For the first time, the Roman army was equipped with uniform weapons and equipment instead of whatever arms the individual soldiers brought with them. The main infantry carried heavy and light javelins, swords, and large oval—later rectangular—shields. Marius redesigned the heavy javelins so that they would bend after impact in an enemy's shield, thereby impeding his movement and making him easier to kill. After throwing their javelins, Roman soldiers rushed the enemy to use their swords in close-in fighting.

Marius deserves credit for increasing the fighting effectiveness of the Roman army by improving both tactical cohesiveness and flexibility, but his reforms had unforeseen consequences. The kind of client army that he created became a source of political power for unscrupulous commanders that destabilized the Republic politically. Marius himself, however, was too traditional to use a client army to maintain his own career. He lost his political importance soon after 100 B.C. because he was no longer commanding armies and had alienated many supporters by deferring to the upper class. His enemies among the *optimates* capitalized on his missteps to block him from exercising further political influence. Nevertheless, Marius had established a precedent for a general to achieve supreme political power by treating the soldiers as personal clients. Other leaders later on would extend this precedent to its logical conclusion: the general ruling Rome by himself, not as a member of a shared government in the old tradition of the Republic.

Long-standing tensions between Rome and its Italian allies erupted into war in the early first century B.C. By Roman tradition, these allies shared in the rewards of military victory. Since they were not Roman citizens, however, they had no voice in decisions concerning Roman domestic or foreign policy. This political disability made them increasingly unhappy as wealth from conquest piled up in Italy in the late Republic. The allies wanted a bigger share in the growing prosperity of the upper classes. Gaius Gracchus had seen the wisdom for the state of extending Roman citizenship to its loyal allies in Italy (and would, of course, also have increased his own power when the grateful new citizens became his clients). His enemies, however, had defeated Gracchus's proposal by convincing Roman voters that they would harm their own political and economic interests by granting citizenship to the Italian allies.

The allies' discontent finally erupted into violence in the Social War of 91 B.C.–87 B.C. (so called because the Latin word for "ally" is *socius*). The Italians formed a confederacy to fight Rome, minting their own coins to finance their violent rebellion. One ancient source claims 300,000 Italians died in battle. The Romans won the war, but the allies prevailed in the end because, to secure the peace, the Romans granted the Italians the citizenship for which they had begun their revolt. From then on, the freeborn peoples of Italy south of the Po River enjoyed the privileges of Roman citizenship. Most importantly, if their men made their way to

Rome, they could vote in the assemblies. The bloodshed of the Social War was the unfortunate price paid to reestablish Rome's early principle of seeking strength by admitting outsiders to membership in its community.

Rome's troubles as a ruler over others increased in this same period when provincials in Asia Minor rebelled. King Mithradates VI of Pontus was able to convince them to rebel above all because they so bitterly resented the notorious Roman tax collectors. The Roman state did not have officials to collect taxes. Instead, it subcontracted that task to private entrepreneurs through annual auctions. Whoever bid the largest amount for the revenue of a particular province received a contract to collect its taxes for that year. The contractor promised to deliver that amount to Rome and was then entitled to keep as profit whatever surplus could be squeezed out of the provincials. Groups of Romans from the equestrian class formed private companies to compete for these provincial tax contracts. The harder these tax collectors pressed the locals, the more money they made. And press they did. It is no wonder, then, that Mithradates found a sympathetic ear in Asia Minor for his charge that the Romans were "an affliction on the entire world" (Sallust, *Histories* 4 frag. 69). A superb organizer, he arranged for the rebels to launch a simultaneous surprise attack on Romans in many locations in Asia Minor on a preestablished date. They succeeded spectacularly, murdering tens of thousands in a single day. This crisis led to the First Mithradatic War (88 B.C.–85 B.C.), which Rome won only with great difficulty. It took two more wars before Mithradates's threat to Roman domination in this part of the world was finally ended.

The Social War and the threat from Mithradates brought to power a ruthless Roman noble, Lucius Cornelius Sulla, whose career further undermined the stabilizing effect of Roman tradition in keeping the community together. Sulla came from a patrician family that had lost much of its status and wealth. Anxious to restore his line's prestige and prosperity, Sulla first schemed to advance his career while serving under Marius against Jugurtha in North Africa. His military success against the allies in the Social War then propelled him to the prominence that he coveted: he won election as consul in 88 B.C. The Senate promptly rewarded him with the command against Mithradates in Asia Minor.

Marius, jealous of his former subordinate, plotted to have Sulla's command transferred to himself. Sulla's reaction to this setback showed that he understood the source of power that Marius had made possible by creating a client army. Instead of accepting the loss of the command, Sulla did the unthinkable: he marched his Roman army to attack Rome itself. All his officers except one, Lucullus, deserted him in horror at this treason. Sulla's ordinary soldiers, by contrast, all obeyed him. Neither they

Figure 14. This painting depicts soldiers armed in the style of the Samnites, an Italian people famous for their valor in war. Distinctive armor was important to warriors not just for combat but also to demonstrate their status and honor. Wikimedia Commons.

nor their commander shrank from starting a civil war. Capturing Rome with his Roman citizen troops, Sulla brutally killed or exiled his opponents. His men went on a rampage in the capital city. He then led them off to campaign in Asia Minor, ignoring a summons to stand trial.

After Sulla left Italy, Marius and his friends retook power in Rome and embarked on their own reign of terror. By employing violence to avenge violence, they bluntly demonstrated that Roman politics had become a literal war at home. Marius soon died, but his friends held undisputed power until 83 B.C., when Sulla returned to Italy after a successful campaign in Asia Minor. Another civil war followed when Sulla's enemies joined some of the Italians, especially the Samnites from central and southern Italy, to resist him. The climactic battle of the war took place in late 82 B.C. at the Colline Gate of Rome. The Samnite general whipped his troops into a frenzy against Sulla by shouting, "The final day is at hand for the Romans! These wolves that have so ravaged the freedom of the Italian peoples will never vanish until we have cut down the forest that harbors them" (Velleius Paterculus, *The Roman Histories* 17.2).

Unfortunately for the Samnites, they lost this battle and the war. Sulla then proceeded to exterminate them and give their territory to his supporters. He also terrorized his opponents at Rome by using a martial law measure called "proscription." This tactic meant posting a list of the names of people who were accused of treasonable crimes. Anyone could then hunt down and kill these people, with no trial necessary. The property of the "proscribed" was confiscated and distributed to the murderers. Sulla's supporters therefore added to the list the names of perfectly innocent citizens whose wealth they simply wanted to seize, under the pretext that they were punishing traitors. Terrified by Sulla's ruthlessness, the senators appointed him dictator, but without any limitation of term. This appointment was of course completely contrary to the Republic's tradition of limiting this office to short-term national emergencies.

Sulla used his unprecedented dictatorship to legitimize his reorganization of Roman government. He claimed that he was returning the Republic to the heart of its tradition by giving control to the "best people." He therefore made the Senate into the supreme power in the state. He also changed the composition of juries so that equestrians no longer judged senators. He severely weakened the office of plebeian tribune by prohibiting the tribunes from offering legislation without the prior approval of the Senate and barring any man who became a tribune from holding any other office thereafter. Minimum age limits were imposed for holding the various posts in the ladder of offices.

Convinced by an old prophecy that he had only a short time to live, Sulla retired to private life in 79 B.C. He in fact died the next year. His violent career had starkly revealed the changes in Roman social and political traditions by the time of the late Republic. First, success in war had come to mean profits for commanders and ordinary soldiers alike, primarily from selling prisoners of war into slavery and seizing booty. This profit incentive for waging war made it much harder to resolve problems peacefully. Many Romans were so poor that they preferred war to a life without prospects. Sulla's troops in 88 B.C. did not want to disband when the governing elite ordered them to do so because they had their eyes on the riches they hoped to win in a war against Mithradates. Second, the extension of the patron-client system to the military meant that poor soldiers felt stronger ties of obligation to their general, who acted as their patron, than to their country. Sulla's men obeyed his order to march on their own capital because they owed obedience to him as their patron and could expect benefits in return. Sulla benefited them by permitting the plundering of Rome and of the vast riches of Asia Minor.

Finally, the overwhelming desire on the part of the upper class to achieve public status worked both for and against the stability of the Republic. When this attitude motivated important men to seek office to promote the welfare of the population as a whole—the traditional ideal of a public career—it was a powerful force for social peace and general prosperity. But pushed to its logical extreme, as in the case of Sulla, an ambitious Roman's concern with personal standing based on individual prestige and wealth could overshadow all considerations of public service. Sulla in 88 B.C. simply could not bear to lose the glory and status that a victory over Mithradates would bring. He therefore chose to initiate a civil war rather than to see his cherished status diminished. For all these reasons, the Republic was doomed once its leaders and their followers abandoned the "way of the elders" that valued respect for the common peace and prosperity and for shared government above personal gain and individual political power. For all these reasons, Sulla's career reveals how the Republic's social and political traditions contained the seeds of its own destruction, as the balance of values between individual success and communal well-being that was supposed to guarantee Rome's safety and prosperity dissolved into violent conflict among Romans.

POMPEY THE GREAT AND JULIUS CAESAR

The famous generals whose ambitions sparked the war among Romans that destroyed the Republic took Sulla's career as their model: while proclaiming they were working to preserve the state, they sought power for themselves above all else. Gnaeus Pompey (106 B.C.–48 B.C.) was the first of these leaders. Pompey forced his way into the ranks of Roman leaders in 83 B.C. when Sulla was first returning to Italy. Only twenty-three years old, far too young for leadership according to Roman tradition, Pompey gathered a private army from his father's clients in Italy to join Sulla in his campaign to return to power in the capital. When Pompey defeated Sulla's remaining enemies, who had fled to Sicily and North Africa, Sulla in 81 B.C. reluctantly allowed Pompey the extraordinary honor of celebrating a triumph. The celebration of a triumph by such a young man, who had never held even a single public office, shattered the Republic's ancient tradition that men had to climb the ladder of offices before achieving such prominence. Pompey did not have to wait his turn for honor or earn his reward only after years of service. Because he was so powerful, he could demand his glory from Sulla on the spot. As Pompey brashly said to the older Sulla, "More people worship the rising than the setting sun" (Plutarch, *Life of Pompey* 14). The completely irregular nature of Pompey's career betrayed the flimsiness of Sulla's vision of the Roman state. Sulla had proclaimed a return to the rule of the "best people" and, according to him, Rome's finest political traditions. Instead, he had fashioned a regime controlled by violence and power politics.

The history of the rest of Pompey's career shows how the traditional checks and balances of politics in the Republic failed. After helping suppress a rebellion in Spain and a massive slave revolt in Italy led by the escaped gladiator Spartacus, Pompey demanded and received election as a consul for 70 B.C., well before he had reached the legal age of forty-two. Three years later, he was voted a command with unprecedented powers to fight the pirates currently infesting the shipping lanes of the Mediterranean Sea. He smashed them in a matter of months. This success made him wildly popular with the urban poor at Rome, who depended on a steady flow of grain imported by sea and subsidized by the state; with the wealthy merchants, who depended on safe sea transport for their goods; and with coastal communities everywhere, which suffered from the pirates' raids. The next year the command against Mithradates, who was still causing trouble in Asia Minor, was taken away from the general Lucullus so it could be given to Pompey. Lucullus had made himself unpopular with his troops by curbing their looting of the province and with the tax collectors by regulating their extortion of the defenseless provincials. Pompey proceeded to conquer Asia Minor and other eastern lands in a series of bold campaigns. He marched as far south as Jerusalem, the capital and religious center of the Jews, which he captured in 63 B.C. When Pompey then annexed Syria as a province, he initiated Rome's formal control of that part of southwestern Asia.

Pompey's conquests in the eastern Mediterranean were spectacular. People compared him to Alexander the Great, and he was awarded the name Magnus, making him "Pompey the Great." He boasted that he had caused Rome's revenues from its provinces to skyrocket, and distributed money equal to twelve and a half years' pay to his soldiers as their share of the booty. During his time in the east he operated largely on his own initiative. He never consulted the Senate when he made new political arrangements for the territory that he had conquered. For all practical purposes, he behaved like an independent king and not an official of the Roman Republic. Early in his career, he expressed the attitude that he relied on throughout his life: when some foreigners objected to his treatment as unjust, he replied, "Stop quoting the laws to us. We carry swords" (Plutarch, *Life of Pompey* 10).

The great military successes that Pompey won made his upper-class rivals at Rome both resent and fear him. Principal among them were two highly ambitious men, the fabulously wealthy Marcus Licinius Crassus, who had defeated the rebel slave leader Spartacus, and the young Julius Caesar (100–44 B.C.). To gain support against Pompey, they promoted themselves as *populares*, leaders dedicated to improving the lives of ordinary people. There was much to improve. The population of the city of Rome had soared to perhaps a million persons. Hundreds of thousands of its residents lived crowded together in shabby apartment buildings no better than slums. Work was hard to find. Many people subsisted on the grain distributed by the government. The streets of the city were dangerous, and Rome had no police force. To make matters worse, economic conditions by the 60s B.C. had become especially precarious, probably as the result of a bust following a boom in the value of property. Sulla's confiscations of land and buildings by proscription had evidently created a much more speculative real estate market. Now, the market was flooded with mortgaged properties for sale, and prices were crashing. Credit seems to have been in short supply at this very time when those in financial difficulties over their property were trying to borrow their way back to respectability. Whatever their exact cause, these financial problems made life difficult and stressful even for many members of the equestrian and senatorial classes.

The conspiracy of Lucius Sergius Catilina in 63 B.C. reveals to what lengths the problems of debt and poverty could drive desperate members of the upper class. Catiline, as he is known, was a debt-ridden noble who rallied around himself a band of fellow upper-class debtors and victims of Sulla's confiscations. Frustrated in his attempts to win election as a consul, he planned to use violence to achieve political power, with the announced goal of then redistributing wealth and property to his supporters after achieving victory. Cicero, one of the two consuls in 63 B.C., thwarted the plotters before they could murder him and the other consul. Catiline and his co-conspirators probably never had a realistic chance of redressing their grievances, even if they had seized the state, because the only way to redistribute property would have been to kill currently solvent property owners. Nevertheless, their futile effort demonstrates the level of violence that became typical of Roman politics in the mid-first century B.C.

When Pompey returned to Rome from the eastern Mediterranean in 62 B.C., the "best people" among the political leaders refused, out of jealousy of his fame, to support his territorial arrangements or authorize the distribution of land as a reward to the veterans of his army. This setback forced Pompey to make a political alliance with Crassus and Caesar. These three in 60 B.C. formed an informal troika, commonly called the First Triumvirate ("Association of Three Men") to advance their own interests. They succeeded. Pompey got laws to confirm his eastern arrangements and give land to his veterans. Caesar was made consul for 59 B.C., receiving a special extended command in Gaul. Crassus got financial breaks for the Roman tax collectors in Asia Minor, whose support helped guarantee his political prominence and in whose profitable business he had a stake. This coalition of former political opponents provided each triumvir (member of the triumvirate) a means to achieve his own ambitions: Pompey wanted status from fulfilling his role as patron to his troops and to the territories that he had conquered, Caesar had an enormous ambition to gain the highest political office and the chance to win glory and booty from foreigners, and Crassus wanted to help his clients and himself financially so that he could remain politically competitive with the other two, whose reputations as generals far exceeded his. The First Triumvirate was a political creation that ignored the "Roman constitution." It was formed only for the advantage of its members. Because they shared no common philosophy of governing, however, the triumvirs' cooperation was destined to last only as long as they continued to profit personally from this tradition-shattering arrangement.

Recognizing the instability of their coalition, the triumvirs used a time-tested tactic to try to give it permanence: they contracted politically motivated marriages among one another. Women were the pawns traded back and forth in these alliances. In 59 B.C., Caesar married his daughter Julia to Pompey. She had been engaged to another man, but her father made this marriage take precedence over her previous commitment in order to create a bond between himself and Pompey. Pompey simultaneously soothed Julia's jilted fiancé by having the man marry Pompey's daughter, who had been engaged to yet somebody else. Through these marital machinations, the two powerful antagonists now had a common interest: the fate of Julia, Caesar's only daughter and Pompey's new wife. (He had divorced his second wife after Caesar allegedly had seduced her.) Despite their arranged marriage, Pompey and Julia by all reports fell deeply in love. So long as Julia lived, Pompey's affection for her helped to restrain him from an outright break with her father, Caesar. But when she died in childbirth in 54 B.C. (and her baby soon after), the bond linking Pompey and Caesar ruptured beyond repair.

Julius Caesar was born to one of Rome's most distinguished families; it claimed the goddess Venus as an ancestor. The intensity of Caesar's ambitions matched the luster of his origins. He borrowed and spent huge sums of money to promote his political career and compete with Pompey to be Rome's premier leader. As triumvir he left Rome to take up a command in Gaul in 58 B.C. For the next nine years he attacked people after people throughout what is now France, the western part of Germany, and even the southern end of Britain. The value of the slaves and booty that his army won was so huge that he was able not only to pay off his enormous debts but also enrich his soldiers. For this reason, his troops loved him, but also for his easy manner when talking with them and his willingness to undergo all the hardships and deprivations that they experienced on military campaign. His political rivals at Rome feared him even more as his military successes in Gaul mounted, while his supporters tried to prepare the ground for a safe and triumphant return to Rome.

The rivalry between Caesar's friends and enemies at Rome culminated in bloodshed. By the mid-fifties B.C., politically motivated gangs of young men roamed the city's streets, prowling for opponents to beat or murder. The street fighting reached such a pitch in 53 B.C. that it was impossible to hold elections, and no consuls were chosen for the year. The triumvirate fell apart that same year with the death of Crassus. In an attempt to win the military glory his career lacked, Crassus had led a Roman army across the Euphrates River to fight the Parthians, an Iranian people whose military aristocracy headed by a king ruled a vast territory stretching from the Euphrates to the Indus River. When Crassus died in battle at Carrhae in northern Mesopotamia, the alliance between Pompey and Caesar also came to an end. In 52 B.C., Caesar's enemies succeeded in having Pompey appointed as sole consul for the year, an outrage against the traditions and values of the "Roman constitution." When Caesar prepared to return to Rome in 49 B.C., he too wanted a special arrangement to protect himself: to be made consul for 48 B.C.

The response of the Senate to Caesar's demand was to order him to surrender his command. Instead, Caesar, like Sulla before him, led his army against Rome. As he crossed the Rubicon River in northern Italy in early 49 B.C., he uttered (in Greek) the words that signaled the start of a civil war: "Let's roll the dice!" (Plutarch, *Life of Julius Caesar* 39, *Life of Pompey* 60; Appian, *Civil War* 2.35; Suetonius, *Life of Julius Caesar* 32 has "The die is cast!"). His troops followed him without hesitation, and most of the people of the towns and countryside of Italy cheered him on enthusiastically. He had many backers in Rome, too, especially those to whom he had lent money or given political support. Some of those who were glad to hear of his coming were ruined nobles, who hoped to recoup their once-great fortunes by backing Caesar against the rich. These were in fact the people whom Caesar had always refused to help politically or financially, saying to them, "What you need is a civil war!" (Suetonius, *Life of Julius Caesar* 27).

The enthusiastic response of the masses to Caesar's advance surprised Pompey and the rest of Caesar's enemies in the Senate. In a panic, they transported the soldiers loyal to them to Greece for training before facing Caesar's more experienced troops. Caesar entered Rome peacefully, but soon departed to defeat the army that his enemies had in Spain. In 48 B.C. he then sailed across the Adriatic Sea to Greece to force a decisive battle with Pompey. There he nearly lost the war when Pompey cut off his supplies with a blockade. But Caesar's loyal soldiers stuck with him even when they were reduced to eating awful bread made from forest grasses and roots mixed with milk. When Caesar's men ran up to Pompey's outposts and threw some of their primitive food over the wall while shouting out that they would never stop fighting so long as the earth produced roots for them to gnaw, Pompey said in horror, "I am fighting wild animals!" (Suetonius, *Life of Julius Caesar* 68). He prevented the food from being shown to his troops, fearing that his men would lose their courage if they found how out how tough Caesar's soldiers were.

The high morale of Caesar's army and Pompey's surprisingly weak generalship eventually combined to bring Caesar a crushing victory at the battle of Pharsalus in central Greece in 48 B.C. Pompey fled to Egypt, where he was treacherously murdered by the ministers of the boy-king Ptolemy XIII, who had earlier exiled his sister and wife, Queen Cleopatra VII, and had supported Pompey in the war. Caesar won a difficult campaign in Egypt that ended with the drowning of the pharaoh in the Nile and the return to the Egyptian throne of Cleopatra, who had begun a love affair with the Roman conqueror. He next had to spend three years in hard fighting against enemies in Asia Minor, North Africa, and Spain. In writing to a friend about one of his victories in this period of frequent battles, he penned his famous three words: *Veni, vidi, vici* ("I came, I saw, I conquered!" Suetonius, *Life of Julius Caesar* 37). By 45 B.C. there was no one left to face him on the battlefield.

The field of politics proved to be more dangerous for Julius Caesar than the battlefield. After his victory in the civil war, Caesar faced the dilemma of how to govern a politically fractured Rome. The problem confronting him had deep roots. Recent experience seemed to show that only a sole ruler could put an end to the chaotic violence of the divided politics of first-century B.C. Rome. The oldest upper-class tradition of the Republic, however, was hatred for monarchy. Cato the Elder had expressed this feeling best: "A king," he quipped, "is a beast that feeds on human flesh" (Plutarch, *Life of Cato the Elder* 8).

Caesar's solution to the dilemma was to rule as a king in everything but name. He began by having himself appointed dictator in 48 B.C. By 44 B.C., he had removed any limitation on his term in this traditionally temporary office, becoming, as his coins expressed it, "Dictator Always" (*dictator perpetuo*; see Crawford nos. 480/6ff.). He insisted that "I am called Caesar, not King" (Plutarch, *Life of Julius Caesar* 60), but the distinction was truly meaningless. As dictator without any limit of time to his term in the office, he personally controlled the government despite the appearance of normal procedures. It is unclear what kind of government Caesar expected to exist in the long term. With no son of his own, in September 45 B.C. he had made a new will designating his grandnephew Gaius Octavius (63 B.C.-A.D. 14) his heir and adopted son. As was customary upon adoption, the young man changed the ending of his name Octavius to Octavian, the name by which he is known today in the period before he eventually became Rome's first emperor as Augustus. Whether Caesar himself somehow expected Octavius in time to take over as ruler of Rome is not recorded.

In the meantime, elections for offices continued, but Caesar determined the results by recommending candidates to the assemblies, which his supporters dominated. Naturally his recommendations were followed. His policies as Rome's sole ruler were ambitious and broad. He reduced debt moderately, limited the number of people eligible for subsidized grain, initiated a large program of public works including the construction of public libraries, established colonies for his veterans in Italy and abroad, rebuilt and repopulated Corinth and Carthage to become commercial centers, proclaimed standard constitutions for Italian towns, and extended citizenship to non-Romans, such as the Gauls in northern Italy. He also admitted non-Italians to the Senate when he expanded its membership from six hundred to nine hundred. Unlike Sulla, he did not proscribe his enemies. Instead, he prided himself on his clemency, whose recipients were, by Roman tradition, obliged to become his grateful clients. In return, Caesar received unprecedented honors, such as a special golden seat in the Senate House and the renaming of the seventh month of the year after him (*Julius*, hence its name, July). He also regularized the Roman calendar by initiating a year of 365 days, which was based on an ancient Egyptian calendar and forms the basis for the modern calendar.

Julius Caesar's dictatorship and his honors pleased most ordinary people but outraged the "best people." This upper-class group saw themselves as largely excluded from power and dominated by one of their own, who, they believed, had deserted to the other side in the perpetual conflict between the Republic's rich and poor. A band of nobles conspired to

Figure 15. A coin shows Brutus, one of the conspirators who murdered Julius Caesar, and symbols of the "liberation" they claimed to perform on the Ides of March 44 B.C. The daggers implied that violence was justified to remove a tyrant, while the cap symbolized the freedom from tyranny that the conspirators believed they restored through their deed. Photo courtesy of Classical Numismatic Group, Inc./www.cngcoins.com.

stab Caesar to death in 44 B.C. on 15 March (the Ides of March, as that day was called in the Roman calendar). The "Liberators," as the conspirators against Caesar called themselves, had no specific plans for governing Rome following the murder. They apparently believed that the traditional political system of the Republic would somehow resume without any further action on their part and without more violence. This faith can only be called simple-minded, to say the least. These self-styled champions of traditional Roman liberty were ignoring the disruptive effect of the turbulent history of the previous forty years from the time of Sulla. In fact, rioting broke out at the funeral of Caesar when the masses vented their anger against the upper class that had robbed them of their hero. Far from presenting a united front, the nobles resumed their struggles with one another to secure political power. Another civil war of great ferocity began following Caesar's death. The Republic, plainly, had been damaged beyond repair by this date. From the ashes of this struggle gradually emerged the disguised monarchy—that we call the Roman Empire but the Romans still called the Republic—under which the rest of Rome's history would unroll in the centuries to come.

It seems fitting to close with a glance at the stark realism of literature and of sculptural portraiture in this violent period because it can hardly be an accident that they appear to reflect the strain and the sadness of social and political life in a Republic that was committing suicide. Historians must necessarily be cautious about postulating overly specific connections between authors' and artists' works and the events of their times because the sources of creativity are so diverse. There is no doubt, however, that contemporary literature directly reflected on the catastrophe of the late Republic. In the work of other creative artists, such as sculptors of portraits, we can suspect a connection to the tumultuous and depressing conditions of the times.

Contemporary references to events and leading personalities in Rome appear in the poems of Catullus (c. 84 B.C.–54 B.C.). He moved to Rome from his home in the province of Cisalpine Gaul in northern Italy, where his family had been prominent enough to host Julius Caesar when he had been governor there. That connection did not prevent Catullus from including Caesar among the politicians of the era whose sexual behavior he made fun of with his witty and explicit poetry. Catullus also wrote poems on more timeless themes, love above all. He employed a literary style popular among a circle of poets who modeled their Latin poems on the elegant Greek poetry of Hellenistic-era authors such as Callimachus. Catullus's most famous series of love poems concerned his passion for a married woman named Lesbia, whom he begged to think only of the

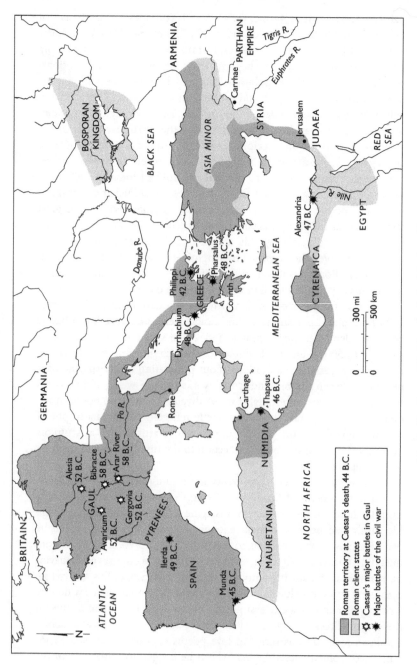

ATLANTIC
OCEAN

BRITAIN

GERMANIA

Alesia
52 B.C. ☆
GAUL   Bibracte
Avaricum 58 B.C. ☆
52 B.C. ☆ Arar River
Gergovia 58 B.C.
52 B.C. ☆

Ilerda
49 B.C. ★
SPAIN

Munda
45 B.C. ★

PYRENEES

Po R.

Rome

Carthage
NUMIDIA
Thapsus
46 B.C. ★

MAURETANIA

NORTH AFRICA

Danube R.

BOSPORAN
KINGDOM

BLACK SEA

ASIA MINOR

GREECE
Philippi
42 B.C. ★
Pharsalus
48 B.C. ★
Corinth
Dyrrhachium
48 B.C. ★

MEDITERRANEAN SEA

CYRENAICA

ARMENIA

Carrhae •

PARTHIAN
EMPIRE

Tigris R.

Euphrates R.

SYRIA

Jerusalem •
JUDAEA

Nile R.

Alexandria
47 B.C.

EGYPT

RED
SEA

N

Roman territory at Caesar's death, 44 B.C.

Roman client states

☆ Caesar's major battles in Gaul

★ Major battles of the civil war

300 mi
0

500 km
0

Map 6. The Roman World at the End of the Republic

pleasures of the present: "Let us live, my Lesbia, and love, and value at one penny all the talk of stern old men. Suns can set and rise again: we, when once our brief light has set, must sleep one never-ending night. Give me a thousand kisses, then a hundred, then a thousand more . . ." (Poem 5). Catullus's call to live for the moment, paying no attention to conventional moral standards, suited this period when the turmoil at Rome could make the concerns of ordinary life seem irrelevant.

The many prose works of Cicero, the master of rhetoric, also often directly concerned events of his time. Fifty-eight of his speeches survive in the revised versions he published, and their eloquence and clarity established the style that later European prose authors tried to match when writing polished Latin—the common language of government, theology, literature, and science throughout Europe for the next thousand years and more. Cicero also wrote many letters to his family and friends in which he commented frankly on political infighting and his motives in pursuing his own self-interest. The nine hundred surviving letters offer a vivid portrait of Cicero's political ideas, joys, sorrows, worries, pride, and love for his daughter. For no other figure from the ancient world do we have such copious and revealing personal material.

During periods when Cicero had to withdraw temporarily from public affairs because his political opponents threatened his safety, he wrote numerous works on political science, philosophy, ethics, and theology. Taking his inspiration mainly from Greek philosophers, Cicero adapted their ideas to Roman life and infused his writings on these topics with a deep understanding of the need to appreciate the uniqueness of each human personality. His doctrine of *humanitas* ("humanness, the quality of humanity") combined various strands of Greek philosophy, especially Stoicism, to express an ideal for human life based on generous and honest treatment of others and an abiding commitment to morality derived from natural law (the rights that exist for all people by nature, independent of the differing laws and customs of different societies). This ideal exercised a powerful and enduring influence on later Western ethical philosophy. Cicero's philosophical thought and the style of his Latin prose, not his political career, made him a central figure in the transmission to later ages of perhaps the most attractive ideal to come from ancient Greece and Rome.

The poet Lucretius (c. 94 B.C.–55 B.C.) provides an example of an author indirectly reflecting the uncertainty and violence of his times. By explaining the nature of matter as composed of tiny, invisible particles called atoms, his long poem *On the Nature of Things* sought to end people's fear of death, which, in his words, served only to feed "the running sores of life." Death, his poem taught, simply meant the dissolving of the union of atoms, which had come together temporarily to make up a person's body. There could be no eternal punishment or pain after death, indeed no existence at all, because a person's soul, itself made up of atoms, perished along with the body. Lucretius took this so-called atomic theory of the nature of existence from the work of the Greek philosopher Epicurus (341 B.C.–270 B.C.), whose views on the atomic character of matter were in turn derived from the work of the fifth-century B.C. thinkers Leucippus and Democritus. Although we do not know when he began to compose his poem, Lucretius was still working on it at Rome during the 50s B.C., when politically motivated violence added a powerful new threat to life in Rome. Romans in Lucretius's time had good reason to need reassurance that death had no sting.

We can also speculate that the starkly realistic style of Roman portraiture of men in the first century B.C. expressed the recognition of life's harshness in this violence-plagued period. The many Roman portraits of individual men that survive from this era did not try to hide unflattering facial features and expressions. Long noses, receding chins, deep wrinkles, bald heads, tired and worn faces—all these appeared in sculpted portraits. The Roman upper-class tradition of making death masks of ancestors and displaying them in their homes presumably contributed to this style of portraiture. Portraits of women from the period, by contrast, were generally more idealized, and children were not portrayed until the early Empire. Since either the men depicted by the portraits or their families paid for these portraits in stone, they must have wanted their hard experience of life to show in their faces. It is hard not to imagine that this insistence on realism mirrored the toll exacted on men who participated in the brutal arena of politics in the late Republic. These men had lived in the period that saw the final corruption of the finest values and ideals of the Republic. In their time a new ideal had emerged: that a Roman leader could never have too much glory or too much money, goals that trumped the tradition of public service to the commonwealth. The strain on their faces reflected the stress and sadness that the destruction of the Republic inflicted on so many Romans.

6

From Republic to Empire

The Roman Empire—the name commonly used today for the system of government that replaced the Republic—was born in blood: fourteen years of civil war followed Caesar's assassination in 44 B.C., until Octavian finally came off victorious over every rival. A few years later, in 27 B.C.—the same date as he took the new name Augustus—he founded a new political system that prevented a renewal of the violence. He said he was restoring and improving the Republic and was not a monarch; modern historians regard the government of the Roman Empire as a disguised monarchy and refer to its rulers as "emperors." Whatever one calls Augustus's system of rule, it is undeniable that he ended decades of civil war by concentrating power in the hands of one ruler—himself—and reinventing the traditional value of loyalty. Under his system, citizens directed their faithfulness to the ruler and his family as the embodiment of the Roman state. Augustus retained traditional institutions of Roman government—the Senate, the ladder of offices, assemblies, courts—while ruling as an emperor but without claiming that title. Instead, he masked the new reality by referring to his position as that of *princeps* ("First Man"), not "king" or "dictator" (Tacitus, *Annals* 1.9). Augustus justified his transformation of the Republic by cloaking it in tradition, explain-

TIMELINE (DATES B.C. AND A.D. AS INDICATED)

43 B.C.: Octavian, nineteen years old, forces the Senate to recognize him as consul; Octavian, Lepidus, and Mark Antony form the Second Triumvirate to dominate Roman government.

42 B.C.: The Triumvirs defeat the self-proclaimed "Liberators" (the conspirators against Julius Caesar) at Philippi in Greece.

32 B.C.: To combat the alliance of Cleopatra and Antony, Octavian has the citizens in Italy and the western provinces swear an oath of loyalty to him personally.

31 B.C.: Octavian's fleet defeats the navy of Cleopatra and Antony in the sea battle of Actium off the northwestern coast of Greece.

27 B.C.: Octavian creates the Principate as the "Restored Republic," which we call the Roman Empire; the Senate honors him with the title *Augustus* ("Divinely Favored"); Augustus stations soldiers (the Praetorian Guard) in Rome for the first time in Roman history.

19 B.C.: On his deathbed Vergil asks for the *Aeneid* to be destroyed, but Augustus has the epic poem preserved.

8 B.C.: Augustus exiles the poet Ovid for his scandalous poetry.

2 B.C.: The Senate honors Augustus with the title "Father of his Country"; the Forum of Augustus opens in the center of Rome.

A.D. 9: Varus is defeated in Germany with the loss of three legions, ending Augustus's plans for northern expansion.

A.D. 14: Augustus dies after forty-one years as *princeps* ("First Man"), the position that we call "Roman emperor."

ing that his changes rebuilt the old system to the way it could and should have existed.

Augustus established his "new old Republic" gradually; inventing tradition takes time. He began his career as a young man who stopped at nothing in pursuing vengeance and power; he ended it as an old man who had brought peace to Rome at home, created a professional standing army, established a limit to Rome's provincial territory that its military could successfully defend, beautified the capital city, supported painters and sculptors, improved the life of the urban masses, used all available media to communicate an image of himself as a successful and generous ruler, and tried to reshape Roman attitudes toward marriage and offspring to preserve the upper class. The changes that he introduced to Roman life have led historians to give the label "the Augustan Age" to the opening decades of the Roman Empire. Despite centuries of scholarship, it is still difficult to understand fully Augustus's motives for doing what he did.

THE "RESTORATION" OF THE REPUBLIC

The civil wars to decide who would govern Rome following Caesar's murder provided the historical context for the transformation of the Republic into the Empire. The original competitors for power in this war were Mark Antony and Lepidus, both experienced generals, and Octavian (not yet known as Augustus), Caesar's nineteen-year-old grandnephew and a military novice, whose new identity as Caesar's son earned him the loyalty of those who had loved Caesar, especially his soldiers. As a student in Greece in 44 B.C., Octavian could compete with Antony and Lepidus only because his adoptive father's military veterans supported him, expecting him to give them rewards from their dead general's riches. Octavian led them to fight against Antony in northern Italy, but after an initial victory he marched men to Rome. The teenager, with his troops at his back, demanded to be made consul for 43 B.C., despite having never before held any public office. As with Pompey, fear made the senators grant Octavian this greatest of exceptions from the tradition of the ladder of offices.

Soon thereafter Octavian joined forces with Antony and Lepidus to wage yet more civil war against various rivals in Italy. They defeated all opposition, especially the "Liberators." In November 43 B.C., the trio formed the so-called Second Triumvirate, which they forced the Senate to recognize as an official emergency arrangement for reconstituting the state. They ruthlessly used Sulla's tactic of proscription to suppress their enemies, even betraying their own family members as they made deals with each other about whom to murder. They defeated the army of the "Liberators" at the battle of Philippi in northern Greece in 42 B.C. Antony and Octavian then conspired to push Lepidus into a lesser role, placating him with the governorship of northern Africa but depriving him of any real say in determining the future of Rome.

Octavian and Antony essentially divided the control of Roman territory between themselves, with Octavian controlling Italy and the west and Antony the eastern Mediterranean territories, including the rich land of Egypt. Over the following years these two then gradually turned openly hostile to one another. Antony joined forces with Cleopatra VII, the queen of Egypt. Through her wit and intelligence, she made Antony her ally and her lover. In response to this formidable alliance, Octavian rallied Romans by claiming Antony planned to make Cleopatra their foreign ruler. He

Figure 16. This coin depicts Cleopatra VII, queen of Egypt, and Mark Antony, Roman general, whom Octavian (the future Augustus) defeated in the sea battle of Actium in 31 B.C. Greek kings after Alexander the Great had customarily put their portraits on coins, but under the Republic no Roman leader had done so before Julius Caesar; the Roman emperors made it a tradition to have their portraits on the front sides of their coins. Photo courtesy of Classical Numismatic Group, Inc./www.cngcoins.com.

transformed the residents of Italy and the western provinces into his clients by having them swear an oath of loyalty to him in 32 B.C. Octavian's victory over Cleopatra and Antony at a naval battle off Actium in northwest Greece in 31 B.C. won the war. The lovers fled to Egypt, where they committed suicide in 30 B.C.; Cleopatra famously ended her life by allowing a poisonous snake, a symbol of royal authority, to bite her. Octavian's capture of the resource-rich kingdom of Egypt made him Rome's unrivaled leader and its wealthiest citizen by far.

After distributing land to army veterans to create settlements loyal to him, Octavian in 27 B.C. announced publicly that he was restoring the Republic. He proclaimed that it was up to the Senate and the Roman people to decide how to preserve their government from this point forward. Recognizing that Octavian possessed overwhelming power in this unprecedented situation, the Senate begged him to do whatever was necessary to safeguard the restored Republic. To recognize his special status, they bestowed on him the honorary name of *Augustus* ("Divinely Favored"), which he accepted. Octavian had originally thought of changing his name to Romulus, to emphasize that he was a second founder of Rome, but he decided that the name of a king, no matter how treasured, was too politically dangerous.

The system of rule devised by Augustus is today called the Principate, from his title as *princeps*. This choice of "First Man" as a title was a brilliant move. In the Republic, that honorary designation had been awarded to the senator with the highest status, the leader other senators looked to for guidance. By using this title, Augustus implicitly claimed to carry on one of the Republic's most valued traditions. Moreover, to appear to continue the Republic's respect for the Senate, he insisted that he served as princeps only at the request of the senators. Periodically, he had them renew a formal approval of his status by granting him the powers of a consul and a tribune without holding the offices. In this way, the compliant senators granted the princeps what amounted to the power of an emperor, but they camouflaged the concession by claiming that this was all just a restoration, and that the Principate system was indeed an improvement in keeping with the traditions of the Republic. The ceremony of rule also remained traditional: Augustus dressed and acted like a regular citizen, not a monarch ranked socially above everyone else. His new powers were described in terms familiar to and respected by citizens, conveying the sense that nothing much was changing. In truth, Augustus revised the basic power structure of Roman politics: no official before him could ever have possessed the powers of both consul and tribune simultaneously.

In the years after 27 B.C., the continuing annual elections of consuls and other officials, the existence of the Senate, and the passing of legislation in the Assemblies maintained the appearance of a Republic. In reality, Augustus exercised power because he controlled the army and the treasury. Augustus reconfigured these institutions to secure his power: he changed the army from a citizen militia into a permanent, standing force and used imperial revenues to guarantee the soldiers' pay. He established regular lengths of service for soldiers and a substantial bonus at retirement. To pay the added costs, Augustus imposed an inheritance tax. This direct tax on citizens, a rarity in Roman history, affected the rich, who deeply resented it.

Augustus's changes made clear the ruler's role as the army's patron. The soldiers in gratitude obeyed and protected him. He sent a military expedition to expand Roman rule into what it is today Germany, but the mission's three legions were wiped out in a disastrous ambush in A.D. 9 in the Teutoburg Forest. Augustus, in despair over his fear of rebellions and attacks and the damage from losing so many men, stopped shaving or cutting his hair for months, wandering around his house in Rome and banging his head against a door while screaming against the expedition's fallen commander: "Quinctilius Varus, give me back my legions!" (Suetonius, *Life of Augustus* 23). Concluding that further expansion was too dangerous, he now concentrated on having the army defend the existing perimeter of the Empire. Later emperors never gave up the dream of winning booty and glory by extending Roman territory, but none was ever able to maintain control of substantial new areas for long. Most of the army was stationed far from Rome in the provinces to provide security against internal rebellions or invasions from outside the imperial frontier zones. In the long run, as we will see, this transformation of the army into what amounted to a large-scale garrison force was to have terrible consequences for the financial stability of the Roman Empire.

Beginning in 27 B.C., for the first time in Roman history Augustus also stationed soldiers in Rome itself, called praetorians from their original role of being stationed as bodyguards close to a commander's tent (*praetorium*) in the field. These troops formed the main imperial guard, though the emperor also had a small force of German mercenaries as his personal protectors, loyal only to him. The Praetorian Guard, along with these foreign bodyguards, provided a visible reminder that the ruler's superiority was in reality guaranteed by the threat of force, not just by his moral authority derived from his respect for traditional Roman values.

Communicating the emperor's image as a successful leader and a generous patron was essential in promoting the stability of the new system. Augustus brilliantly used media as small as coins and as large as buildings to achieve this goal. As the only mass-produced source of official messages, coins could function something like the political advertising on modern billboards or bumper stickers. Augustus's coins proclaimed slogans such as "Restorer of Liberty" to remind people of his claim to have brought back the Republic, or "Roads Have Been Built," to emphasize his spending his own funds to pay for highway construction.

Augustus's building program in Rome proved his commitment to the traditional obligation of the rich to use their money for the public good. He paid for huge and highly decorated buildings, using the vast fortune he had inherited from Julius Caesar and then increased through the confiscations of the civil wars and replenished with the spoils that he won in Egypt. These building projects certainly improved public facilities, but more than that, they communicated an image of the emperor as pious, caring, and generous. The huge new forum (a public square near the old Roman Forum) that Augustus paid for in the center of the city illustrates his brilliant skill in sending messages with bricks, stone, and statues. The Forum of Augustus, formally opened in 2 B.C., centered on a temple to Mars, the Roman god of war, and Venus, the Roman goddess of love, whom he claimed as his divine ancestor. Augustus built the temple to thank the gods for the victory against the forces of Caesar's assassins. He displayed Julius Caesar's sword in the temple as a memorial to his adoptive father. Two-story colonnades stretched out from the temple like wings, sheltering statues of famous Roman heroes, to serve as inspirations to citizens. The Forum of Augustus also provided practical space for religious services and the ceremonies marking the passage into adulthood of upper-class boys. Most of all, it also showed the emperor's devotion to the gods who protected Rome in war and the begetting of offspring, respect for history's moral lessons, and unselfishness in spending money for public purposes. Augustus built his personal house on the Palatine Hill, where he lived in well-publicized simplicity and modesty as an "ordinary citizen." Later emperors failed to follow his example, building mammoth palaces on the same hill, overlooking the Circus Maximus. There chariot racing, one of Rome's favorite forms of public entertainment, took place before crowds of as many as two hundred thousand spectators.

Augustus himself produced a document that stands as the most significant single piece of evidence for understanding the image that he wished to present. During his long rule, he worked on a long written statement describing his accomplishments. He ordered this document to be widely published after his death, and versions were therefore inscribed in public places around the empire. Known today as the *Res Gestae* ("Things Done; Achievements"), it was a first-person description of his deeds as Rome's

Figure 17. This cameo portrays Augustus, the first Roman emperor, in the company of the gods, with scenes below of Roman soldiers piling up weapons of conquered barbarians. The two-level image expresses the supreme status that Augustus claimed and the superior power that his rule bestowed on Rome. Andreas Praefcke/Wikimedia Commons.

leader and his huge personal spending for the common good. He consistently emphasized that his spectacular career had been in keeping with the traditions of the Republic: as a teenager he organized a personal army to avenge his (second) father and defend the liberty of the Republic; as victor in the civil war he refused the title of dictator when it was offered. The only position he held was that of princeps; he spent gigantic amounts of his own money to help the people; and he gained his leading position in the state not through formal power but only from the great respect that he earned for his display of traditional virtues.

Historians disagree concerning Augustus's motives. Opinions range

from condemning him as a cynical despot bent on suppressing the free-
doms of the Republic, to praising him as a well-intentioned reformer with
no choice but to impose a disguised monarchy to stabilize a world crippled by anarchy. Perhaps the answer is that Augustus was a revolutionary
bound by tradition. His problem was not new in Roman political history: how to balance society's need for peace, its traditional commitment
to its citizens' freedom of action, and his own personal ambitions. Augustus's solution was to employ traditional values to make changes, as seen
in his reinvention of the meaning of princeps. Above all, he officially
transferred the traditional paternalism of social relations—the patron-client
system—to politics by making the emperor everyone's (and especially
the army's) most important patron, with the moral authority to guide
their lives. This process culminated with his being named "Father of his
Country" in 2 B.C., the greatest honor Rome could grant. Coins were
minted carrying this title, to proclaim the honor as widely as possible.
The title implied that Romans had a ruler who governed them like a father: presiding alone at the head of the family, stern but caring, expecting obedience and loyalty from his children, and obligated to nurture
them in return. The goal of such an arrangement was stability and order,
not political freedom.

Despite several serious illnesses, Augustus ruled until his death at age
seventy-five in A.D. 14. The great length of his reign (forty-one years)
helped make permanent his changes in Roman government. As the historian Tacitus observed a century later, Augustus lived so long that by the
time he died, "almost no one was still alive who had seen the Republic"
(*Annals* 1.3). Through his longevity, support from the army, and crafty
manipulation of the traditional vocabulary of politics to disguise his
power, Augustus restored stability to Roman society and transformed the
Republic into the Empire.

ROME IN AUGUSTUS'S TIME

Augustus built legitimacy for his new government not only by communicating the image of a generous ruler but also by taking action to
improve the lives of ordinary people. The most pressing social problems
were in Rome itself, now a teeming city of more than a million inhabitants, many of whom had too little to eat. This population was vast for the
ancient world; no European city would have nearly this many people
again until London in the 1700s. So many people meant overcrowding. The
streets were packed: "One man jabs me with his elbow, another whacks
me with a pole; my legs are smeared with mud, and big feet step on me

from all sides" was one later resident's description of walking in Rome (Juvenal, *Satires* 3.245–248). To ease congestion, carts and wagons were banned from the streets in daytime. This regulation made nights noisy with the creaking of axles and the shouting of drivers caught in traffic jams.

Most people lived in small apartments in multistoried buildings called "islands" (*insulae*). Outnumbering separate houses by more than twenty-five to one, these apartment buildings had first floors that usually housed shops, bars, and simple restaurants. Graffiti of all kinds—political endorsements, rewards for the return of stolen property, personal insults, sexy rhymes, and advertising of all kinds—filled their exterior walls. The higher the floor in the building was, the cheaper the apartment. Well-off tenants occupied the lower stories. The poorest people lived high above in single rooms rented by the day, or even in slum shacks built from scrap. Some wealthier families had piped-in water, but most apartment residents had to lug buckets of drinking and cooking water up the stairs from one of the hundreds of public fountains and basins in the city's streets.

Since Rome's residents generated about sixty tons of human waste every day, sanitation was an enormous challenge. Most lodgings had no separate bathrooms, and so residents had to walk to one of Rome's many public latrines, or use a bucket for a toilet at home. Apartment dwellers either flung the smelly contents of these containers out the window, or carried the buckets down to the streets to be emptied by people who made their living collecting excrement to sell to farmers for fertilizer. Officials tried to ensure that waste was disposed of outside the city's residential areas, but there were too few personnel to enforce the regulations consistently. Archaeological excavation has uncovered hundreds of deep pits on the Esquiline Hill that had been filled with a decomposing mixture of dead bodies, animal carcasses, and sewage of all sorts not far from the city center. The area was lined with signs with warnings such as, "Gaius Sentius, son of Gaius, as praetor and by order of the Senate, has set up this line of boundary stones, to mark the area that must be kept absolutely free from dirt and animal carcasses and human corpses. It is also strictly forbidden to burn corpses here" (Lanciani, pp. 64–67). The impossibility of keeping the city clean meant that flies buzzed everywhere, and people often had stomach trouble from contaminated food and water.

To keep clean, people used public baths. Since admission fees were low, almost everyone could afford to go to these establishments daily. Scores of bath buildings were located in the city, serving like modern health clubs as centers for exercising and socializing as well as washing. Bath patrons progressed through a series of increasingly warm, humid areas until they reached a sauna-like room. Bathers swam naked in their choice of hot or cold pools. Women had full access to the public baths; the sexes bathed apart, either in separate rooms or at different times of the day.

As in all ancient cities, unsanitary conditions prevailed despite the many baths, fountains with running water, and the ongoing efforts of officials to keep the streets clean. Since bathing was thought to be particularly valuable for sick people, the baths actually contributed to the spread of communicable diseases. Furthermore, although the government built a sewer system, its contents emptied untreated into the city's Tiber River. The technology for sanitary disposal of waste simply did not exist. People regularly left human and animal corpses in the streets, to be gnawed by vultures and dogs. The poor were not the only people affected by such conditions: a stray mutt once brought a human hand to the table where Vespasian (a future emperor) was eating lunch. Flies buzzing everywhere and a lack of mechanical refrigeration contributed to frequent gastrointestinal ailments. The most popular jewelry of the time was a necklace believed to prevent stomach trouble. Although the wealthy could not eliminate such discomforts, they made their lives more pleasant with luxuries such as snow rushed from the mountains to ice their drinks and slaves to clean their airy houses, which were built around courtyards and gardens behind high walls for privacy.

Augustus did all he could to promote the safety and health of all the people of Rome. He divided the city into fourteen regions and 265 wards, appointing ex-slaves as the leaders of "citizen watch" groups to be on the alert for traffic problems, assaults and robberies, and fires. These local officials also built loyalty to the new regime by sponsoring sacrifices at altars built in the streets to honor Augustus's Lares (the household spirits of his ancestors). Still, unpredictable hazards characterized much of city life in the crowded capital. The inhabitants living on the upper stories of apartment buildings, too poor to own slaves to do the dirty work of the household, threw broken crockery and toilet waste out their windows, raining their garbage down like missiles on unwary pedestrians below. "If you are walking to a dinner party in Rome," one poet remarked, "you would be foolish not to make out your will first. For every open window is a source of potential disaster" (Juvenal, *Satires* 3.272–274). The "islands" could be dangerous to their inhabitants as well as to people in the streets because the buildings were in constant danger of collapsing. Roman engineers, despite their expertise in using concrete, brick, and stone as durable building materials, lacked the technology to calculate precisely how much stress their constructions could stand. The real problem, how-

ever, was that builders trying to cut costs paid little attention to engineering safeguards, which led Augustus to impose a height limit of seventy
feet on new apartment buildings. Often built in low-lying areas because
the sunny hilltops were occupied by the homes of the rich, apartment
buildings were also susceptible to floods. Fire presented an even greater
risk. One of Augustus's many services to the urban masses was to provide
Rome with the first public fire department in European history. He also
established Rome's first police force, despite his reported fondness for
stopping to watch the brawls that frequently broke out in Rome's jam-
packed streets. The rich hired security guards to protect themselves and
their homes.

Augustus's most important service to the urban masses was to assure
them adequate and affordable food. By using his personal fortune to pay
for imported grain to feed the hungry, he prevented food riots and demonstrated his respect for the Roman value of patrons supporting their clients. Government distribution of low-cost or free grain to at least some
of Rome's poor had been a tradition for decades, but the number of male
recipients in Augustus's welfare system totaled 250,000. Because many of
these men had families, this statistic suggests that as many as 700,000
people depended on Augustus's regime for their dietary staple. Poor people usually made the grain, which was not well suited for baking bread,
into a watery porridge, which they washed down with inexpensive wine.
If they were lucky, they might also have some beans, leeks, or a few meat
scraps. The rich, as we learn from the ancient cookbook of Apicius, ate
more delectable dishes, such as spiced roast pork or lobster, often fla-
vored with sweet-and-sour sauce concocted from honey and vinegar.

Wealthy people had increasingly come to prefer spending money on
such luxuries instead of on raising families. Feeling that the expense and
trouble of having children threatened its high standard of living, the elite
failed to reproduce itself sufficiently. Children became so rare among this
social class that Augustus passed laws designed to strengthen marriages
and encourage more births by granting special legal privileges to the
parents of three or more children. He made adultery a criminal offense
as another attempt to protect marriage. So seriously did Augustus support
these reforms that he exiled his own daughter—his only child—and a
granddaughter for their extramarital sex scandals. His legislation had little effect, however, and the prestigious old families withered away under
the empire. Demographic research suggests that three-quarters of the families of senatorial status died out in every generation. New people from
below the senatorial class who won the emperors' favor continuously took
their places in the social hierarchy.

Slaves occupied the lowest rung in society's hierarchy and provided the basis of the imperial work force. Since Roman law still granted citizenship to freed slaves, their descendants, if they became wealthy, could rise to be members of the social elite. This possibility for upward social mobility over the long run gave slaves hope, which they needed to survive the often harsh conditions of enslavement. The slave ancestry of many ordinary Romans gave them some sympathy for current slaves, to judge from a riot that broke out in Rome in A.D. 61. A rich and prominent member of the social elite had been murdered by one of his slaves, and Roman tradition called for all the rest of his slaves to be executed, too, on the assumption that they should have known about and stopped the crime against their master. In this case, the murdered man was so wealthy that his household included some four hundred slaves, and a huge outcry arose over the proposal to put so many innocent people to death. The issue was even debated in the Senate, but the harsh tradition was upheld. When in response crowds set fires in the streets and threw stones at officials, Emperor Nero had to use soldiers to cordon off the execution site from the outraged mob of citizens (Tacitus, *Annals* 42–45).

Slavery in agriculture and manufacturing meant a grueling existence. Most such workers were men, although women might assist the foremen who managed gangs of rural laborers. Apuleius in a vivid novel offers this grim description of slaves at work in a flourmill: "Through the holes in their ragged clothes you could see the scars from whippings all over their bodies. Some wore only loincloths. Letters had been branded on their foreheads and irons manacled their ankles" (*The Golden Ass* 9.12). Worse than the mills were the mines, where the foremen constantly flogged the miners to keep them working in a life-threatening environment.

Household slaves had an easier physical existence, especially the many servants owned by the imperial family. Although households had more male slaves than female, many domestic slaves were women, working as nurses, maids, kitchen help, and clothes makers. Some male slaves ran businesses for their masters, and they were often allowed to keep part of the profits as an incentive. Women had less opportunity to earn money. Masters sometimes granted tips for sexual favors, to both female and male slaves. Female slave prostitutes, who were mostly owned by men, could sometimes make enough money to live in a small amount of physical comfort. Slaves who saved enough money would sometimes buy slaves themselves, thereby creating their own hierarchy. A man might buy a woman for a mate, and the couple could then have a semblance of family life, though legal marriage was impossible because they remained their master's property, as did their children. If truly fortunate, slaves could save enough to buy themselves from their masters, or they could be freed in their masters' wills. Some inscriptions on tombstones testify to affectionate feelings masters had for slaves, but even household servants could suffer miserable lives if their masters were cruel. They had no defense against harsh treatment. Even if they attacked their owners only to defend themselves against abuse, their punishment was death.

The most publicly visible slaves were gladiators: men and women who fought with weapons in public competitions. Not all gladiators were slaves, however. Prisoners of war and condemned criminals could be forced to fight, and free people also voluntarily enrolled themselves as gladiators in return for pay and celebrity. Early in the first century A.D., the Senate became alarmed at the number of citizens willingly entering this less than honorable occupation and banned members of the elite and all freeborn women under twenty years old from competing. Women, perhaps daughters trained by their gladiator fathers, had first competed during the Republic. They continued to fight in public until the emperor Septimius Severus (ruled A.D. 193–211) successfully banned their appearance.

Gladiatorial shows originated as part of the ceremonies at expensive funerals; the combats became so popular that by the time of the Empire they provided entertainment at public festivals in large arenas seating tens of thousands of spectators. The most famous arena in Rome was the Colosseum, created by the emperor Vespasian and completed by his son Titus in A.D. 80. This stone amphitheater holding some fifty thousand spectators was built near the spot where there had stood a huge statue of the emperor Nero. (The statue had soared more than a hundred feet high, and as a "colossus" gave its name to the amphitheater.)

Gladiatorial combat was not always, or even often, fought to the death (except between condemned criminals) because trained gladiators were so valuable. Killing one off represented a substantial loss for the organizers of the shows. In the rare fights to the death, the crowd could shout for the defeated fighter to be spared if he or she had shown special courage. To make the fights more unpredictable, gladiators fought with different kinds of weapons. One popular match pitted a lightly armored fighter, called a "net man" because he used a net and a trident, against a more heavily armored "fish man," so named from the design of his helmet crest. Betting was fierce, and crowds could be rowdy. One critic blasted Roman sports fans: "Look at the mob coming to the show—already they're out of their minds! Aggressive, thoughtless, already screaming about their bets! They all share the same suspense, the same madness, the same voice" (Tertullian, *On Spectacles* 16). Mosaics—pictures composed from small brightly colored tiles, a favorite form of art that Romans loved

Figure 18. The gladiators shown in this mosaic are armed and armored according to their different styles of fighting and their names are recorded. The most exciting gladiatorial matches often involved a heavily armored, slower-moving fighter against a lightly protected but more mobile opponent. Scala/Art Resource, NY.

to place on their floors—provide vivid images of gladiators fighting that reveal the strong emotional response these contests provoked.

Expensive gladiatorial shows became the rage under the Empire as the people came to expect this kind of spectacular entertainment from their imperial patrons. Augustus paid for more than five thousand pairs of gladiators to fight in spectacular festivals. The programs of these extravagant events also included chariot races, mock naval battles on artificial lakes, fights between humans and savage beasts, displays of exotic African animals that sometimes mangled condemned criminals as a form of capital punishment, and theatrical productions. Mimes were the most popular form of theater. These dramas of everyday life employed actresses to play female roles, as did the sexually explicit farces that were also popular with Rome's audiences. The city's largest theater, whose seating rising on arches held about twenty thousand people, was the Theater of Marcellus, named by the emperor Augustus in memory of his dead nephew.

As the Roman emperors over time abandoned Augustus's stance as an accessible ruler and distanced themselves from ordinary people, gladiatorial shows, chariot races, and theater productions became the only venues in which the masses could communicate their discontents to the emperors, who were expected to attend the shows or send a high-ranking representative. On more than one occasion the poor rioted at festivals to express their unhappiness about a shortfall in the free grain supply.

EDUCATION, LITERATURE, AND SCULPTURE
IN THE EARLY EMPIRE

Education changed beginning in the time of Augustus so that, like coins, architectural monuments, and public entertainments, it, too, would now serve the goals of legitimizing and strengthening the transformed system of government. Rhetoric remained education's central subject, but it lost its traditional political bite. Under the Republic, the ability to make persuasive speeches criticizing opponents had been such a powerful weapon that it could catapult someone like Cicero, who lacked social and military distinction, to political prominence. Now, the emperor's supremacy ruled out open political debate and freedom of speech. Under these new circumstances, ambitious men required rhetorical skills only for private legal cases, trials of government officials, and speeches in praise of the emperor on the numerous public occasions that communicated his image as an effective and generous ruler. Since political criticism was too risky, rhetorical training had less and less to do with politics. Instead of learning to make speeches on national policy, students now learned how to make an impression as a clever speaker by practicing on topics such as "a rape victim's alternatives," or "cures for the plague," using an exaggerated style designed to attract attention to the speaker's skill rather than to offer frank opinions on political matters (Tacitus, *Dialogue on Orators* 35.5).

Education remained a privilege of the wealthy. Rome still had no publicly financed schools, so the poor were lucky to pick up rudimentary literacy from their busy parents. Even wealthier people valued education more for its practical skills than for general knowledge or its effect on character, now that making money replaced politics as the preferred—and safe—form of social competition for men. A character in a satirical literary work of the mid-first century A.D. expressed this utilitarian attitude toward education succinctly: "I didn't study geometry and literary criticism and worthless junk like that. I just learned how to read the letters on signs and how to work out percentages, and I learned weights, measures, and the values of the different kinds of coins" (Petronius, *Satyricon* 58).

Although the Roman ideal called for mothers to teach their offspring, servants or hired teachers usually looked after the children of rich families under the Empire. The children attended private elementary schools from the ages of seven to eleven to learn reading, writing, and basic arithmetic. Some children went on to the next three years of school, in which they were introduced to literature, history, and grammar. Only a few boys advanced to the study of rhetoric.

Advanced studies concerned literature, history, ethical philosophy, law, and dialectic (determining the truth by identifying contradictions in arguments). Mathematics and science were little studied except for practical use; Roman engineers and architects became extremely proficient at calculation. Rich men and women would pursue their interests in books by having slaves read aloud to them. Reading required manual dexterity as well as literacy because books, instead of being bound page by page, consisted of continuous scrolls made from the papyrus reed or animal skin. A reader had to unroll the scroll with one hand while simultaneously rolling it up with the other.

Literature and sculpture also took a new direction under Augustus, helping to communicate a positive image of the ruler, though not without conflict between the emperor and some authors and artists. So much literature blossomed at this time that modern critics regard the time of Augustus as the Golden Age of Latin literature (as opposed to the empire's political Golden Age, which historians place in the second century A.D.). Augustus himself wrote poetry, and he supported this flourishing in literature by acting as the patron of a circle of writers and artists. His favorites, Horace (65 B.C.–8 B.C.) and Vergil (or Virgil, 70 B.C.–19 B.C.), supported his new system of government. Horace entranced audiences with the supple rhythms and subtle humor of his short poems on public and private subjects. His poem celebrating Augustus's victory over Antony and Cleopatra at Actium became famous for its opening line "Now it's time to start drinking!" (Odes 1.37).

Vergil became the most popular Augustan poet in later times for his long poem, the Aeneid, which he wrote both to please the emperor and to give him advice (very politely). An epic inspired by Homeric poetry, it told the legend of the Trojan Aeneas, said to be the most distant ancestor of the Romans. Vergil limited the poem's praise of the Roman state by expressing, through the many tragic deaths of its story, a profound recognition of the price to be paid for success. The Aeneid therefore underscored the complex mix of gain and loss that followed Augustus's transformation of politics and society. Above all, it expressed a moral code for emperors to follow: be merciful to the conquered but bring down the arrogant. Vergil had read portions of the Aeneid to Augustus and his family with great success, but on his deathbed in 19 B.C. he is reported to have asked his friends to burn the poem because he had not finished revising the text. Augustus ordered it preserved.

Authors with a more independent streak had to be careful. The historian Livy (54 B.C.–A.D. 17) composed an enormous history of Rome that did not hide the ruthless actions of Augustus and his supporters. The emperor reprimanded Livy for his frankness but did not punish him, most likely because the history also made clear that Rome's success and stability depended on maintaining traditional values of loyalty and self-sacrifice.

The poet Ovid (43 B.C.–A.D. 17) fared worse. With mocking wit, his erotic poems *Ars Amatoria* and *Amores* (*Art of Love* and *Love Affairs*) implicitly made fun of the emperor's moral legislation, offering tongue-in-cheek tips for conducting illicit love affairs and picking up other men's wives at festivals. Ovid's *Metamorphoses* (*Transformations*) reimagined myths of bizarre supernatural changes of shapes, with people becoming animals and confusions between the human and the divine, thereby undermining the tradition of accepting social hierarchy as natural and stable. In 8 B.C., Augustus coldly expressed his disapproval by exiling Ovid to a dreary town on the Black Sea, perhaps also in response to Ovid's involvement in a sex scandal surrounding the emperor's daughter.

Sculpture also responded to the emperor's wishes. In the late Republic, sculpted portraits had realistically emphasized the hard wear and tear of human experience. Sculpture after Augustus became emperor began to display a much more idealized style, reminiscent of classical Greek art, or Lysippus's fourth-century B.C. portrait of Alexander the Great. In famous works of art such as the Prima Porta statue of Augustus (now in the Vatican Museum in Rome), or the sculpted panels on the Altar of Augustan Peace (now reconstructed in a museum next to the Tiber River), the emperor had himself portrayed as calm and dignified rather than anxious and sick, as he in truth often was. As with his monumental architecture, Augustus used sculpture to project a serene image of himself as the always-in-charge restorer of the world.

Much of the poetry and the portraiture of the new empire therefore reflected Augustus's much-publicized image of himself: the great father selflessly and generously restoring peace and prosperity to his war-torn people. He hoped that this image would persuade Romans to accept a new way of being governed, without their focusing on the hidden costs of the change. Augustus was certainly a generous patron to Rome's poor, and he forced the rich to make financial contributions to pay for the standing army and public works. But underneath his benevolence lay a vein of ruthlessness. Many people, including friends and even relatives, had been murdered in the proscriptions of 43 B.C. Others lost their homes in the confiscations that provided land for his army veterans. Perhaps most tellingly, it was Augustus's power as the army's commander and patron that guaranteed the "Roman peace." The open debate and shared decision-making by citizens that had been the most cherished ideals of the Republic had been lost—this was the price to be paid for social and political order under the Empire.

7

From the Julio-Claudians to the Empire's Golden Age

Augustus's transformation of Roman government brought two centuries of relatively calm prosperity referred to as the Roman Peace (*Pax Romana*). Historians rank the second century A.D. as the Golden Age of the Roman Empire. As a de facto monarchy, however, the "Restored Republic" always faced the threat of a violent struggle for power among the elite. In fact, it seemed likely that a civil war might erupt after Augustus died because there was no precedent for how to pass on rule under this new system. Augustus's fiction that the Republic still existed meant that the rulership did not automatically pass to a son as his successor, as it would in an acknowledged kingdom. At the same time, he wanted to determine who would become Rome's next ruler and make it someone close to him. Having no son of his own, he adopted Tiberius, an adult son of his wife Livia by her previous marriage. Tiberius was famous for his brilliant military record, and Augustus informed the Senate that the army wanted this adoptive son to be in line to become the next princeps. The senators prudently confirmed Augustus's choice in this position after the first emperor died. Members of Augustus's family—known as the Julio-Claudians from the names of the family lineages of Augustus (the Julians) and Tiberius (the Claudians)—continued to fill the post of "First

TIMELINE (ALL DATES A.D.)

14–37: Tiberius, the first Roman emperor of the Julio-Claudian dynasty, rules until his (probably) natural death.

23: Tiberius builds a permanent camp in Rome for the Praetorian Guard.

37–41: Gaius (Caligula) rules as Roman emperor until he is murdered.

41: The Praetorian Guard blocks the Senate from reestablishing the old Republic and makes Claudius the emperor.

41–54: Claudius rules as Roman emperor until he is murdered.

54–68: Nero rules as Roman emperor until he commits suicide; his death ends the Julio-Claudian dynasty.

69: Vespasian wins a civil war and creates the Flavian dynasty of emperors; he rules until his natural death in 79.

70: Titus, Vespasian's son, captures Jerusalem, ending a four-year Jewish rebellion.

79–81: Titus rules as Roman emperor until his natural death.

79: The volcano Vesuvius erupts, burying Pompeii and Herculaneum in southern Italy.

80: Titus has the Colosseum finished at Rome.

81–96: Domitian, Vespasian's son, rules until he is murdered.

96–180: The Five Good Emperors (Nerva, Trajan, Hadrian, Antoninus Pius, and Marcus Aurelius) rule during the Roman Empire's political Golden Age.

113: Trajan erects his sculpted victory column at Rome.

125: Hadrian finishes construction on the domed Pantheon in Rome.

Late second century: The sculpted victory column of Marcus Aurelius is erected at Rome.

Man"—thereby becoming "emperors"—for the next half-century, always with the formal approval of the Senate.

The goals of the Julio-Claudian dynasty (the succession of rulers related to one another) included preventing unrest, building loyalty, and financing their administrations. These emperors oversaw a vast territory of provinces populated by a mix of Roman citizens and local populations. Therefore, the emperors took special care of the army, encouraged religious rituals dedicated to the welfare of the imperial household, and promoted Roman law and culture as universal standards while allowing as much local freedom as possible. Their subjects expected the emperors to be generous patrons rewarding their faithful loyalty to the regime, but the difficulties of long-range communication and the low level of technology limited the emperors' ability to care for the inhabitants of the empire.

The greatest challenge facing the Julio-Claudian emperors after Augustus—Tiberius, Gaius (Caligula), Claudius, and Nero—was how to keep the Principate functioning peacefully and prosperously. With nothing to guide them except Augustus's example, they had to protect Roman territory from foreign enemies, prevent the elite from conspiring to replace them, keep the people content, and resist the personal temptations of supreme power. Some emperors governed better than others, but by the end of Nero's reign, no Roman seriously believed that family dynasties of emperors would not continue to rule the Roman Empire. To understand how this great change took place, it is necessary to survey briefly the reigns of the Julio-Claudian emperors following Augustus.

IMPERIAL DYNASTIES

Tiberius (42 B.C.–A.D. 37) held power for twenty-three years after Augustus's death in A.D. 14 because he had the most important qualifications for succeeding as princeps: a family connection to Augustus and a brilliant record as a general earning him the respect of the army. He paid a steep personal price for becoming Augustus's successor as emperor: to strengthen their family ties, his new father had forced Tiberius to divorce his beloved wife, Vipsania, to marry Augustus's daughter, Julia. This political marriage proved disastrously unhappy. Tiberius never recovered from this sadness, and he was a reluctant ruler, so bitter at his fate that he spent the last decade of his life as a recluse in a palace at the top of a cliff on the island of Capri near Naples, never again returning to Rome.

Despite Tiberius's infamously bitter frame of mind and his deep unpopularity with the Roman populace, his long reign provided the stable transition period that the Empire needed to become established as a compromise in governing between the emperor and the elite. Despite ruling essentially as a monarch, the emperor still needed the cooperation of the upper class as officials in the imperial administration, commanders in the army, and leaders and financial contributors in local communities in the provinces. So long as this compromise endured, the Empire could thrive and both sides could enjoy status and respect. On the one hand, the elite could continue to bask in the prestige of their traditional roles as consuls, praetors, senators, and high-ranking priests. On the other, the emperors could make their superior status clear by deciding who

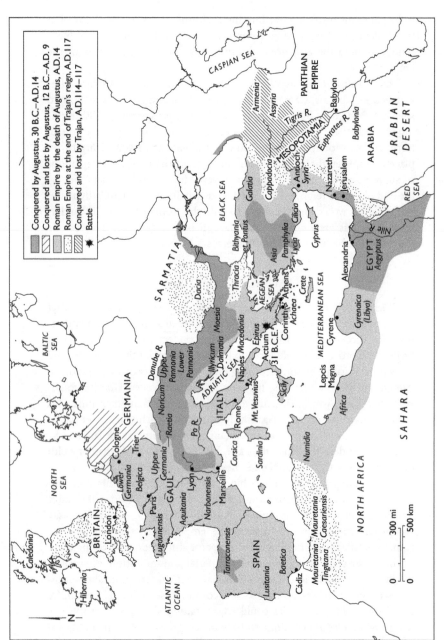

Legend:
- Conquered by Augustus, 30 B.C.–A.D.14
- Conquered and lost by Augustus, 12 B.C.–A.D. 9
- Roman Empire by the death of Augustus, A.D.14
- Roman Empire at the end of Trajan's reign, A.D.117
- Conquered and lost by Trajan, A.D.114–117
- Battle

CALEDONIA
HIBERNIA
BRITAIN
London
NORTH SEA
BALTIC SEA
GERMANIA
Cologne
Trier
Paris
Lower Germania
Upper Germania
Belgica
GAUL
Aquitania
Lugdunensis
Lyon
Narbonensis
Marseille
SPAIN
Tarraconensis
Lusitania
Baetica
Cádiz
ATLANTIC OCEAN
Corsica
Sardinia
ITALY
Rome
Naples
Mt Vesuvius
Sicily
Po R.
Raetia
Noricum
Upper Pannonia
Lower Pannonia
Danube R.
SARMATIA
Dacia
Illyricum
Dalmatia
Moesia
Epirus
Actium 31 B.C.E.
ADRIATIC SEA
Macedonia
Thracia
AEGEAN SEA
Athens
Corinth
Achaea
Crete
BLACK SEA
Bithynia et Pontus
Galatia
Asia
Pamphylia
Lycia
Cyprus
Cilicia
CASPIAN SEA
Armenia
Assyria
PARTHIAN EMPIRE
Cappadocia
MESOPOTAMIA
Tigris R.
Euphrates R.
Babylon
Babylonia
Antioch
Syria
Nazareth
Jerusalem
ARABIA
ARABIAN DESERT
RED SEA
EGYPT
Aegyptus
Nile R.
Alexandria
Cyrene
Cyrenaica (Libya)
MEDITERRANEAN SEA
Lepcis Magna
Africa
Numidia
Mauretania Caesariensis
Mauretania Tingitana
NORTH AFRICA
SAHARA

0 300 mi
0 500 km

Map 7. Roman Expansion During the Early Empire

would fill these positions, assuming the power formerly held by the Assemblies. These meetings soon became rubberstamps for the emperors' wishes and eventually withered away. In sum, the government of the Empire was a negotiated settlement between members of the upper class. In A.D. 23 Tiberius also built a permanent camp in the city for the Praetorian Guard, making it easier to use them in supporting him with force if necessary. He died in his bed of natural causes, it seems, although there was a rumor that he was smothered. He was so unpopular that the news of his death caused rejoicing in the streets.

The next Julio-Claudian emperor, Gaius, known as Caligula (A.D. 12–41), had a fatal shortcoming: he enjoyed his power too much and never made a career as a military leader. Tiberius had chosen him as his successor because he was the great-grandson of Augustus's sister. Gaius could have been successful because he was wildly popular at first and also knew about soldiering: Caligula means "Baby Boots," the nickname the troops gave him as a child because he wore little leather shoes imitating theirs while he lived in military camps where his father was a commander. Unfortunately, he soon showed that he lacked the personality for leadership when given unbridled power; what he did possess were extravagant desires for personal dissipation. Ruling through cruelty and violence, he overspent from the treasury to humor his cravings and, to raise money, imposed new sales taxes on everything from the fast food sold in Rome's many take-out shops to each sex act performed by a prostitute. Caligula outraged the value of dignified conduct expected of a member of the social elite by appearing on stage as a singer and actor, fighting mock gladiatorial combats, appearing in public in women's clothing or costumes imitating gods, and, it seems likely, having sexual affairs with his sisters. His abuses finally went too far: two soldiers in the Praetorian Guard murdered him in A.D. 41 to avenge his insults to them.

The murder of Caligula threatened to end the Julio-Claudian dynasty because Gaius had no son and his violent behavior had frightened everyone around him. When his murder was announced, some senators proclaimed that it was time to bring back the original Republic and true liberty. The Praetorian Guard overthrew this plan, however, because they wanted emperors to continue so as to be their patrons. The soldiers in the city therefore literally dragged Augustus's relative Claudius (10 B.C.–A.D. 54), now fifty years old and never considered to be capable of rule, to their camp and forced the Senate to acknowledge him as the new ruler. The threat to use force to get what they wanted made it clear that the soldiers, whether praetorians in Rome or troops in the legions, would always insist on having an emperor. It also revealed that any senatorial yearnings for the return of a true Republic had no chance of being ever fulfilled.

Claudius surprised everyone by ruling competently overall. He set a crucial precedent for imperial rule by enrolling men from a province (Transalpine Gaul, meaning southeastern France) in the Senate for the first time. This change opened the way for the growing importance of provincials as the emperors' clients, whose role was to help keep the empire peaceful and prosperous. Claudius also changed imperial government by employing freed slaves as powerful administrators; since they owed their great advancement to the emperor, they could be expected to be loyal.

Claudius's wife Agrippina poisoned him in A.D. 54 because she wanted Nero (A.D. 37–68), her teenaged son by a previous husband, to become emperor instead of Claudius's own son. Nero, like Caligula, succumbed to the glorious temptations of absolute power. Having received no military training or preparation for governing, Nero had a passion for music and acting, not for administering an empire. The spectacular public festivals he put on and the cash he distributed to the masses in Rome kept him popular with the poor, although a giant fire in the city in A.D. 64 aroused suspicions that he might have ordered the conflagration to clear the way for new building projects. Nero spent outrageous sums on his pleasures. To raise more money, he trumped up charges of treason against wealthy men and women to seize their property. Alarmed and outraged, commanders in the provinces turned against him and supported rebellion, as did many senators. When one of the praetorians' commanders bribed them to desert the emperor, Nero had no defense left. Fearing arrest and execution, Nero shouted in dismay, "To die! And such a great artist!" Not long after he had a servant help him cut his own throat (Suetonius, *Life of Nero* 49).

With no successor to the childless Nero in the palace, a civil war began in A.D. 68 between different rivals to the throne. The winner of the conflict among four rivals for the throne in the following "Year of the Four Emperors" (A.D. 69) was the general Vespasian (A.D. 9–79). He installed his family, the Flavians, as the new imperial dynasty to succeed the Julio-Claudians. To create political legitimacy for this new regime, Vespasian had the Senate recognize him as ruler with a detailed statement of the powers that he held, which were made into a law and explicitly said to come down to him from the precedents of the powers of his worthy predecessors as "First Men" (a list that excluded Caligula and Nero). To encourage loyalty in the provinces, he encouraged the elites there to take part in the so-called "imperial cult" (rituals that focused on sacrificing

Figure 19. This street at Herculaneum, preserved by the eruption of Vesuvius in A.D. 79, is lined by multistoried and balconied houses typical of Roman towns. Windows and porches in the upper stories provided light, ventilation, and space to combat the crowding and smells of the streets below. Alinari/Art Resource, NY.

animals to the traditional gods for the welfare of the emperor and his family and, in some cases, actual worship of the emperor).

Vespasian built on local traditions in the eastern provinces in promoting the imperial cult. The deification of the current ruler seemed normal to the provincials there because they had been honoring local kings as divinities for centuries, going back to the time of Alexander the Great in the late fourth century B.C. The imperial cult communicated the same image of the emperor to the people of the provinces as the city's architecture and sculpture did to the people of Rome: he was larger than life, worthy of loyal respect, and the source of benefactions as their patron. Because emperor worship had already become better established in the eastern part of the empire under Augustus, Vespasian concentrated on strengthening it in the provinces of Spain, southern France, and North Africa. Italy, however, still had no temples to the living emperor, and traditional Romans there scorned the imperial cult as a provincial peculiarity. Vespasian, known for his wit, even skeptically muttered as he lay dying in A.D. 79, "Poor me! I'm afraid I'm becoming a god" (Suetonius, *Life of Vespasian* 23).

Vespasian's sons Titus (A.D. 39–81) and Domitian (A.D. 51–96) continued the dynasty, dealing with two problems that would increasingly occupy future emperors: improving life for people throughout the empire to prevent disorder, and defending against invasions from peoples on the frontiers. Titus had become famous in A.D. 70 for defeating a four-year rebellion by Jews in what is today Israel and capturing Jerusalem, where the Jewish Temple, the ritual center of Judaism, was burned down in the attack, never to be rebuilt. In his brief time as emperor (A.D. 79–81), Titus sent relief to the communities damaged by the volcanic eruption of Mount Vesuvius in A.D. 79; the gigantic quantity of ash and volcanic mud spewed out by the exploding mountain preserved large parts of the neighboring towns of Pompeii and Herculaneum. This disaster that killed and displaced so many people made those sites into uniquely rich sources for us because it froze in time so many specimens of the architecture, painting, and mosaics of the era.

Titus also provided the public with a state-of-the-art site for lavish public entertainments by finishing Rome's Colosseum (or Coliseum) in A.D. 80, outfitting it with giant awnings to shade the crowd. Following his brother's death from natural causes, Domitian as emperor (A.D. 81–96) led the army north to the Rhine and Danube River areas to fight off Germanic invaders, the beginning of a danger that was going to plague the empire for centuries. His arrogance made him disliked at home. For example, in communicating his wishes in writing and in conversation he customarily said, "Our Master and God, myself, orders you to do this" (Suetonius, *Life of Domitian* 13). He also emphasized his superiority over everyone else by expanding the imperial palace on the Palatine Hill to more than 350,000 square feet. Fearing Domitian was going to eliminate them, a group of conspirators from his court murdered him after fifteen years of rule.

EMPERORS AND FINANCE IN THE EMPIRE'S GOLDEN AGE

By now, the murder of an emperor meant only that a new one needed to be found who satisfied the army, not that the system of government

Figure 20. Soldiers on a victory column erected by Emperor Marcus Aurelius in Rome have equipment typical of the Roman army in the early Empire. The continuous sculpted bands winding around this and similar monuments provide a wide array of scenes of the imperial army in battle, in camp, and on parade. Barosaurus Lentus/Wikimedia Commons.

might change. As the historian Tacitus (A.D. 56–118) wrote, emperors had become like the weather; their extravagance and greed for domination had to be endured just as drought or floods did (*Histories* 4.74). A better political climate prevailed in the empire under the next five emperors—Nerva (ruled A.D. 96–98), Trajan (ruled 98–117), Hadrian (ruled 117–138), Antoninus Pius (ruled 138–161), and Marcus Aurelius (ruled 161–180). Historians have designated their reigns as the empire's political Golden Age because these rulers provided peace and quiet for nearly a century. Of course, "peace" is a relative term in Roman history: Trajan fought fierce campaigns that expanded Roman power northward across the Danube River into Dacia (today Romania) and eastward into Mesopotamia (Iraq), Hadrian punished a second Jewish revolt by turning Jerusalem into a military colony, and Aurelius spent many miserable years protecting the Danube region from outside attacks.

Still, the idea of a Golden Age under the "Five Good Emperors" makes sense, at least compared to the violence of the late Republic and the murderous history of the Julio-Claudians. These five rulers succeeded each other without assassination or conspiracy—indeed, the first four, having no sons, used the Roman tradition of adopting adults to find the best possible successor. Moreover, adequate revenue was coming in through taxes, the army remained obedient, and overseas trade reached its greatest heights. Chinese records even show that a group of Roman merchants apparently claiming to bring the greetings of the Roman emperor reached the court of the Han emperor during the reign of Marcus Aurelius (Schoff, pp. 276–277). These reigns marked the longest stretch in Roman history without a civil war since the second century B.C.

The peace and the prosperity of the second century A.D. depended on defense by a loyal and efficient military, public-spiritedness among provincial elites in local administration and tax collection, the spread of common laws and culture to promote unity throughout huge and diverse territories, and a healthy population reproducing itself. The great size of the Roman Empire, combined with the enduring conditions of ancient life, meant that emperors had less control over these factors than they would have liked.

In theory, Rome's military goal remained infinite expansion. Vergil in the *Aeneid* (2.179) had expressed this notion by portraying Jupiter, the king of the gods, as promising the Romans "rule without limit." In reality, the empire's territory never expanded much beyond what Augustus had established, encircling the Mediterranean Sea; Trajan's conquest of Mesopotamia had to be given up by Hadrian as too difficult to defend. Most emperors had to concentrate on defense and maintaining internal order, only dreaming of further conquest.

Most provinces were stable and peaceful in this period and had no need for garrisons of troops. Roman soldiers were therefore a rare sight in many places. Even Gaul, which in Julius Caesar's time had resisted Roman control with a suicidal frenzy, was, according to a contemporary witness, "kept in order by 1,200 troops—hardly more soldiers than it has towns" (Josephus, *The Jewish War* 2.373). Most Roman troops were concentrated on the northern and eastern fringes of the empire, where powerful and sometimes hostile neighbors lived just beyond the boundaries and the distance from the center weakened the local residents' loyalty to the imperial government.

Now that Rome was no longer fighting wars of conquest, it became difficult to pay the costs of the military. In the past, successful foreign wars had been an engine of prosperity because they brought in huge amounts of capital through booty, indemnities, and prisoners of war sold into slavery. Conquered territory converted into provinces also provided additional tax revenues. Now, there were no longer any such opportunities to increase the government's income, but the standing army still had to be paid regularly to maintain its loyalty. To fulfill their obligations as patrons of the army, emperors supplemented soldiers' regular pay with substantial bonuses on special occasions. The financial rewards made a military career desirable, and enlistment counted as a privilege restricted to free male citizens. The army also included many auxiliary units of noncitizens fighting as cavalry, archers, and slingers. Serving under Roman commanders, the auxiliaries learned the Latin language and Roman customs. Upon discharge, they received Roman citizenship. In this way, the army served as an instrument for spreading a common way of life.

A tax on agricultural land in the provinces (Italy was exempt) provided the principal source of revenue for imperial government and defense. The provincial administration cost relatively little because the number of officials was small compared to the size of the empire being governed: no more than several hundred government officials governed a population of around 50 million. As under the Republic, governors with small personal staffs ran the provinces, which eventually numbered about forty. In Rome, the emperor employed a substantial palace staff, while officials called prefects managed the city itself.

The tax system required public service by the provincial elites in order to work; the empire's revenues absolutely depended on these members of the upper class. They collected taxes as a required duty as unsalaried officials (*curiales*) on their city's council (*curia*). In this decentralized system, these wealthy people were personally responsible for sending each year's amount of tax to the central administration. If there was any shortfall, the officials had to make up the difference from their own pockets. Most emperors under the early Empire attempted to keep taxes from rising. As Tiberius put it once when refusing a request for tax increases from provincial governors, "I want you to shear my sheep, not skin them alive" (Suetonius, *Life of Tiberius* 32). Over time, however, the government's need for more revenue grew more insistent, and the provincial elites found themselves hard-pressed to deliver.

The elites' responsibility for tax collection could make civic office expensive, but the prestige and influence with the emperor that the positions carried made many provincials willing to shoulder the cost. Some received priesthoods in the imperial cult as a reward, an honor open to both men and women. *Curiales* could hope that the emperors would respond to their requests for special help for their areas, for example after an earthquake or a flood.

This system of financing the empire worked because it was rooted in the tradition of the patron-client system: the local social elites were the patrons of their communities but the clients of the emperors. As long as there were enough rich and public-spirited provincials responding to this value system that offered status as its reward, the empire could function by fostering the ancient Roman ideal of privileging communal values over individual comfort. The system was increasingly coming under pressure, however, because the costs of national defense kept rising, reflecting the need to defend against the growing threats from external enemies along the frontiers.

STABILITY AND CHANGE IN THE EMPIRE'S GOLDEN AGE

The Roman Empire changed the Mediterranean world profoundly but unevenly in a process that historians label "Romanization," meaning the adoption of Roman culture by non-Romans. The empire's provinces contained a wide diversity of peoples speaking different languages, observing different customs, dressing in distinctive styles, and worshiping various divinities. In the remote countryside, stability in life and customs prevailed because Roman conquest had little effect on local people. In the many places where new cities sprang up, however, change stemming from Roman influence was easy to see. These communities grew from the settlements of army veterans the emperors had sprinkled throughout the provinces, or they sprouted spontaneously around Roman forts. These settlements became particularly influential in Western Europe, permanently rooting Latin (and the languages that would emerge from it) and Roman law and customs there. Prominent modern cities such as Trier and Cologne near Germany's western border started as Roman towns. Over time, the social and cultural distinctions weakened between the provinces and Italy, the Roman heartland. Eventually, emperors came from the provinces. Trajan, whose family had settled in Spain, was the first.

Romanization raised the standard of living for many provincials as transportation improved with the building of more roads and bridges and long aqueducts supplied fresh water to cities. Trade increased, including direct commercial interaction with markets as far away as India and China, where Roman merchants began to sail to find goods to import to Europe. Taxes on this international trade became a major source of revenue for the imperial government. Agriculture in the provinces flourished under the peaceful conditions secured by the army. Where troops were stationed in the provinces, their need for supplies meant new business for farmers and merchants. That the provincials for the

Figure 21. This gigantic stone bridge carried an aqueduct bringing fresh water from sources in the hills miles away to a large town in Gaul (today France). Engineers carefully calculated the proper slope for the channel so that water flowed continuously downhill to the urban center at a steady but manageable rate. Ad Meskens/Wikimedia Commons.

most part lived more prosperously under Roman rule than they ever had before made it easier for them to accept Romanization. In addition, Romanization was not a one-way street culturally. In western provinces as diverse as Gaul, Britain, and North Africa, interaction between provincials and Romans produced new, mixed cultural traditions, especially in religion and art. This process led to a gradual merging of Roman and local culture, not the unilateral imposition of the conquerors' way of life on provincials.

Romanization had less effect on the eastern provinces, which largely retained their Greek and western Asian character. When Romans had gradually taken over the region during the second and first centuries B.C., they found stable urban cultures there that had been flourishing for thousands of years. Huge cities such as Alexandria in Egypt and Antioch in Syria rivaled Rome in size and splendor. In fact, they boasted more individual houses for the well-to-do, fewer blocks of high-rise tenements, and equally magnificent temples. While retaining their local languages and customs, the eastern social elites easily accepted the "emperor as patron, themselves as clients" nature of provincial governance: they had long ago become accustomed to such a system through the comparable paternalistic relationships that had characterized the kingdoms under whose governments they had lived before the arrival of the Romans. The willing cooperation of these local, non-Roman elites in the task of governing the empire was crucial for its stability and prosperity.

In much of the eastern empire, then, daily life continued to follow traditional local models. The emperors lacked any notion of themselves as missionaries who had to impose Roman civilization on foreigners. Rather, they saw themselves primarily as preservers of law and social order. Therefore, they were happy for long-standing forms of eastern civic life and government to continue largely unchanged, so long as they promoted social stability and therefore internal peace.

The continuing vitality of Greek culture and language in bustling eastern cities contributed to a flourishing in literature in that language. New trends were especially notable in Greek prose. Second-century A.D. authors such as Chariton and Achilles Tatius wrote romantic adventure novels that began the enduring popularity of that kind of story as entertainment. Lucian (A.D. 117–180) composed satires and fantasies that fiercely mocked stuffy people, frauds, and old-fashioned gods. The essayist and philosopher Plutarch (A.D. 50–120) wrote biographies that matched Greek and Roman leaders in comparative studies of their characters. His keen moral sense and lively taste for anecdotes made him favorite reading for centuries. Shakespeare based several plays on Plutarch's biographies.

Latin literature thrived as well. In fact, scholars rank the late first and early second centuries A.D. as its "Silver Age," second in its production of masterpieces only to the literature of the Augustan literary Golden Age. The most famous Latin authors of this later time wrote with acid wit, verve, and imagination. The historian Tacitus (A.D. 56–120) composed a biting narrative of the Julio-Claudians, laying bare the ruthlessness of Augustus and the personal weaknesses of his successors. The satiric poet Juvenal (A.D. 65–130) skewered pretentious Romans and grasping provincials, while hilariously bemoaning the indignities of living broke in the city. Apuleius (A.D. 125–170) scandalized readers with his *Golden Ass*, a lusty novel about a man turned into a donkey, who then miraculously regains his body and his soul through salvation by the kindly Egyptian goddess Isis.

Large-scale architecture flourished in Rome during the first centuries of the Empire because the emperors saw large-scale building projects as a way to win public goodwill and broadcast their image as successful and caring rulers. For instance, the emperor Domitian in the first century A.D. built a stadium with a running track for athletic events to provide another large venue for public entertainment. Even more popular than these contests were the many theatrical performances, from drama to mime, that filled the Roman calendar of events.

The most impressive surviving example of these imperial monuments comes from the Golden Age of the second century A.D. This is the giant domed building called the Pantheon (meaning "All the Gods"; the building's precise function remains unclear). Like Domitian's stadium, the Pantheon was located just outside Rome's center in the area known as the Field of Mars (Campus Martius). The emperor Hadrian had the Pantheon constructed from A.D. 118 to 125, on the site of earlier buildings that had burned down. The diameter of its rotunda is the same (nearly 150 feet) as the height of its dome, making its interior space a perfect half-sphere. It has stood for nearly two thousand years largely intact because Roman engineers made its outer brick structure so thick and interlocking. Hadrian also built himself a dazzling estate on the outskirts of Rome (today near the town of Tivoli), whose countless rooms, many statues, and architectural design were meant to recall the most famous monuments of the Greek and Roman world that he had seen on his many trips around the empire. We can be sure that it contained many paintings as well because that form of art remained immensely popular, but as elsewhere the passage of time has destroyed artistic creations such as paintings that were made from organic materials.

In financing such massive construction, Hadrian was following in the steps of his predecessor in the early second century A.D., the emperor Trajan. A successful general, Trajan in A.D. 113 erected a tall, sculpted column near the Roman Forum to tell the story of his war against the Dacians ("barbarians," as the Romans called them, from the northern frontier of the empire along the Danube River). The column reached nearly 130 feet high, with an interior spiral staircase carved out from its solid stone and, at the top, a statue of the emperor (later replaced by the statue of St. Peter that stands there today). A band of sculpted scenes illustrating preparations for the war, its battles, and much other detail spirals upward around the column, presenting a filmstrip in stone, as it were, to portray the emperor's success. Its images provide our best evidence for what Roman soldiers and their equipment looked like. This column, the best-preserved such monument in Rome, stood at one end of the large forum that Trajan also built. This vast public space had a complex archi-

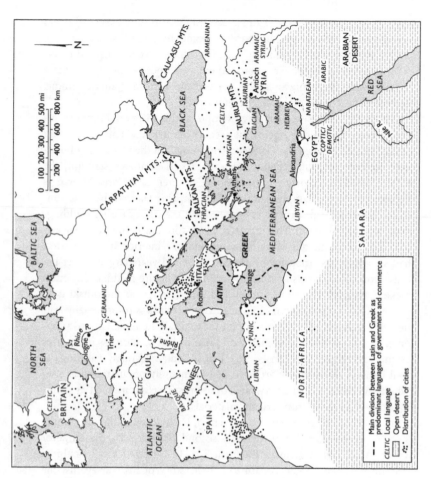

Map 8. Spoken Languages Around the Roman World

tecture, including the largest basilica (a meeting hall, especially for court cases) yet erected in Rome. The basilica's multistoried design had an interior ceiling some 80 feet high. Rising along the hillside next to Trajan's forum was the set of buildings known as Trajan's Market, a labyrinth of commercial spaces built on three different street levels.

The aqueducts built to bring an endless supply of fresh water to the capital city constituted a category of architecture that greatly benefited the people of Rome. Rome's earliest aqueduct had been built in the second century B.C., but the emperors vastly increased the public water supply by constructing channels carried atop ranks of arches that stretched for miles and miles to bring water from the surrounding hills to pour out through countless and constantly-flowing fountains scattered around the city (many still functioning today). Gravity-fed for their entire length, the aqueducts produced a steady stream of moving water. This resource provided everyone in Rome, poor as well as rich, with water safe to drink, and a flow sufficient to fill the pools of the public baths and rinse out the public toilets. The emperors also improved the supply of food for the city by continuing development of its port, located west of Rome on the coast in the town of Ostia. With some buildings preserved to more than one story, the impressive remains of ancient Ostia testify to the thriving commercial activity associated with the import-export business conducted in the port of ancient Rome.

Unlike Augustus in his outrage at the sexy poems of Ovid, his successors did not worry that scandalous literature posed a threat to the social order they worked constantly to maintain. They did, however, believe that law was crucial. Indeed, Romans prided themselves on their ability to order their society through law. As Vergil had expressed it, their mission was "to establish law and order within a framework of peace" (*Aeneid* 6.851–853). The principles and practices that characterized Roman law influenced most systems of law in modern Europe. Roman law's most distinctive characteristic was the recognition of the principle of equity, which meant accomplishing what was "good and fair," even if the letter of the law had to be ignored to do so. This principle led legal thinkers to insist, for example, that the intent of parties in a mutually agreeable deal outweighed the words of their contract, and that the burden of proof lay with the accuser rather than the accused. The emperor Trajan ruled that no one should be convicted on the grounds of suspicion alone because it was better for a guilty person to go unpunished than for an innocent person to be condemned.

The Roman desire for social order led their system of law to specify formal distinctions among people and divide them into classes defined by wealth and status. As always, the elites constituted a tiny portion of the population under the Empire. Only about one in every fifty thousand had enough money to qualify for the senatorial class, the highest status in Roman society, while about one in a thousand belonged to the equestrian class, the next rank in the social hierarchy. Different purple stripes on clothing advertised these statuses. The third-highest order consisted of local officials in provincial towns.

Those outside the social elite faced greater disadvantages than just snobbery. An old distinction that had originated in the Republic between "worthier people" and "humbler people" hardened under the Principate; by the third century A.D. it was recognized throughout the system of Roman law. The law institutionalized such distinctions because an orderly existence for everyone was thought to depend on maintaining these differences. The "better people" included senators, equestrians, curiales, and retired army veterans. Everybody else (except for slaves, who counted as property, not people) made up the vastly larger group of "humbler people." This second group, the majority of the population, faced the gravest disadvantage of their inferior status in trials: the law imposed harsher penalties on them for the same crimes. "Humbler people" convicted of capital crimes were regularly executed by being crucified or torn apart by wild animals before a crowd of spectators. "Better people" rarely suffered the death penalty. If they were condemned, they received a quicker and more dignified execution by the sword. "Humbler people" could also be tortured in criminal investigations, even if they were citizens. Romans regarded these differences as fair on the grounds that a person's higher status reflected a higher level of genuine merit. As the upper-class provincial governor Pliny the Younger expressed it, "nothing is less equitable than equality itself" (Letters 9.5).

Nothing mattered more to the empire's stability and prosperity than the population continuing to reproduce itself steadily and healthily. Concern over children therefore characterized marriage. Pliny the Younger once sent the following report to the grandfather of his third wife, Calpurnia: "You will be very sad to learn that your granddaughter has suffered a miscarriage. She is a young girl and did not realize she was pregnant. As a result she was more active than she should have been and paid a high price for her lack of knowledge by falling seriously ill" (Letters 8.10). Romans saw a loss of a pregnancy not only as a family tragedy but also a loss to society.

Without antibiotics or antiseptic surgery techniques, ancient medicine could do little to promote healthy childbirth. Complications during and after delivery could easily lead to the mother's death because doctors could not cure infections or stop internal bleeding. They did possess carefully crafted instruments for surgery and for physical examinations, but they did not know about the transmission of disease by microorganisms, and they were badly mistaken about the process of reproduction. Gynecologists erroneously recommended the days just before and after menstruation as the best time to become pregnant. As in Greek medicine, treatments were mainly limited to potions based on plants and other organic materials; some of these natural remedies were effective, but others were at best placebos, such as the drink of wild boar's manure boiled in vinegar customarily given to chariot drivers who had been injured in crashes. Many doctors were freedmen from Greece and other provinces, usually with only informal training. People considered medical occupations to have low status, unless the practitioner served the emperor or other members of the upper class.

As in earlier times, girls often married in their early teens, giving them a longer time to bear children. Because so many children died young, families had to produce numerous offspring to keep from disappearing. The tombstone of Veturia, a soldier's wife married at eleven, tells a typical story, here in the form of a poem singing her praises: "Here I lie, having lived for twenty-seven years. I was married to the same man for sixteen years and bore six children, five of whom died before I did" (*Corpus Inscriptionum Latinarum* 3.3572 = *Carmina Epigraphica Latina* 558). Although marriages were usually arranged between spouses who hardly knew each other, husbands and wives could grow to admire and love each other in a partnership devoted to family. The butcher Lucius Aurelius Hermia erected a gravestone to his wife inscribed with this poem that she is imagined as speaking after death: "Alive, I was named Aurelia Philematium. I was chaste, modest, knowing nothing about the crowd, faithful to my husband. My husband, also a freedman, like me, I have left, alas! He was more than a parent to me. He took me to his bosom when I was seven. At forty years old I am in the power of death. He thrived through my carefully doing my duty in everything" (*Corpus Inscriptionum Latinarum* 1.2.1221 = *Inscriptiones Latinae Selectae* 7472).

The emphasis on childbearing in marriage brought many health hazards to women, but to remain single and childless represented social failure for a Roman girl. Once children were born, both their mothers and servants took care of them. Women who could afford childcare routinely had their babies attended to and breast-fed by wet-nurses. Following ancient tradition, Romans continued to practice exposure (abandoning imperfect and unwanted babies), more so for infant girls than boys.

Both public and private sources did their best to support reproduction. The emperors donated financial support for children whose families were too poor to keep them. Wealthy people sometimes adopted children in their communities. One North African man gave enough money to support three hundred boys and three hundred girls each year until they grew up. The differing values placed on male and female children were evident in these welfare programs: boys often received more aid than girls. In the end, however, human intervention could barely affect this most essential process of life, leaving the empire vulnerable to devastation by epidemics. It is no wonder, then, that Romans believed their fates ultimately lay in the lap of the gods.

8

From Jesus to Crisis in the Early Empire

The Roman Empire was home to many different forms of religion, from the worship of the many gods of polytheism, to the newly important imperial cult, to the monotheism of Judaism. Almost everyone believed in the power of the divine and that it deeply affected their everyday lives, but there was a great diversity of specific religious beliefs and practices. That variety increased in the first century A.D. when Christianity began as a splinter group within Judaism in Judea, where Jews were allowed to practice their religion under Roman provincial rule. The emergence of Christianity would turn out to be the most significant long-term change for the history of the world to come from the history of ancient Rome.

Only a relatively small group of people embraced the new movement in the beginning; it was centuries before Christians became numerous. Believers in the new faith faced constant suspicion and hostility. Virtually every book of the biblical New Testament refers to the resistance that Christians encountered. Their numbers grew, if only gradually, as more people drew inspiration from stories of the charismatic career of Jesus, Christians' belief in his role as a savior of humanity, their sense of mission, and the strong bonds of community they developed. Another source of strength was

TIMELINE (ALL DATES A.D.)

30: Jesus is executed in Jerusalem.

64: Emperor Nero blames Christians for a huge fire in Rome.

65 (?): Paul of Tarsus is executed in Rome.

112 (?): The Roman provincial governor Pliny executes Christians in Asia Minor for refusing to sacrifice to the cult of the emperor.

Mid-second century: Roman emperors fight wars against Germanic barbarian invaders on the empire's northern frontier in central Europe.

Late second century: The prophetesses Prisca and Maximilla preach an apocalyptic message.

193–211: Septimius Severus rules as Roman emperor and drains the imperial treasury to pay the army.

203: Perpetua is executed as a Christian martyr in Carthage.

212: Caracalla, son of Septimius Severus, extends Roman citizenship to almost everyone except slaves to try to increase government tax collections.

249 (?): Origen writes his *Against Celsus* to refute the philosopher Celsus's criticisms of Christianity.

Mid-third century: The empire is in crisis from civil war, barbarian invasions, economic troubles, and epidemic disease.

260: Emperor Valerian is captured in Syria by Shapur I, the ruler of Sasanian Persia.

260–268: Emperor Gallienus stops attacks on Christians and restores church property.

the new religion's inclusion of women and slaves, which allowed it to draw members from the entire population.

The new religion was based on the life and teachings of Jesus (4 B.C.–A.D. 30). The background of Christianity lay, however, in Jewish history from long before. Harsh Roman rule in the homeland of Jesus had made the people restless and the provincial authorities anxious about rebellion. His career therefore unrolled in an unsettled environment, and his execution reflected Roman readiness to eliminate any perceived threat to peace and social order. When, after the death of Jesus, devoted followers, above all Paul of Tarsus (A.D. 5–65), preached the message that understanding the significance of Jesus was the source of salvation and spread their teachings beyond the Jewish community at the eastern end of the

Mediterranean Sea to include non-Jews, Christianity took its first step into a wider, and unwelcoming, world.

For Rome's rulers, Christianity presented a problem because it seemed to them to place individuals' commitment to their faith above the traditional Roman value of loyalty and public service to the state. When in the third century A.D. a severe political and economic crisis struck the empire, the emperors responded in the traditional way: they looked for the people whose actions must have, the rulers believed, provoked the anger of the gods against Rome. The ones they settled on to punish for having harmed the community by angering the gods were the Christians.

CHRISTIANITY'S ORIGINS

The creation of Christianity had deep roots in the history of the Jews. Their harsh experiences of oppression under the rule of others raised the most difficult question about divine justice: How could a just God allow the wicked to prosper and the righteous to suffer? Nearly two hundred years before Jesus' birth, persecution by the Seleucid king Antiochus IV (ruled 175 B.C.–164 B.C.) had provoked the Jews into a long and bloody revolt. The desperateness of this struggle pushed them to develop their version of apocalypticism ("revealing what is hidden"). According to this worldview, evil powers, divine and human, controlled the present world. This hateful regime would soon end, however, when God and his agents would reveal their plan to conquer the forces of evil by sending a deliverer, an "anointed one," to win a great battle. A final judgment would follow, to bring eternal punishment to the wicked and eternal reward to the righteous. Apocalypticism became immensely popular, especially among the Jews living in Judea under Roman rule. Eventually, it inspired not only Jews but Christians and Muslims as well.

Apocalyptic yearnings fired the imaginations of many Jews in Judea at the time of Jesus' birth about 4 B.C. because they were unhappy with the political situation under Roman rule and disagreed among themselves about what form Judaism should take in such troubled times. Some Jews favored subjecting themselves to their overlords, while others preached rejection of the non-Jewish world and its spiritual corruption. The Jews' local ruler, installed by the Romans, was Herod the Great (ruled 37 B.C.–4 B.C.). His flamboyant taste for a Greek style of life, which outraged Jewish law, made him unpopular with many locals, despite his magnificent rebuilding of the holiest Jewish shrine, the great temple in Jerusalem. When a decade of unrest followed his death, Augustus punished the Jews

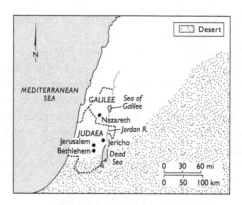

Map 9. Palestine in the Era of Jesus

by sending rulers directly from Rome to oversee their local leaders, and by imposing high taxes. By Jesus' lifetime, then, his homeland had become a powder keg threatening to explode.

Jesus began his career as a teacher and healer in his native region of Galilee during the reign of Tiberius (ruled A.D. 14–37). The New Testament Gospels, first written between about A.D. 70 and 90, offer the earliest accounts of his life. Jesus himself wrote nothing down, and others' accounts of his words and deeds are varied and controversial. Jesus taught not by direct instruction but by telling stories and parables that challenged people to think about what he meant. Lively discussion therefore surrounded him wherever he went.

The Gospels begin the story of his public ministry with his baptism by John the Baptist, who preached a message of the need for repentance before God's soon-to-arrive final judgment on the world. John was executed by the Jewish leader Herod Antipas, a son of Herod the Great, whom the Romans supported; Antipas feared John's apocalyptic preaching might instigate riots.

After John's death, Jesus continued his mission by proclaiming the imminence of God's kingdom and the need to prepare spiritually for its coming. He accepted the designation of Messiah, but his complex apocalypticism did not preach immediate revolt against the Romans. Instead, he revealed that God's true kingdom was not to be found on the earth but in heaven. He stressed that salvation in this kingdom was open to everyone, regardless of his or her social status or apparent sinfulness. He welcomed women and the poor, traveling around the local countryside to spread his teachings. His emphasis on God's love for people as his children and their overriding responsibility to love one another was consistent with Jewish religious teachings, as in the interpretation of the Scriptures by the rabbi Hillel (active 30 B.C.–A.D. 9).

An educated Jew who perhaps knew Greek as well as Aramaic, the local tongue, Jesus realized that he had to reach the urban crowds to make a truly great impact. Therefore, he left the villages where he had begun his career and took his message to the region's main towns and cities. His miraculous healings and exorcisms combined with his powerful preaching to create a sensation. His notoriety attracted the attention of the authorities, who automatically assumed that he aspired to political power. Fearing Jesus might start a Jewish revolt, the Roman regional governor Pontius Pilate (ruled A.D. 26–36) ordered his crucifixion in Jerusalem in A.D. 30, the usual punishment for threatening the peace in Roman-ruled territory.

In contrast to the fate of other suspected rebels whom the Romans executed, Jesus's influence emphatically lived on after his punishment. His followers reported that God had miraculously raised him from the dead, and they set about convincing other Jews that he was the promised Messiah, who would soon return to judge the world and usher in God's kingdom. At this point those who believed this had no thought of starting a new religion. They considered themselves faithful Jews and continued to follow the commandments of Jewish law.

A radical change took place with the conversion of Paul of Tarsus, a pious Jew with Roman citizenship who had formerly persecuted those who accepted Jesus as the Messiah. After a religious vision that he interpreted as a direct revelation from Jesus, Paul became a believer, or a Christian (follower of Christ), as members of the new movement came to be known. Paul made it his mission to tell as many people as possible that accepting Jesus's death as the ultimate sacrifice for the sins of humanity was the only way to be righteous in the eyes of God. Those who accepted Jesus as divine and followed his teachings could expect to attain salvation in the world to come. Paul's teachings and his strenuous efforts to spread his ideas among people outside Judea led to the creation of Christianity as a new religion.

Although Paul stressed the necessity of ethical behavior, especially avoiding sexual immorality and not worshiping traditional Greco-Roman gods, he also taught that there was no need to keep all the provisions of Jewish law. Seeking to bring Christianity outside the Jewish community, he directed his efforts to the non-Jews of Syria, Asia Minor, and Greece. To make conversion easier, he did not require the males who entered the movement to undergo the Jewish initiation rite of circum-

cision. This tenet, along with his teachings that his congregations did not
have to observe Jewish dietary restrictions or festivals, led to tensions
with the followers of Jesus living in Jerusalem, who still believed Christians had to follow Jewish law. Although Paul preached that Christians
should follow traditional social rules in everyday life in the current world,
including the distinction between free people and slaves, the controversy
generated by his appearances in many cities in the eastern provinces of
the empire led Roman authorities to arrest him as a criminal trouble-
maker and execute him about A.D. 65.

Paul's mission was only one part of the turmoil afflicting the Jewish
community in this period. Hatred of Roman rule finally provoked the
Jews to revolt in A.D. 66, with disastrous results. After defeating the rebels in A.D. 70 in a bloody siege that saw the Jewish Temple destroyed by
fire, Titus sold most of the city's population into slavery. Without a temple to serve as the center of their ancestral rituals, Jews had to reinvent
the practices of their religion. In the aftermath of this catastrophe, the
distancing of Christianity from Judaism that Paul had begun gained mo-
mentum, giving birth to a separate religion. His impact on the movement
can be gauged by the number of his letters—thirteen—that were included
in the collection of twenty-seven Christian writings that became the New
Testament. Followers of Jesus came to regard these writings as having
equal authority with the Jewish Bible, which they now called the Old
Testament. Since teachers like Paul preached mainly in the cities, where
the crowds were, congregations of Christians began to spring up among
non-Jewish, urban, middle-class men and women, with a few richer and
poorer members. Women as well as men could hold offices in these congregations. Indeed, the first head of a congregation attested in the New
Testament was a woman.

CHALLENGES TO A NEW RELIGION

Christianity had to overcome serious challenges to become a new religion separate from Judaism. The emperors found Christians baffling and
irritating. Since, unlike Jews, Christians followed a novel faith rather than
a traditional religion handed down from their ancestors, they enjoyed no
special treatment under Roman law. The Romans traditionally respected
different customs and beliefs if they were ancient, but they were deeply
suspicious of any new creed. Romans also looked down on Christians
because Jesus, their divine savior, had been crucified as a criminal by the
government. Christians' worship rituals also aroused hostility because they
led to accusations of cannibalism and sexual promiscuity arising from

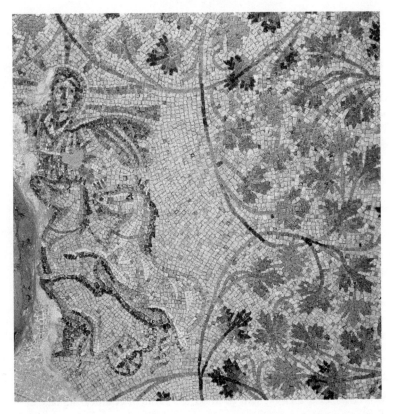

Figure 22. A mosaic portrays Christ riding in a chariot through the sky with light rays extending from his head, in the style of traditional depictions of the sun god. Early Christian art frequently took its models from the image traditions of Greek and Roman religion. Scala/Art Resource, NY.

Christians' ritual of eating the body and drinking the blood of Jesus during their central rite, which they called the Love Feast. In short, they seemed a dangerous threat to traditional social order. Roman officials, suspecting Christians of being politically subversive, could prosecute them for treason, especially for refusing to participate in the imperial cult.

It made sense to Roman officials, therefore, to blame Christians for public disasters. When a large part of Rome burned in A.D. 64, Nero punished them for arson. As Tacitus reports (*Annals* 15.44), Nero had Christians "covered with the skins of wild animals and mauled to death by dogs, or fastened to crosses and set on fire to provide light at night."

The harshness of this punishment ironically earned the Christians some sympathy from Rome's population. After this persecution, the government acted against Christians only intermittently. No law specifically forbade their religion, but they made easy prey for officials, who could punish them in the name of maintaining public order. The action of Pliny as a provincial governor in Asia Minor illustrated their predicament. About A.D. 112 he asked some people accused of practicing this new religion if they were indeed Christians, urging those who admitted it to reconsider. Those who denied it, as well as those who stated they no longer believed, he freed after they sacrificed to the imperial cult and cursed Christ. He executed those who persisted in their faith.

From the official point of view, Christians had no right to retain their religion if it created disturbances. As a letter from Emperor Trajan to Pliny made clear, however, the emperors had no policy of tracking them down. Christians concerned the government only when authorities noticed their refusal to participate in official sacrifices or non-Christians complained about them. Ordinary Romans felt hostile toward Christians mostly because they feared that tolerating them would bring down upon everyone the wrath of the gods of traditional Roman religion. Christians' refusal to participate in the imperial cult caused the most concern. Because they denied the existence of the old gods and the divine associations of the emperor, they seemed sure to provoke the gods to punish the world with natural catastrophes. Tertullian (A.D. 160–220), a Christian scholar from North Africa, described this thinking (*Apology* 40): "If the Tiber River overflows, or if the Nile fails to flood; if a drought or an earthquake or a famine or a plague hits, then everyone immediately shouts, 'To the lions with the Christians!'"

In response to official hostility, intellectuals such as Tertullian and Justin (A.D. 100–165) defended their cause by arguing that Romans had nothing to fear from Christians. Far from spreading immorality and subversion, these writers insisted, the Christian religion taught an elevated moral code and respect for authority. It was not a foreign superstition, but rather the true philosophy that combined the best features of Judaism and Greek thought and was thus a fitting religion for their diverse world. As Tertullian pointed out (*Apology* 30), though Christians could not worship the emperors, they did "pray to the true God for their safety. We pray for a fortunate life for them, a secure rule, safety for their families, a courageous army, a loyal Senate, a virtuous people, a world of peace."

Official hostility to Christians had the opposite effect to its intention of suppressing the new religion; as Tertullian remarked (*Apology* 50), "the blood of the martyrs is the seed of the Church." Some Christians re-

garded public trials and executions as an opportunity to become wit-
nesses ("martyrs" in Greek) to their faith. Their firm conviction that their
deaths would take them directly to paradise allowed them to face excru-
ciating tortures with courage; some even tried for martyrdom. Ignatius
(A.D. 35–107), bishop of Antioch, begged the Rome congregation, which
was becoming the most prominent one, not to ask the emperor to show
him mercy after his arrest (*Epistle to the Romans* 4): "Let me be food for the
wild animals (in the arena) through whom I can reach God," he pleaded.
"I am God's wheat, to be ground up by the teeth of beasts so that I may
be found pure bread of Christ."

Women as well as men could show their determination as martyrs. In
A.D. 203, Vibia Perpetua, wealthy and twenty-two years old, nursed her
infant in a Carthage jail while awaiting execution; she had received the
death sentence for refusing to sacrifice an animal to the gods for the emperor's health and safety. One morning the jailer dragged her off to the
city's main square, where a crowd had gathered. Perpetua described in
her diary what happened when the local governor made a last, public
attempt to get her to save her life:

> My father came carrying my son, crying "Perform the sacrifice; take
> pity on your baby!" Then the governor said, "Think of your old fa-
> ther; show pity for your little child! Offer the sacrifice for the welfare
> of the imperial family." "I refuse," I answered. "Are you a Christian?"
> asked the governor. "Yes." When my father would not stop trying to
> change my mind, the governor ordered him flung to the earth and
> whipped with a rod. I felt sorry for my father; it seemed they were
> beating me. I pitied his pathetic old age (*The Passion of Saints Perpetua and
> Felicity* 6).

Perpetua's punishment was then carried out: gored by a wild bull and
stabbed by a gladiator, she died professing her faith. She was later recognized as a saint. Stories such as Perpetua's proclaimed the martyrs' courage
to inspire other Christians to stand up to hostility from non-Christians.
They also helped to attract new members and to shape the identity of this
new religion as a faith that gave its believers the spiritual power to endure great suffering.

Christians in the first century A.D. expected Jesus to return to pass
final judgment on the world during their lifetimes. When this hope was
not met, by the second century they began transforming their religion
from an apocalyptic Jewish sect expecting the immediate end of the
world into one that could survive over the long term. To do this, they
had to create organizations with leaders tasked to build connections be-

tween congregations, work for order and unity among often-fractious
groups, and reconcile diverse beliefs about their new faith, including disagreements about the role of women in the congregations.

Order and unity were hard for Christians to achieve because they constantly and fiercely disagreed about what they should believe and how
they should live. The bitterest arguments came over how they should follow God's command to imitate his love for them by loving each other
with tenderness and compassion. Some insisted that it was necessary to
withdraw from the everyday world to escape its evil. Others believed they
could strive to live by Christ's teachings while retaining their jobs and
ordinary lives. Many Christians questioned whether they could serve as
soldiers without betraying their religious beliefs because the army regularly participated in its patron's cult. This dilemma raised the further
issue of whether Christians could remain loyal subjects of the emperor.
Controversy over such issues raged in the many congregations that had
arisen by the second century around the Mediterranean, from Gaul to
Africa to Mesopotamia.

The appointment of bishops as a hierarchy of leaders with authority
to define doctrine and conduct was the most important institutional
development to deal with this disunity. This hierarchy was intended to
combat the splintering effect of the differing and competing versions of
the new religion and to promote "communion" among congregations,
an important value of early Christianity. Bishops had the power to define
what was orthodoxy (true doctrine as determined by councils of themselves) and what was heresy (from the Greek word meaning "private
choice"). Most importantly, they decided who could participate in worship, especially the Eucharist, or Lord's Supper, which many Christians
regarded as necessary for achieving eternal life. Exclusion meant losing
salvation. For all practical purposes, the meetings of the bishops of different cities constituted the final authority in the church's organization.
This loose organization became the early Catholic Church.

Christians could not agree on the role women should play in the
church and its hierarchy. In the earliest congregations, women held leadership positions, an innovation that contributed to Roman officials' suspicion of Christianity. When bishops began to be chosen, however,
women were usually relegated to inferior positions. This demotion reflected Paul's view that in Christianity women should be subordinate to
men; he also reaffirmed the view of his times that slaves should be subordinate to their masters.

Some congregations took a long time to accept this demotion of female believers; women still commanded positions of authority in some

groups in the second and third centuries A.D. The late second-century prophetesses Prisca and Maximilla, for example, proclaimed the apocalyptic message of Montanus that the Heavenly Jerusalem would soon descend in Asia Minor. Second-century Christians could also find inspiration for women as leaders in written accounts of devout believers such as Thecla. As a young woman, she canceled her engagement to a prominent noble in order to join Paul in preaching and founding churches. Thecla's courage overruled her mother's sadness at her refusal to marry: "My daughter, like a spider bound at the window by that man's words, is controlled by a new desire and a terrible passion" (*The Acts of Paul and Thecla* 9). Even when leadership posts were closed off to them, many women still chose a life of celibacy to serve the church. Their commitment to chastity as proof of their devotion to Christ gave these women the power to control their own bodies by removing their sexuality from the control of men. It also bestowed social status upon them, as women with a special closeness to God. By rejecting the traditional roles of wife and mother in favor of spiritual celebrity, celibate Christian women achieved a measure of independence and authority generally denied to them in the outside world.

TRADITIONAL RELIGION AND PHILOSOPHY

Diverse ideas and rituals also characterized the old polytheism of Greco-Roman religion, just as in the new faith of Christianity. Even two centuries after Jesus's death the overwhelming majority of religious people were still polytheists, worshiping numerous different gods and goddesses. What polytheists did agree on was that the empire's success and prosperity demonstrated that the old gods favored and protected their community and that the imperial cult added to their safety.

The religious beliefs and rituals of traditional religion in ancient Rome were meant to offer worship to all the divinities that could affect human life and thereby win divine favor for the worshipers and their community. The deities ranged from the central gods of the state cults, such as Jupiter and Minerva, to local spirits thought to inhabit forests, rivers, and springs. In the third century A.D., the emperors imitated the ancient pharaohs of Egypt by officially introducing worship of the sun as the supreme deity of the empire. Several popular new religious cults also emerged as the empire's diverse regions mingled their traditions. The Iranian god Mithras developed a large following among merchants and soldiers as the god of the morning light, a superhuman hero requiring ethical conduct and truthful dealings from his followers. Since Mithraism excluded women, this restriction put it at a disadvantage in expanding its membership.

The cult of the Egyptian goddess Isis best reveals how traditional religion could provide believers with a religious experience that aroused strong personal emotions and demanded a moral way of life. The worship of Isis had already attracted Romans by the time of Augustus. He tried to suppress it because it was Cleopatra's religion, but Isis's widely known reputation as a kind and compassionate goddess who cared for the suffering of each of her followers made her cult too popular to crush. Her image was that of a loving mother, and in art she was often shown nursing her son. The Egyptians even said that it was her tears for her starving people that caused the Nile to flood every year and bring good harvests to the land. A central doctrine of the cult of Isis concerned the death and resurrection of her husband, Osiris. Isis promised her followers a similar hope for life after death for themselves. Her cult was open to both men and women. A preserved wall painting found at Pompeii in Italy shows people of both dark- and light-skinned races officiating at her rituals, reflecting the diversity of the population of Egypt where her worship originated.

Isis required her believers to behave morally. Inscriptions put up for all to read expressed her high standards by referring to her own civilizing accomplishments: "I put down the rule of tyrants; I put an end to murders; I forced women to be loved by men; I caused what is right to be mightier than gold and silver" (Burstein, no. 112). The hero of Apuleius's novel, whom Isis rescued from a life of pain, humiliation, and immorality, expressed his intense joy after having been spiritually reborn by the goddess (*The Golden Ass* 11.25): "O holy and eternal guardian of the human race, who always cherishes mortals and blesses them, you care for the troubles of miserable humans with a sweet mother's love. Neither day nor night, nor any moment of time, ever passes by without your blessings." Other traditional cults also required their worshipers to lead morally upright lives. Inscriptions from villages in Asia Minor record ordinary people's confessions to sins, such as sexual transgressions, for which their local god had imposed harsh penance on them. In this way, their polytheist religion guided their moral lives.

Religion was not the exclusive guide to life in the Roman Empire. Many people believed that philosophic principles also helped them to understand the nature of human existence and how best to live. Stoicism, derived from the teachings of the Greek philosopher Zeno (335 B.C.– 263 B.C.), was the most popular philosophy among Romans. Stoic values emphasized self-discipline above all else, and their code of personal ethics

Figure 23. This Roman statue depicts Isis, the Egyptian goddess whose cult became extremely popular in the empire; she is holding objects used in her worship. Worshipers prized her as a source of salvation and protection— a kind and caring mother with divine powers. Marie-Lan Nguyen/Wikimedia Commons.

left no room for out-of-control conduct. As the first-century A.D. author Seneca put it in a moral essay on controlling one's rage, "It is easier to prevent harmful emotions from entering the soul than it is to control them once they have entered" (*On Anger* 1.7.2). Stoicism taught that a single creative force incorporating reason, nature, and divinity guided the universe. Humans shared in the essence of this universal force and found

happiness and patience by living in accordance with it. The emperor
Marcus Aurelius in his Meditations, written while he was on military campaign on the cold northern frontier of the empire, bluntly expressed the
Stoic belief that people exist for each other: "Either make others better,
or just put up with them," he insisted (Meditations 8.59). Furthermore, he
repeatedly stressed, people owed obligations to society as part of the natural order; the conduct of every moral person needed to reflect this truth.
The Stoic philosopher Musonius Rufus insisted that this principle was
just as true for women as for men, and he supported philosophic education for both genders.

Other systems of philosophy, especially those rooted in the thought of
Plato (429 B.C.–347 B.C.), challenged Christian intellectuals to defend
their new faith. About A.D. 176, for example, Celsus published a wide-
ranging attack on Christianity reflecting his ideas as a follower of Plato.
His essay On the True Doctrine revealed what educated non-Christians knew
about the new faith and their varied reasons for rejecting it. As his arguments show, they had difficulty understanding the basic ideas of Christian belief in this period, to say nothing of the diversity of competing
"orthodox" and "heretical" versions. In his criticism of Christianity, Celsus paid no attention to accusations of evil and immoral conduct by
Christians, although this type of slander had become common. Instead, he
concentrated on philosophical arguments, such as the Platonic insistence
on the immateriality of the soul as contrasted to the Christian belief in
bodily resurrection on the Day of Judgment. In short, Celsus accused
Christians of intellectual deficiency rather than immorality.

Celsus's work achieved great notoriety as a formidable challenge to
Christianity on intellectual and philosophical grounds. So strong and
enduring was its influence that even seventy years later a well-known
teacher and philosopher, Origen (A.D. 185–255), composed a work entitled Against Celsus (Contra Celsum) to refute Celsus's arguments. Origen insisted that Christianity was both true and superior to traditional philosophy as a guide to correct living.

At about the same time, however, traditional religious belief achieved
its most intellectual formulation in the works of Plotinus (A.D. 205–270).
Plotinus's spiritual philosophy, called Neoplatonism because it developed
new doctrines based on Plato's philosophy, influenced many educated
Christians as well as traditional believers. The religious doctrines of Neoplatonism focused on the human longing to return to the abstract universal Good from which human existence was derived. By turning away
from the life of the body through the intellectual pursuit of philosophy,
individual souls could ascend to the level of the universal soul. In this

way, individuals could become unified with the whole that expressed the true meaning of existence. This mystical union with what the Christians would call God could be achieved only through strenuous self-discipline in personal morality as well as in intellectual life. Neoplatonism's stress on spiritual purity gave it a powerful appeal.

Stoicism, the worship of Isis, Neoplatonism—all these manifestations of traditional philosophy and religion paralleled Christianity in providing guidance, comfort, and hope to people through good times or bad. By the third century A.D., then, thoughtful people had various options of what to believe in to help them survive the harshness of ancient life. The seriousness of the competition for adherents among these different belief systems is reflected in the growing emphasis on the complex history of religion, especially Christianity, found in the sources that have survived until today.

CRISIS IN THE THIRD CENTURY A.D.

Life became much harsher for many Romans across the empire in the third century A.D. Some regions suffered less than others, but multiple disasters combined to create a crisis for government and society. The invasions that outsiders had long been conducting on the northern and eastern frontiers had forced the emperors to expand the army, but the increased need for military pay and supplies strained imperial finances because, with no more successful conquests, the army had become a source of negative instead of positive cash flow to the treasury. The nonmilitary economy did not expand sufficiently to provide revenues to make up the difference. In short, the emperors' need for revenue had grown faster than the empire's tax base. This discrepancy fueled a crisis in national defense because the emperors' desperate schemes to raise money to pay and equip the troops damaged the economy and eroded public confidence in the empire's security. The unrest that resulted encouraged ambitious generals to repeat the crimes that had destroyed the Republic, leading personal armies to seize power. Civil war once again ravaged Rome, lasting for decades in the middle of the century and destabilizing the Principate system of government.

Emperors concerned with national defense had been leading campaigns to repel invaders since the reign of Domitian in the first century A.D. The most aggressive attackers were the loosely organized Germanic bands that often crossed the Danube and Rhine rivers from the north to raid the provinces there. These invaders had begun to mount damaging attacks during the reign of Antoninus Pius (A.D. 138–161) and then greatly escalated the pressure in the rule of Marcus Aurelius (A.D. 161–180). Constant fighting against the Roman army allowed these originally disorganized warrior bands to develop greater military cohesiveness. This change made them much more effective and laid the basis for the enormous military challenges that they would later present to the Roman Empire in the fourth and fifth centuries.

Respecting the great fighting spirit of Germanic warriors, the emperors began hiring them as auxiliary soldiers for the Roman army and settling them on the frontiers as buffers against other invaders. This recruitment of foreign soldiers became a key resource in national defense; it had the unintended consequence of allowing the Germans to experience the comparative comfort and prosperity of Roman life on a daily basis. This development over time increased the tendency for these "barbarians" to want to stay in the empire's territory permanently. This tendency in turn put in motion a long-term pattern of change that was eventually going to alter the shape and structure of the empire forever, even foreshadowing the territorial outlines of the nation states of modern Europe.

The emperors tried to meet the increasing threat of invasion by expanding the number of regular and auxiliary soldiers. By around A.D. 200, the army had 100,000 more troops than under Augustus, enrolling perhaps as many as 350,000 to 400,000 men. It was crucial to guarantee regular pay to keep these men content because their career was rugged. Training constantly, soldiers had to be fit enough to carry forty-pound packs up to twenty miles in five hours, swimming rivers in their way. Since on the march they built a fortified camp every night, they carried all the makings of a wooden-walled city with them everywhere they went. As one writer reported after seeing Roman soldiers in action, "infantrymen were little different from loaded pack mules" (Josephus, The Jewish War 3.95). Huge quantities of supplies were required to support the army. At one temporary fort in a frontier area, archaeologists found a supply of a million iron nails—ten tons' worth. The same encampment required seventeen miles of planks and logs for its buildings and fortifications. To outfit a single legion of five to six thousand men with tents required fifty-four thousand calves' hides.

To make matters worse, inflation had driven up prices. A principal cause of inflation under the early Empire may have been, ironically, the long period of "Roman Peace" that had promoted increased demand for the economy's relatively static production of goods and services. Over time, some emperors responded to inflated prices by debasing the most important form of official currency—the silver coins issued under the ruler's name. Debasement of the coinage involved putting less silver in each coin without reducing its face value to reflect the lower quantity of precious metal and therefore the lower intrinsic value of the money. With this technique, emperors hoped to create more cash from the same amount of precious metal. This attempt to cut government costs for purchasing goods and services soon became a dismal failure. Merchants, who were not fooled, simply raised prices to make up for the loss in value from the debased currency, leading to hyperinflation of prices. By the end of the second century A.D., these pressures had imposed a permanent shortfall in the imperial balance sheet. Still, the soldiers demanded that their patrons, the emperors, pay them well. The stage was set for a full-blown financial crisis in the imperial government.

Emperor Septimius Severus (A.D. 145–211) and his sons Caracalla and Geta set the catastrophe into final motion. These emperors from the Severan family fatally drained the treasury to satisfy the army. In addition, the sons' murderous rivalry with each other and reckless spending further destabilized the empire. An experienced military man who came from Punic ancestors in the large North African city of Lepcis Magna (in what is today Libya), Severus seized imperial power in A.D. 193 as a result of a crisis in Rome following the murder of Marcus Aurelius's son Commodus, and defeated rival claimants for power in several years of civil war. To try to win money for his army and glory for his family, Severus vigorously pursued the traditional imperial dream of foreign conquest by launching campaigns beyond the eastern and western ends of the empire in Mesopotamia and Scotland respectively. Unfortunately, these expeditions failed to bring in enough profits to fix the imperial budget deficit.

The soldiers were desperate because inflation had diminished the value of their wages to virtually nothing after the costs of basic supplies and clothing were deducted from their pay, according to long-standing army regulations. The troops therefore routinely expected the emperors as their patrons to provide them with regular bonuses. Severus spent large sums to provide this money, and he also decided to improve their condition over the long term by raising their regular rate of pay by a third. The expanded size of the army made this raise more expensive than the treasury could handle and further increased inflation. The dire financial consequences of his military policy concerned Severus not at all. His deathbed advice to his sons in A.D. 211 was to "stay on good terms with each other, make the soldiers rich, and pay no attention to everyone else" (Cassius Dio, *Roman History* 77.15).

Severus's sons followed this advice only on the last two points. Caracalla (A.D. 188–217) secured sole rule for himself by murdering his brother Geta. Caracalla's violent and profligate reign definitively ended the peace and prosperity of the empire's Golden Age. He increased the soldiers' pay by another 40 to 50 percent and also spent gigantic sums on grandiose building projects, including the largest public baths Rome had ever seen, covering blocks and blocks of the city. Caracalla's extravagant spending put unbearable pressure on the local provincial officials responsible for collecting taxes and on the citizens whom they pressed to pay ever-greater amounts. In short, he wrecked the imperial budget and paved the way for ruinous inflation in the coming decades.

In A.D. 212 Caracalla took his most famous step to try to resolve the budget crisis: he granted Roman citizenship to almost every man and woman in the empire except slaves. Because only citizens paid inheritance taxes and fees for freeing slaves, an increase in citizens meant an increase in revenues, most of which was earmarked for the army. But too much was never enough for Caracalla. Those close to him whispered that he was insane. Once when his mother upbraided him for his excesses he replied, "Never mind," as he drew his sword, "we shall not run out of money as long as I have this" (Cassius Dio, *Roman History* 78.10). In 217 the commander of Caracalla's bodyguards murdered him to make himself emperor.

A combination of human and natural disasters following the rule of the Severan emperors brought on the climax of the third-century crisis in the Roman Empire. First, political instability accompanied the imperial government's accelerating financial weakness. For almost seventy years in the mid-third century A.D., a parade of emperors and pretenders fought over power. Nearly thirty men held or claimed the throne, often several at a time, during these decades of near-anarchy. Their only qualification was their ability to command troops and to reward them for loyalty to themselves instead of the state.

The nearly constant civil wars of the mid-third century exacted a tremendous toll on the population and the economy. Insecurity combined with hyperinflation to make life miserable in much of the empire. Agriculture withered as farmers found it impossible to keep up normal production in wartime, when battling armies damaged their crops searching for food. City council members faced constantly escalating demands for tax revenues from the swiftly changing emperors. The constant financial pressure destroyed local elites' willingness to support their communities.

Foreign enemies took advantage of this period of crisis to attack, especially from the east and the north. Roman fortunes hit bottom when Shapur I, king of the Sasanian Empire of Persia, captured the emperor Valerian (ruled A.D. 253–260) in Syria in A.D. 260. Even the tough and

Figure 24. A Persian cameo shows Shapur I, a Sasanian king, accepting the surrender of the Roman emperor Valerian in A.D. 260. The Sasanian Empire rivaled those of Rome and of China as the world's most powerful of that era. Marie-Lan Nguyen/Wikimedia Commons.

experienced emperor Aurelian (ruled A.D. 270–275) could manage only defensive operations, such as recovering Egypt and Asia Minor from Zenobia, the warrior queen of Palmyra in Syria. Aurelian also encircled Rome with a massive wall more than eleven miles long to ward off surprise attacks from Germanic tribes, who were already smashing their way into Italy from the north. The Aurelian Wall snaked its way among Rome's hills, at one point incorporating one of Rome's most idiosyncratic monuments, the marble-faced pyramid that the wealthy Roman official C. Cestius built to be his tomb at the end of the first century B.C. Sections of the Aurelianic wall and its towers and gates can still be seen looming high above the streets at various places in modern Rome, such as at the Porta San Sebastiano opening onto the Appian Way.

Natural disasters compounded the crisis when devastating earthquakes and virulent epidemics struck the Mediterranean region in the middle of the century. The population declined significantly as food supplies became less dependable, civil war killed soldiers and civilians alike, and infection flared over large regions. The loss of population meant fewer soldiers for the army, whose efficiency as a defense force and internal provincial se-

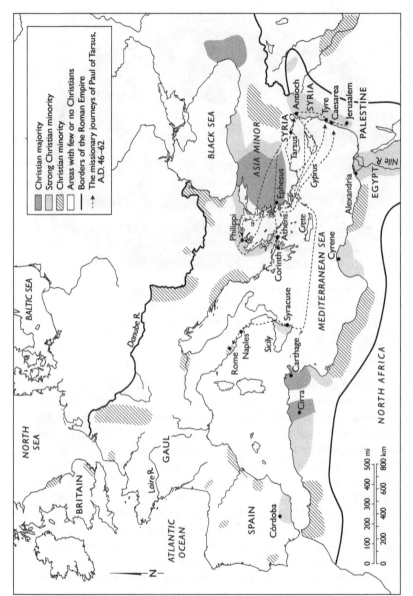

Map 10. Significant Populations of Christians, Late Third Century A.D.

Legend:
- Christian majority
- Strong Christian minority
- Christian minority
- Areas with few or no Christians
- Borders of the Roman Empire
- The missionary journeys of Paul of Tarsus, A.D. 46–62

Labels:
NORTH SEA, BALTIC SEA, BRITAIN, GAUL, Loire R., Danube R., BLACK SEA, SPAIN, Córdoba, ATLANTIC OCEAN, Rome, Naples, Sicily, Syracuse, Carthage, Cirta, NORTH AFRICA, MEDITERRANEAN SEA, Philippi, Corinth, Athens, Crete, Cyrene, ASIA MINOR, Ephesus, Tarsus, SYRIA, Antioch, Cyprus, Tyre, Caesarea, Jerusalem, PALESTINE, Alexandria, EGYPT, Nile R.

Scale: 0 100 200 300 400 500 mi
0 200 400 600 800 km

curity corps had already deteriorated seriously from political and financial chaos. More frontier areas of the empire therefore became vulnerable to raids, while roving bands of robbers also became more and more common inside the borders as economic conditions worsened. This deadly mix of troubles brought the empire to the brink of collapse. By this time, Romans once again desperately needed to refocus their values and transform their political system to keep their government and society from disintegrating.

Believers in traditional Roman religion explained these horrible times in the traditional way: the state gods were angry. But why? One obvious possibility seemed to be the growing presence of Christians, who denied the existence of Rome's gods and refused to participate in their worship. Therefore, the emperor Decius (ruled A.D. 249–251) conducted violent and, for the first time, systematically organized persecutions to eliminate this contaminated group and restore the goodwill of the gods. Decius ordered all inhabitants of the empire to prove their loyalty to the welfare of the state by participating in a sacrifice to its gods. Christians who refused were executed. Supporting the new emperor's claim to be the defender of Rome's protective cults and the freedom that polytheists believed that their ancestral rituals secured for Rome, the citizens of an Italian town in a public inscription praised Decius as "the Restorer of the Sacred Rites and of Liberty" (Babcock 1962). On the other side of the persecution, Cyprian, a convert from paganism who had become bishop of Carthage, urged Christians to be ready for martyrdom at the hands of the Antichrist (*Letters* 55).

These widespread persecutions did not stop the civil war, economic failure, and diseases that had precipitated the empire's protracted crisis. The emperor Gallienus (ruled A.D. 260–268) acted to restore religious peace to the empire by stopping the attacks on Christians and allowing bishops to recover church property that had been confiscated. This policy reduced overt tensions between Christians and the imperial government for the rest of the century. By the 280s A.D., however, no one could deny that the empire was tottering on the edge of the abyss financially and politically.

9

From Persecution to Christianization in the Later Empire

Remarkably, the empire was to be dragged back to safety in the same way it had begun: by creating a new form of authoritarian leadership, this time to replace the Principate, which had replaced the Republic. When Diocletian became emperor (ruled A.D. 284–305), he rescued the empire from its crisis by replacing the Principate with a more openly autocratic system of rule. As Roman emperor, Diocletian used his exceptional talent for leadership to reestablish centralized political and military authority. His administrative and financial reforms changed the shape and finances of the empire, while his persecution of Christians failed to prevent the new faith from becoming the official religion of the Roman Empire in the fourth century A.D., the time in which Roman history reaches the chronological period that modern historians often refer to as the "later Empire."

Emperor Constantine's conversion to Christianity in the early fourth century A.D. is understandably seen as a turning point in the history of Rome. He set the empire on a gradual path to Christianization, meaning the formal recognition of the new religion both as the official religion of the state and of the majority of the population. The process of Christianizing the Roman Empire was slow and tense, as Constantine's policy of religious toleration did not change people's minds about how

TIMELINE (ALL DATES A.D.)

284–306: Diocletian rules as Roman emperor and establishes the Dominate, ending the political crisis of the third century.

285: Antony becomes a Christian monk living alone in the Egyptian desert.

301: Diocletian imposes price and wage controls in a failed attempt to control inflation.

303: Diocletian begins the Great Persecution of Christians to try to restore the "peace of the gods."

306–337: Constantine rules as Roman emperor.

312: Constantine wins the battle of the Milvian Bridge in Rome and proclaims himself a Christian.

313: Constantine announces a policy of religious toleration.

321: Constantine makes Sunday the Lord's Day.

324–330: Constantine builds a new capital, Constantinople (today Istanbul), on the site of ancient Byzantium.

325: Constantine holds the Council of Nicea to try to end disputes over Christian doctrine.

349: St. Peter's Basilica in Rome is completed.

361–363: Emperor Julian tries (and fails) to reestablish traditional polytheism as the state's leading religion.

382: The Altar of Victory is removed from the Senate House in Rome.

386: Augustine converts to Christianity.

391: Emperor Theodosius makes Christianity the official religion by successfully banning pagan sacrifices.

415: The pagan philosopher Hypatia is murdered by Christians in Alexandria.

wrong—and therefore dangerous—the people were who worshiped differently from themselves. Christians thought that traditional believers were idolaters and atheists; traditional believers feared Christians threatened the goodwill of the gods of the official state cults that they saw as protecting the empire.

RESCUING THE EMPIRE

No one could have predicted Diocletian's spectacular imperial career: he originated as an uneducated military man from the rough region of

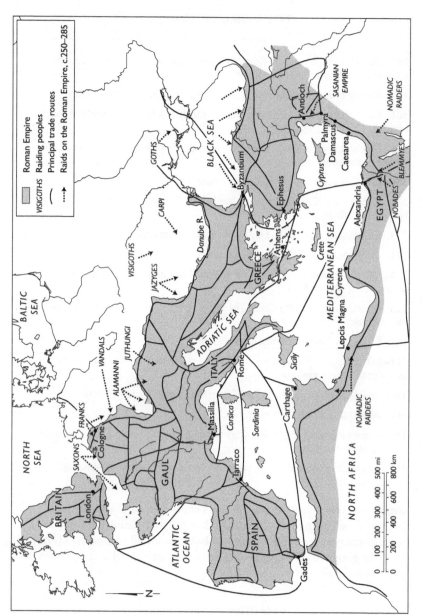

Map 11. The Roman Empire in the Third-Century A.D. Crisis

Dalmatia in the Balkans. His courage and intelligence propelled him through the ranks until with the backing of the army he was recognized as the emperor in A.D. 284. He ended the third-century A.D. crisis by imposing the most autocratic system of rule the Roman world had yet seen.

Relying on the military's support, he had himself formally recognized as *dominus* ("Master"—the term slaves called their owners) instead of "First Man." For this reason, historians refer to the system of Roman imperial government from Diocletian onward as the Dominate. The Dominate's system of blatant autocracy—rulers openly claiming and exercising absolute power—eliminated any pretense of shared authority between the emperor and the Roman elite. Senators, consuls, and other traces of traditions of the Republic continued to exist—including the name "Republic" for the government—but these survivals from long ago were kept on only to give a façade of traditional political legitimacy to the new autocratic system. The emperors of the Dominate would increasingly choose their imperial officials from the lower ranks of society based on their competence and loyalty to the ruler, instead of automatically taking high-ranking administrators from the upper class.

As "Masters" the emperors developed new ways to display their supremacy. Abandoning the precedent set by Augustus of wearing plain, everyday clothes, the rulers in the Dominate dressed in jeweled robes, wore dazzling crowns, and surrounded themselves with courtiers and ceremony. To show the difference between the "Master" and ordinary people, a series of veils separated the palace's waiting rooms from the inner space where the ruler held audiences. Officials marked their rank in the fiercely hierarchical imperial administration with grandiose titles such as "Most Perfect" and showed off their status with special shoes and belts. In its style and propaganda, the Dominate's imperial court more closely resembled that of the Great King of Persia a thousand years earlier and that of the contemporary Sasanian kingdom in Persia than that of the first Roman emperor. Following ancient Persian custom, people seeking favors from the "Master" had to throw themselves at his feet like slaves and kiss the gem-encrusted hem of his golden robe. The architecture of the Dominate also reflected the image of its rulers as all-powerful autocrats. When Diocletian built a public bath in Rome, it dwarfed its rivals with soaring vaults and domes covering a space over three thousand feet long on each side.

The Dominate also developed a theological framework for legitimizing its rule. Religious language was used to mark the emperor's special status above everybody else. The title *et deus* ("and God"), for example, could be added to "Master" as a mark of supreme honor. Diocletian also adopted the title *Jovius*, proclaiming himself descended from Jupiter (Jove), the chief Roman god. When two hundred years earlier the Flavian emperor Domitian had tried to call himself "Master and God," this display of pride had helped turn opinion against him. Now, these titles became usual, expressing the sense of complete respect and awe that emperors now expected from their subjects and demonstrating that imperial government on earth replicated the hierarchy of the gods.

The Dominate's emperors asserted their autocracy most aggressively in law and punishments for crime. Their word alone made law; the Assemblies of the Republic were no longer operating as sources of legislation. Relying on a personal staff that isolated them from the outside world, the emperors rarely sought advice from the elite, as earlier rulers had traditionally done. Moreover, their concern to maintain order convinced them to increase the severity of punishment for crimes to brutal levels. Thus Emperor Constantine in A.D. 331 ordered officials to "stop their greedy hands" or be punished by having their hands cut off by the sword (Theodosian Code 1.16.7). Serious criminals could be tied in a leather sack with snakes and drowned in a river. The guardians of a young girl who had allowed a lover to seduce her were punished by having molten lead poured into their mouths. Punishments grew especially harsh for the large segment of the population legally designated as "humbler people," but the "better people" generally escaped harsh treatment. In this way, the Dominate's autocracy strengthened the divisions between the poorer and the richer sections of the population.

Despite Diocletian's success in making himself into an autocrat, he concluded that the empire was too large to administer and defend from a single center. He therefore subdivided the rule of the empire to try to hold it together. In a daring innovation, he effectively split imperial territory in two by creating one administrative region in the west and another in the east. This essentially created a Western Roman Empire and an Eastern Roman Empire, though this division was not yet formally recognized. He then subdivided these regions in two, appointing four "partners" in rule to govern cooperatively, each controlling a separate district, capital city, and military forces. To prevent disunity, the most senior partner—in this case Diocletian—served as emperor and was supposed to receive the loyalty of the other three co-emperors. This tetrarchy ("rule of four") was meant to keep imperial government from being isolated in Rome, distant from the empire's elongated frontiers where trouble often lurked, and to prevent civil war by identifying successors in an orderly fashion.

The creation of the four regions ended Rome's thousand years as the Romans' capital. Diocletian did not even visit the ancient city until nearly twenty years after becoming emperor. He chose the regions' new capitals

Figure 25. This sculpture shows the tetrarchs whom Emperor Diocletian established to govern the empire. The similar size and style of the depictions of the co-emperors symbolize the close ties and harmony that Diocletian hoped his colleagues would display. Giovanni Dall'Orto/Wikimedia Commons.

for their utility as military command posts: Milan in northern Italy, Sirmium near the Danube River border, Trier near the Rhine River border, and Nicomedia in Asia Minor. Italy became just another section of the empire, on an equal footing with the other provinces and subject to the same taxation system, except for Rome itself; this exemption was the last trace of the city's traditional primacy.

Diocletian's rescue of the empire called for vast revenues, which the third century's hyperinflation had made hard to find. The biggest expense stemmed from expanding the army by 25 per cent. He used his power as sole lawmaker to dictate two reforms meant to improve the financial situation: controlling wages and prices and imposing a new taxation system.

The restrictions on wages and prices resulted from Diocletian's blaming private businesspeople instead of government action—the massive debasement of coinage—for the unheard-of level of inflation in many regions. Inflated prices caused people to hoard whatever they could buy, which only drove up prices even higher. "Hurry, spend all my money you have; buy me any kinds of goods at whatever prices they are available," wrote one official to his servant when he discovered another devaluation was scheduled (Roberts and Turner vol. 4, pp. 92–94, papyrus no. 607). In A.D. 301, Diocletian tried to curb inflation by imposing an elaborate system of wage and price controls in the worst hit areas; he called this preventing "injustice in commerce." His Edict on Maximum Prices, which explicitly blamed high prices on what the emperor regarded as the unlimited greed of profiteers in supplying food, transportation, and many other things, banned hoarding and set ceilings on the amounts that could legally be charged or paid for about a thousand goods and services (Frank vol. 5, pp. 305–421). The edict soon became ineffective, however, because merchants and workers refused to cooperate, and government officials proved unable to force them to follow the new rules, despite the threat of death or exile as the penalty for violations.

Taxation had to be reformed because the government's inability to control inflation had rendered the empire's debased coinage and the taxes collected in it virtually worthless. Therefore, only one way remained to try to increase revenue: collect more taxes in goods as well as in money. Diocletian, followed by Constantine, increased taxation "in kind," meaning that more citizens now had to pay taxes in goods and services rather than only pay with currency. Taxes paid in coin continued, but payments of taxes in kind became a more prominent source of government revenue until the end of the fourth century A.D., when payments were more and more commuted into uncorrupted gold and silver, to make tax collection easier for imperial officials.

Taxes in kind went mostly to support the expanded number of soldiers. Payments of barley, wheat, meat, salt, wine, vegetable oil, horses, camels, mules, and so on provided food and transport animals for the army. The major sources of the payments, whose amounts varied in different regions, were a tax on land, assessed according to its productivity, and a head tax on individuals. There was no regularity to this reformed taxation system because the empire was too large and the administration too small to overcome traditional local variations. In some areas, both men and women from the age of about twelve to sixty-five paid the full tax, while in other places women paid only half the tax assessment, or none at all. Workers in cities perhaps paid taxes only on their property and not themselves, but they also periodically had to labor without pay on public works projects. Their tasks ranged from cleaning the municipal drains to repairing dilapidated buildings. Owners of urban businesses, from shop-keepers to prostitutes, still paid taxes in money. Members of the senatorial class were exempt from ordinary taxes but had to pay special levies.

Diocletian's financial reforms provoked harmful social consequences by restricting freedom and corroding communal values among both poorer and richer citizens. Merchants had to break the law to make a profit to stay in business, while the government increasingly imposed oppressive restrictions to promote tax collection. The emperors could squeeze greater revenues from the population only if agricultural production remained stable, workers remained at their jobs, and the urban elites continued to perform public service. Therefore, imperial law now forced working people to remain where they were and to pass on their occupations to their children. Tenant farmers (*coloni*) completely lost the freedom to move from one landlord's farm to another. Male tenants, as well as their wives in those areas in which women paid taxes, were now legally confined to working a particular plot. Their children were required to continue farming their family's allotted land forever. Over time, many other occupations deemed essential were also made compulsory and hereditary, from transporting grain and baking to serving in the military. The emperors' attempts to increase revenues also produced destabilizing social discontent among poorer citizens. When the tax rate on agricultural land eventually reached one-third of its gross yield, this intolerable burden provoked the rural farming population to open revolt in some areas, especially Spain in the fifth century A.D.

The emperors also decreed burdensome regulations for the propertied classes in the cities and towns. The men and some women from this elite socio-economic level had traditionally served as *curiales* (unsalaried city council members) and spent their own money to support the community. Their financial responsibilities ranged from maintaining the water supply to feeding troops, but their most expensive responsibility was paying for shortfalls in tax collection. The emperors' demands for more and more revenue now made this a crushing duty, compounding the damage to the financial well-being of *curiales* that the third-century crisis had set in motion.

For centuries, the empire's welfare had of course depended on a steady supply of public-spirited members of the social elite enthusiastically filling these crucial local posts in the towns of Italy and the provinces to win the admiration of their neighbors. As the financial pressure increased, this tradition broke down as wealthier people avoided public service to escape being bled dry. So distorted was the situation that compulsory service on a municipal council became one of the punishments for a minor crime. Eventually, to prevent *curiales* from escaping their obligations, imperial policy banned them from moving away from the towns where they had been born. They even had to ask official permission to travel. These laws made members of the elite eager to win exemptions from public service by exploiting their social connections to petition the emperor, by bribing higher officials, or by taking up one of the occupations that freed them from such obligations (the military, imperial administration, or the church). The most desperate *curiales* simply ran away, abandoning home and property when they could no longer fulfill their traditional duties. The restrictions on individual freedom caused by the vise-like pressure for higher taxes thus eroded the communal values that had motivated wealthy Romans for so long.

REGAINING DIVINE GOODWILL

Following the Roman tradition of finding religious explanations for disasters, Diocletian concluded that the gods' anger had caused the great crisis in the empire. To regain the divine goodwill on which Romans believed their safety and prosperity depended, Diocletian called upon citizens to follow the religion that had guided Rome to power and virtue in the past. As he said in an official announcement, "Through the providence of the immortal gods, eminent, wise, and upright men have in their wisdom established good and true principles. It is wrong to oppose these principles or to abandon the ancient religion for some new one" (Hyamson 15.3, pp. 131–133).

This edict specifically concerned believers in a sect formed by the third-century A.D. Iranian prophet Mani, but Christianity as a new religion received the full and violent effect of Diocletian's belief about the cause of the empire's troubles. Blaming Christians' hostility to traditional Roman religion, Diocletian in A.D. 303 launched a massive attack on them known as the Great Persecution. He seized Christians' property, expelled them from his administration, tore down churches, ordered their scriptures burned, and executed them for refusing to participate in official religious rituals. As usual, policy was applied differently in different regions because there was no effective way to police the action or inaction of local officials enforcing orders from the emperor. In the western empire, the violence stopped after about a year. In the eastern empire, it continued for a decade. The public executions of martyrs were so gruesome that they aroused the sympathy of some of their polytheist neighbors. The Great Persecution therefore had an effect contrary to Diocletian's purpose: it undermined the peace and order of society that he intended his reforms to restore.

Constantine (ruled 306–337), Diocletian's successor, changed the empire's religious history forever by converting to Christianity. For the first time ever, a Roman ruler overtly proclaimed his allegiance to the religion that would eventually garner the largest number of adherents of all the world's religions. A century earlier, Abgar VIII, ruler of the small client kingdom of Osrhoëne in northern Mesopotamia, had converted to Christianity, but now the head of the entire Roman world had aligned himself with the new faith. Constantine adopted Christianity for the same reason that Diocletian had persecuted it: in the belief that he was gaining divine protection for the empire and for himself. During the civil war that he had to fight to become emperor after Diocletian, Constantine experienced a dream vision promising him the support of the Christian God. His biographer, Eusebius, reported (*Life of Constantine* 1.28) that Constantine had also seen a vision of Jesus's cross in the sky surrounded by the words, "With this sign you shall win the victory!" When Constantine finally triumphed over his rivals by winning the battle of the Milvian Bridge in Rome in A.D. 312, he proclaimed that the miraculous power of the Christians' God had won him this victory. He therefore declared himself a Christian emperor. Several years later, to celebrate his victory, Constantine erected the famous arch that still stands today near the Colosseum. To provide decoration for it, the emperor ordered sculpted sections to be attached to it that displayed his supreme status, towering over everyone else. Constantine's assertion that divine power lay behind his superiority was traditional for Roman emperors; his linking of that power to the Christian God was new.

Following his conversion to Christianity, Constantine did not outlaw traditional Roman religion or make his personal faith the official religion. Instead, he decreed religious toleration. The best statement of this policy survives in the so-called Edict of Milan of A.D. 313 (Lactantius, *On the Death of the Persecutors* 48). Building on the ideas proclaimed by Emperor Gallienus half a century earlier, this proclamation specified free choice of religion for everyone and referred to the empire's protection by "the highest divinity"—an imprecise term meant to satisfy both Christians and

Figure 26. This coin has a profile of Emperor Constantine and a picture of his battle standard carrying the monogram for Christ (the combined Greek letters chi and rho). This sign, the Christogram, has endured as a symbol of Christianity until the present day. Photo courtesy of Classical Numismatic Group, Inc./www .cngcoins.com.

traditional believers. For Constantine, religious toleration was the correct choice both to regain divine goodwill for the empire and also to prevent social unrest.

Constantine wanted to avoid angering traditional believers if at all possible because they still greatly outnumbered Christians, but he nevertheless did much to promote his newly chosen faith. For example, he began construction on the Basilica of St. John Lateran to be the home church of the bishop of Rome, as well as on an enormous basilica dedicated to St. Peter (finished in A.D. 349 after decades of construction and a center of worship for more than a thousand years until it was torn down in the sixteenth century to make way for the present building). Constantine also returned to Christians all their property that had been seized during Diocletian's persecution, but, to pacify those non-Christians who had bought the confiscated property at auction, the emperor had the treasury compensate them financially for their loss. When in A.D. 321 Constantine made the Lord's Day a holy occasion on which no official business or manufacturing work could be performed, he shrewdly made sure that it corresponded with "Sunday." This name allowed polytheists to believe that a particular day of the week also continued to honor their ancient deity: the sun. Constantine's arch acknowledged the role of divine aid in his victory, but it did not specifically mention the Christian God. And when Constantine in A.D. 324–330 built a new capital, Constantinople, on the site of ancient Byzantium (today Istanbul in Turkey) at the mouth of the Black Sea, he erected many statues of the traditional gods in the city. Most conspicuously of all, he respected Roman tradition by continuing to hold the ancient office of *pontifex maximus* ("highest priest"), which emperors had filled ever since Augustus. Constantine as emperor was engaged in a careful balancing act when it came to the political implications of his publicly chosen new faith because he knew full well that polytheists still outnumbered Christians in the empire's population.

A NEW OFFICIAL RELIGION

By this period, the evidence for Roman history that survives has become much more concerned than before with Christianity. It shows that the Christianization of the empire provoked strong emotional responses because ordinary people cared fervently about religion, which provided their best hope for private and public salvation in a dangerous world over which they had little control. On this point, believers in traditional religion and Christians shared some similar beliefs. Both, for instance, assigned a potent role to spirits and demons as ever-present influences on life. For some people, it seemed safest to reject neither faith. A silver spoon used in the worship of the pagan forest spirit Faunus has been found engraved with a fish; the letters spelling "fish" in Greek (ICHTHYS) were an acronym for "Jesus Christ the Son of God, the Savior" (Johns and Potter no. 67, pp. 119–121).

The overlap between some traditional religious beliefs and Christianity did not, however, mask the even greater differences between polytheists' and Christians' beliefs. They debated passionately about whether there was one God or many, and about what kind of interest the divinity (or divinities) took in the world of humans. Polytheists still participated in frequent festivals and sacrifices to many different gods. Why, they wondered, did these joyous occasions of worship not satisfy everyone's yearnings for personal contact with the power of divinity?

Equally incomprehensible to traditional believers was a creed centered on a savior who had not only failed to overthrow Roman rule, but had even been executed as a common criminal. The traditional gods, by contrast, had bestowed a world empire on their worshipers. Moreover, they pointed out, cults such as that of the goddess Isis and philosophies such as Stoicism insisted that only the pure of heart and mind could be admitted to their fellowship. Christians, by contrast, sought out the impure. Why, wondered perplexed polytheists, would anyone willingly want to associate with acknowledged sinners? In any case, polytheists insisted that Christians had no right to claim they possessed the sole version of religious truth, for no doctrine that provided "a universal path to the liberation of the soul" had ever been found, as the philosopher Porphyry (A.D. 234–305) argued (Augustine, City of God 10.32).

The slow pace of religious transformation revealed how strong traditional religion remained in this period, especially at the highest social levels. In fact, Emperor Julian (ruled A.D. 361–363) rebelled against his family's Christianity and tried to restore polytheism as the leading religion. A deeply pious person, Julian believed in a supreme deity corresponding to Greek philosophical ideas: "This divine and completely beautiful universe, from heaven's highest arch to earth's lowest limit, is tied together by the continuous providence of god, has existed ungenerated eternally, and is imperishable forever" (Oration 4.132C). Julian's policy failed, however, because his religious vision struck most people as too abstract and his public image as too pedantic. When he lectured to a large audience in Antioch, the crowd made fun of his philosopher's beard instead of listening to his message. Still, this "apostate" emperor had his admirers, such as the upper-class army officer and historian Ammianus Marcellinus of Antioch. He documented Julian's strife-filled reign in his detailed work of the history of his own times, drawing on his personal experience at court and on the battlefield to give a vivid description of this turbulent era.

The Christian emperors chipped away at traditional religion by slowly removing polytheism's official privileges and financial support. In A.D. 382 came the highly symbolic gesture of removing the altar and statue of the ancient deity Victory, which had stood in the Senate House in Rome for centuries. Ending government payment for animal sacrifices to the gods was even more damaging. Symmachus (A.D. 340–402), a pagan senator who held the prestigious post of prefect ("mayor") of Rome, objected to what he saw as an outrage to Rome's tradition of religious diversity. Speaking in a last public protest against the new religious order, he argued: "We all have our own way of life and our own way of worship. . . . So vast a mystery cannot be approached by only one path" (*Relatio* 3.10).

Christianity's growing support from the imperial government combined with its religious and social values to help it to gain more and more believers. They were attracted by Christians' strong sense of community in this world, as well as by the promise of salvation in the world to come after death. Wherever Christians traveled or migrated in this period, they could find a warm welcome in the local congregation. The faith also won converts by emphasizing charitable works, such as caring for the poor, widows, and orphans. By the mid-third century A.D., for example, Rome's congregation was supporting fifteen hundred widows and other impoverished persons. Christians' hospitality, fellowship, and philanthropy to one another were enormously important because people at that time had to depend mostly on friends and relatives for advice and practical help. State-sponsored social services were rare and limited. Soldiers also now found it comfortable to convert and continue to serve in the army. Previously, Christian soldiers had sometimes created disciplinary problems by renouncing their military oath. As an infantry officer named Marcellus had said at his court martial in A.D. 298 for refusing to continue his duties, "A Christian fighting for Christ the Lord should not fight in the armies of this world" (*Acts of Marcellus* 4). Once the emperors had become Christians, however, soldiers could justify military duty to themselves as serving the affairs of Christ.

Christianity officially replaced traditional polytheism as the state religion in A.D. 391, when Emperor Theodosius (ruled A.D. 379–395) succeeded where his predecessors had failed: he enforced a ban on animal sacrifices, even if private individuals paid for them. Also rejecting the title of *pontifex maximus*, he made divination by the inspection of the entrails of animals punishable as high treason and closed and confiscated all temples. Many shrines, among them the famous Parthenon in Athens, subsequently became Christian churches. Theodosius did not, however, require anyone to convert to Christianity, and he did not forbid non-Christian schools. The Academy teaching Plato's philosophy in Athens, for instance, continued for another 140 years. Capable non-Christians such as Symmachus continued to find government careers under the Christian emperors. But traditional believers were now the outsiders in an Empire that had officially been transformed into a monarchy devoted to the Christian God. Polytheist adherents continued to exist for a long time and to practice their religion as best they could privately. This was easier to do in remote locations in the countryside than in cities filled with inquisitive neighbors. For this reason, Christians came to refer to traditional believers as "pagans" (*pagani*, the Latin for "country bumpkins").

Tensions between Christians and pagans could generate violence, especially when conflict over political influence was involved. In A.D. 415 in Alexandria in Egypt, for example, Hypatia, the most famous woman scholar of the time and a pagan, was torn to pieces in a church by a Christian mob. Her lectures had gained her a great reputation as a mathematician and expert in the philosophy of Plato. Her fame gave her influence with the Roman official in charge of Alexandria (himself a pagan) and aroused the jealousy of Cyril, the bishop of Alexandria. Rumor had it that Cyril secretly instructed an underling to stir up the crowd that murdered Hypatia (Socrates, *Church History* 7.15).

Judaism posed a special problem for the emperors in an officially Christian empire. Like pagans, Jews rejected the new state religion. On the other hand, Jews seemed entitled to special treatment because Jesus had been a Jew and because previous emperors had allowed Jews to practice their religion, even after Hadrian's refounding of Jerusalem as a Roman colony. Therefore, the Christian emperors compromised by allowing Judaism to continue, while imposing increasing legal restrictions on its adherents. For instance, imperial decrees eventually banned Jews from holding government posts but required them to assume the financial burdens of *curiales* without receiving the honorable status of that rank. In addition, each Jew had to pay a special tax to the imperial treasury every year. By the late sixth century A.D., the law barred Jews from making wills, receiving inheritances, or testifying in court.

Although these developments began the long process that made Jews into second-class citizens in later European history, they did not disable their religion. Magnificent synagogues continued to exist in Palestine, where a few Jews still lived; most of the population had been dispersed throughout the cities of the empire and the lands to the east. The scholarly study of Jewish law and tradition flourished in this period, culminating in the production of the learned texts known as the Palestinian and the Babylonian Talmuds and the scriptural commentaries of the Midrash. These works of religious scholarship laid the foundation for later Jewish life and practice.

The contributions of women continued to be a crucial factor in Christianity's growing strength as the official religion of the Roman state. Women's exclusion from public careers—other than the burdens of curial office—motivated them to become active church participants. The famous Christian theologian Augustine eloquently recognized the value of women in strengthening Christianity in a letter he wrote to the unbaptized husband of a baptized woman: "O you men, who fear all the burdens imposed by baptism! Your women easily surpass you. Chaste and devoted to the faith, it is their presence in large numbers that causes the church to grow" (*Letters* 2*). Some women earned exceptional fame and status by giving their property to their congregation, or by renouncing marriage to dedicate themselves to Christ. Consecrated virgins and widows who chose not to remarry thus joined large donors as especially respected women.

Christianity also grew stronger from its continued success in consolidating a formal leadership hierarchy. By now, a rigid organization based on the authority of bishops—all male—had fully replaced early Christianity's relatively looser, more democratic structure, in which women were also leaders. In the new state-supported church, the extent of the bishops' power grew so much greater that it came to resemble, on a smaller scale of course, that of the emperors. Bishops in the late Empire ruled their flocks almost as monarchs, determining their membership and controlling their finances.

The bishops in the largest cities—Rome, Constantinople, Alexandria, Antioch, Carthage—became the most powerful leaders among their colleagues. The main bishop of Carthage, for example, oversaw at least a hundred local bishops in the surrounding area. Regional councils of bishops exercised supreme authority in appointing new bishops and deciding the doctrinal disputes that increasingly arose.

The bishop of Rome eventually emerged as the church's supreme leader in the western empire. This bishop eventually claimed the title of "Pope" (from *pappas*, a Greek word for "father"), which still designates the head of the Roman Catholic Church. The popes based their claim to preeminence on the passage in the New Testament in which Jesus speaks to the apostle Peter: "You are Peter, and upon this rock I will build my church. . . . I will entrust to you the keys of the kingdom of heaven. Whatever you bind on earth shall be bound in heaven. Whatever you loose on earth shall be loosed in heaven" (Matthew 16: 18–19). Because Peter's name in Greek and Aramaic means "rock" and because he was seen as the first bishop of Rome, later popes claimed that this passage authorized their superior position.

BELIEF AND PRACTICE IN OFFICIAL CHRISTIANITY

Christianity's official status did not bring unity in belief and practice. Disputes centered on what constituted orthodoxy as opposed to heresy. The emperors became the final authority for enforcing orthodox creeds (summaries of beliefs) and could use force to compel agreement when disputes became so heated that disorder or violence resulted.

Subtle theological questions about the nature of the Trinity of Father, Son, and Holy Spirit caused the bitterest disagreements. Arianism, named after Arius of Alexandria (A.D. 260–336), generated tremendous conflict by insisting that God the Father had created Jesus his son from nothing and granted him his special status. Thus, Jesus was not co-eternal with the Father, having been created by him, and divine not on his own, but because God had made him so as his son. Arianism appealed to ordinary people because its subordination of son to father corresponded to the norms of family life. Arius used popular songs to make his views known, and people everywhere became engrossed in the controversy. "When you ask for your change from a shopkeeper," one observer remarked in describing Constantinople, "he lectures you about the Begotten and the Unbegotten. If you ask how much bread costs, the reply is that 'the Father is superior and the Son inferior'; if in a public bath you ask 'Is the water ready for my bath?' the attendant answers that 'the Son is of nothing'" (Gregory of Nyssa, *On the Deity of the Son and the Holy Spirit* in J.-P. Migne, *Patrologia Graeca* vol. 46, col. 557b).

Many Christians became so incensed over this apparent demotion of Jesus that Constantine had to intervene to try to restore order. In A.D. 325 he convened 220 bishops to hold the Council of Nicea to settle the dispute over Arianism. The bishops declared that the Father and the Son were indeed "of one substance" and co-eternal. So fluid were Christian beliefs in this period, however, that Constantine later changed his mind on the doctrine twice, and the heresy lived on; many of the Germanic peoples who later came to live in the empire converted to Arian Christianity.

The disagreements could be complicated. Nestorius, for example, a Syrian who became bishop of Constantinople in A.D. 428, insisted that

Christ paradoxically incarnated two separate beings, one divine and one human. Orthodox doctrine regarded Christ as a single being with a double nature, simultaneously God and man. Expelled by the church hierarchy, Nestorian Christians moved to Persia, where they generally enjoyed the support of its non-Christian rulers. They established communities that still endure in Arabia, India, and China. Similarly, Monophysites—believers in a single divine nature for Christ—founded independent churches in Egypt, Ethiopia, Syria, and Armenia beginning in the sixth century A.D.

No heresy better illustrates the ferocity of Christian disputes than Donatism. Followers of the fourth-century North African priest Donatus insisted that they could not readmit to their congregations any members who had cooperated with imperial authorities to avoid martyrdom during the Great Persecution of Diocletian. Feelings reached such a fever pitch that they violently split families, as in one son's threat against his mother: "I will join Donatus's followers, and I will drink your blood" (Augustine, *Letters* 34.3).

Augustine (A.D. 354–430) became the most important thinker in establishing the western church's orthodoxy as religious truth. The pagan son of a Christian mother and a pagan father in North Africa, he began his career by teaching rhetoric. In A.D. 386, he converted to Christianity under the influence of his mother and Ambrose, the powerful bishop of Milan. In A.D. 395 Augustine became a bishop in his homeland, but his reputation rests not on his church career but on his writings. For the next thousand years Augustine's works would be the most influential doctrinal texts in western Christianity next to the Bible. He wrote so much about religion and philosophy that a later scholar declared: "The man lies who says he has read all your works" (Isidore of Seville, *Carmina* in J.-P. Migne, *Patrologia Latina* vol. 83, col. 1109a).

Augustine in his book *City of God* explained that people were misguided to look for true value in their everyday lives because only life in God's heavenly city had meaning. The imperfect nature of earthly existence demanded secular law and government to prevent anarchy. The doctrine of original sin—a subject of theological debate since at least the second century A.D.—meant that people suffered from a hereditary moral disease turning their will into a disruptive force. This inborn corruption, Augustine argued, required governments to use coercion to suppress evil. Civil government was necessary to impose moral order on the chaos of human life after humanity's fall from grace in the Garden of Eden. The state therefore had a right to compel people to remain united to the church, by force if necessary.

Order in society was so valuable, Augustine insisted, that it could even make the inherently evil practice of slavery into a source of good. Corporal punishment and enslavement were lesser evils than the violent troubles that disorder created. Christians therefore had a duty to obey the emperor and participate in political life. Soldiers, too, had to follow their orders. Torture and the death penalty, on the other hand, had no place in a morally upright government.

Augustine also insisted that sex automatically plunged human beings into sin and that the only pure life was asceticism (a life of denial of all bodily pleasures). Augustine knew from personal experience how difficult this was: he revealed in his autobiographical work *Confessions* that he felt a deep conflict between his sexual desire and his religious philosophy. For years he followed his natural urges and had sex frequently outside marriage, including fathering a son by a mistress. Only long reflection, he explained, gave him the inner strength to pledge his future chastity as a Christian.

Augustine advocated sexual abstinence as the highest course for Christians because he believed Adam and Eve's disobedience in the Garden of Eden had forever ruined the original, perfect harmony God created between the human will and human passions. God punished his disobedient children by making sexual desire a disruptive force that they could never completely control through their will. Although Augustine reaffirmed the value of marriage in God's plan, he added that sexual intercourse even between loving spouses carried the melancholy reminder of humanity's fall from grace. A married couple should "descend with regret" to the duty of procreation, the only acceptable reason for sex (*Sermon on the New Testament* 1.25). Married couples should not take pleasure in intercourse, even when fulfilling their social responsibility to produce children.

This doctrine elevated chastity to the highest level of moral virtue. In the words of the biblical scholar Jerome (A.D. 348–420), living this spotless life counted as "daily martyrdom" (*Letters* 108.32). Sexual renunciation became a badge of honor, as illustrated by the inscription on the tombstone of a thirty-nine-year-old Christian woman in Rome named Simplicia: "She paid no heed to producing children, treading beneath her feet the snares of the body" (*L'Année épigraphique* 1980, no. 138, p. 40). This self-chosen holiness gave women the status to demand more privileges, such as education in Hebrew and Greek to be able to read the Bible for themselves. By the end of the fourth century A.D., the importance of virginity as a Christian virtue had grown so large that congregations began to call for virgin priests and bishops. This demand represented a dramatic change because traditionally virginity had been a state of chastity that Roman society required only of women, before marriage.

Christian asceticism reached its peak in monasticism. Monks (from the Greek *monos*, originally meaning "single, solitary") and nuns (from the Latin *nonna*, originally meaning an older unmarried woman) were men and women who withdrew from society to live a life of extreme self-denial demonstrating their devotion to God. Both polytheism and Judaism had long traditions of a few people living as ascetics, but what made Christian monasticism distinctive was the number of people choosing it and the heroic status that they earned. Christian monks' and nuns' high reputations came from their abandoning ordinary pleasures and comforts. They left behind their families and congregations, renounced sex, worshiped constantly, wore the roughest, often unisex form of clothing, and—most difficult of all, they reported—ate only enough to prevent starvation. Monastic life was a constant spiritual struggle—these religious ascetics frequently dreamed of plentiful, tasty food, more often even than of sex.

The earliest Christian monks emerged in Egypt; among the earliest to make this radical choice in lifestyle was a prosperous farmer named Antony (A.D. 251–356). One day around A.D. 285 he abruptly abandoned all his property after hearing a sermon based on Jesus's admonition to a rich young man to sell his possessions and give the proceeds to the poor (Matthew 19:21). Placing his sister in a community of virgins, Antony spent almost all the rest of his time in a barren existence in the desert as a hermit to demonstrate his heroism for God, leading others to emulate him in choosing this demanding life of deprivation; he was later recognized as a saint.

Monasticism appealed for many reasons, but above all because it gave ordinary people a way to become heroes in the traditional ancient Greek religious sense (human beings with extraordinary achievements, who after their deaths retained the power to help the living). Becoming a Christian ascetic served as a substitute for the glory of martyrdom, which Constantine's conversion had made irrelevant. "Holy women" and "holy men" attracted great attention with feats of pious endurance. Symeon (A.D. 390–459) lived atop a tall pillar for thirty years, preaching to the people gathered at the foot of his perch. Egyptian Christians came to believe that the monks' and nuns' supreme piety as living heroes ensured the annual flooding of the Nile, the duty once associated with the magical power of the ancient pharaohs. Christian ascetics with reputations for exceptional holiness exercised influence even after death. Their relics—body parts or clothing—became treasured sources of protection and healing for worshipers.

The earliest monks and nuns lived alone or in isolated tiny groups,

Figure 27. St. Catherine's Monastery on Mount Sinai was established at the site where Moses was believed to have seen the burning bush; built in the sixth century A.D., it is still operating. ccarlstead/Wikimedia Commons.

but by A.D. 320 larger single-sex communities had sprung up along the Nile River so that Christian ascetics living together in greater numbers could encourage one another along the harsh road to heroic holiness. Some monastic communities imposed military-style discipline, but they differed in allowing contact with the outside world. Some aimed for complete self-sufficiency to avoid interaction with the outside world. Basil ("the Great") of Caesarea (A.D. 330–379), however, started the competing tradition that monks should do good in society. For example, he required his monks to perform charitable service in the outside world, such as ministering to the sick. This practice led to the foundation of the first nonmilitary hospitals, attached to monasteries.

The level of asceticism enforced in monastic communities also varied significantly. The followers of Martin of Tours (A.D. 316–397), an ex-soldier famed for his pious deeds, organized groups famed for their harshness. A milder code of monastic conduct, however, exerted more influence on later worship traditions. Called the Benedictine Rule after its creator, Benedict of Nursia in central Italy (A.D. 480–553), it prescribed a daily routine of prayer, scriptural readings, and manual labor. The Rule divided the day into seven parts, each with a compulsory service of prayers and lessons, but no Mass. The required worship for each part of the day was called the liturgy (literally, "public work" and, by extension, the services of the church). This arrangement became standard practice. Unlike the harsh regulations of Egyptian and Syrian monasticism, Benedict's code did not isolate his monks from the outside world or deprive them of sleep, adequate food, or warm clothing. Although it gave the abbot (the head monk) full authority, it instructed him to listen to what every member of the community, even the youngest monk, had to say before deciding important matters. He was not allowed to beat them for lapses in discipline except when they refused to respond to correction. Nevertheless, monasticism was always a demanding, harsh existence. Jerome, himself a monk in a monastery for men that was located next to one for women, once gave this advice to a mother who decided to send her young daughter to a monastic community: "Let her be brought up in a monastery, let her live among virgins, let her learn to avoid swearing, let her regard lying as an offense against God, let her be ignorant of the world, let her live the angelic life, while in the flesh let her be without the flesh, and let her suppose that all human beings are like herself" (Letters 107.13). When the girl reached adulthood as a virgin, he added, she should avoid the baths so she would not be seen naked or give her body pleasure by dipping in the warm pools. Jerome promised that God would reward the mother with the birth of sons in compensation for the dedication of her daughter.

By the early fifth century A.D., many adults were also joining monastic communities to flee obligations and social restrictions. Parents also gave children to monastic communities to raise as offerings ("oblations") to God and, sometimes, to escape the practical burdens and expenses of child rearing. Adult men would flee military service. Women could sidestep the outside world's restrictions on their ambitions and freedom. Jerome well explained this latter attraction: "[As monks] we evaluate people's virtue not by their gender but by their character, and deem those to be worthy of the greatest glory who have renounced both status and riches" (Letters 127.5). This open-minded attitude helped monasticism attract a steady stream of adult adherents eager to serve God in this world of troubles and achieve salvation in the world of bliss to come.

10

Barbarian Migrations and the Fates of the Empire

The political fate of the Roman Empire altered forever in the fourth century A.D. First, Constantine shifted the center of imperial government and power from Italy to the eastern sector of the empire. Then, at the end of the fourth century A.D., the empire was split permanently into two geographic divisions, forming a western empire and an eastern empire. In the west, migrations of Germanic peoples subsequently transformed the region socially, culturally, and politically by replacing Roman provincial government with their own new kingdoms. These new inhabitants inside the empire's borders lived side by side with Romans, the different groups keeping some of their traditions intact but merging other parts of their cultures. The growing strength of these new regimes in the western section of the empire and the consequent weakening of Roman authority there in the fifth century A.D. led many historians to refer to these events as the "Fall of the Roman Empire."

More recently, however, scholars have reevaluated these developments as a political and social transformation that provided the deep background for important national divisions that came to characterize Europe in much later times. Largely avoiding the disruptions caused by the movements of the barbarians, the eastern empire had a different fate: ruling a traditionally diverse popu-

TIMELINE (ALL DATES A.D.)

Late fourth century: The Roman Empire is divided into eastern and western sections, each ruled by a separate emperor; the Huns' attacks terrorize central Europe.

376: The Visigoths beg the eastern emperor Valens for permission to enter the Roman Empire to escape the Huns.

378: The Visigoths defeat Emperor Valens at the battle of Adrianople (today in European Turkey).

404: Honorius, emperor in the west, makes Ravenna in Italy the western capital instead of Rome.

406: The Vandals break into the Roman Empire in Gaul (today France) and force their way to Spain.

410: The Visigoths under their commander Alaric capture and loot Rome.

418: The western empire allows the Visigoths to establish a kingdom in Gaul.

429: The Vandals seize Roman North Africa.

455: The Vandals attack and plunder Rome.

476: Romulus Augustulus, the last Roman emperor in the west, is deposed by the barbarian Odoacer.

527–565: Justinian rules as eastern Roman emperor and wages war against the Germanic kingdoms in western Europe to try to reunite the old empire.

529: Plato's Academy in Athens closes after a thousand years.

532: Empress Theodora convinces Justinian not to run away during the Nika Riot in Constantinople.

538: Justinian opens the church of the Holy Wisdom (Hagia Sophia) in Constantinople.

540s: An epidemic kills a third of the population in Justinian's empire.

lation speaking many different languages, it continued to exist for another thousand years as the self-identified descendant of ancient Rome, preserving the literature that would help preserve the traditions of classical antiquity and allow future generations to continue to learn from that past.

TRANSFORMING THE WESTERN EMPIRE

Diocletian's tetrarchy did not last, but the principle of dividing imperial rule persisted. Constantine had fought a long civil war at the beginning of his reign to seize unified rule for himself, and he abolished the tetrarchy because he feared disloyal "partners" outside his own family. By the end of his reign, however, he reluctantly conceded that the empire required more than one ruler. Therefore, he designated his three sons as joint successors, hoping that they could share power to preserve the stability that Diocletian's reforms had achieved. A gory rivalry among the brothers ruined any chance of maintaining a unified empire. Their forces took up positions roughly splitting the empire on a north-south line along the western edge of the Balkan Peninsula and Greece. By the end of the fourth century A.D., the empire was finally formally divided in two sections, each with an emperor. On the surface these rulers cooperated, but in reality the empire's western and eastern halves were now launched on separate histories.

The halves' separateness was made clear by each having its own capital city. Constantinople ("City of Constantine"), located near the mouth of the Black Sea, became the capital of the eastern empire after Constantine in A.D. 324 "refounded" the ancient Greek city of Byzantium as "New Rome." He chose the city for its military and commercial possibilities: it lay on an easily fortified peninsula astride principal routes for trade and troop movements. To recall the glory of Rome and thus claim the political legitimacy bestowed by the memory of the old capital, Constantine graced his refounded city with a forum, an imperial palace, a hippodrome for chariot races, and numerous statues of the traditional gods. The eastern emperors inherited Constantine's "new" city as their seat.

Geography determined the site of the capital of the western empire, too. In A.D. 404, the emperor Honorius (ruled 395–423) made Ravenna, a port on Italy's northeastern coast, the permanent western capital. Its walls and marshes protected it from attack by land, while its access to the sea kept it from being starved out in a siege. Ravenna's new status led to great churches with dazzling multicolored mosaics being built there, but as a city it never rivaled Constantinople in size or splendor. Rome itself was now on a long decline that would eventually reduce it almost to the condition of the impoverished village in which the ancient home of the Romans had begun so many centuries before.

Fear as well as poverty motivated the migrations into the Roman Empire of northern "barbarians" (as they seemed to Romans because of their different language, clothing, and customs). Some historians decline to call these movements "migrations," reserving that term to designate organized, large-scale movements of peoples who see themselves as ethnically united groups. The Germanic barbarians of the fourth century A.D. living beyond the frontiers of the Roman Empire were certainly ethnically diverse and fluid in their political and social groupings, but nevertheless it seems

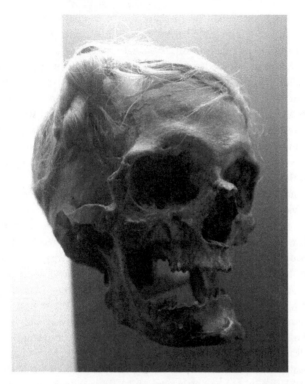

Figure 28. The skull of a Germanic barbarian preserves the topknot hairstyle that served as a marker of identity for his band. In ancient society just as today, how people dressed and kept their hair was as important as clothing in making a statement about their social status. Bullenwächter/Wikimedia Commons.

reasonable to refer to the permanent transfer of these groups of people from one region to another as "migrations." These peoples first migrated into Roman territory as refugees terrified into relocating by the relentless attacks of the Huns. Eager to improve their lives by sharing in the empire's relative prosperity, they wanted to live in the comparative safety and comfort that they saw prevailing in the Roman provinces across the frontiers from their own lands. By the late fourth century A.D., however, the influx of barbarians had swollen to a near flood, at least in the eyes of the imperial administration.

The Roman emperors unintentionally helped provoke the barbarian migrations into imperial territory by heavily recruiting northern warriors to fill out the reduced ranks of the Roman army in response to the third-century A.D. crisis. By the later fourth century, a large number of women and children joined these men in their migrations. They came not in carefully planned invasions but rather fleeing for their lives. Raids by the Huns had forced these Germanic people from their traditional homelands in what is now eastern Europe north of the Danube River. Bands of men, women, and children crossed the Roman frontier into the empire as hordes of squatters. Their prospects for survival were grim because they had no political or military unity, no clear plan of what to do, and not even a shared sense of identity. Loosely organized at best, the only possible tie they (or at least some of them) had in common was the Germanic origin of their diverse languages.

All these peoples felt terror at the coming of the Huns. These famously fierce warriors first appeared in history several centuries earlier as marauders raiding widely over central Asia. Scholars today are uncertain whether, as once thought, the later Huns were descended from the raiding groups called the Xiongnu that disturbed the frontiers of the Chinese Empire for many years before they were finally driven away westward (Sima Qian, Shiji 110). Wherever exactly the Huns may have originated, by the mid-fourth century A.D. they had arrived in the region of central Europe north of the Danube and east of the Rhine rivers. Moving deeper into the Hungarian plain by the 390s, they began raiding southward into the Balkans. The Huns excelled as nomadic warriors on horseback, launching cavalry attacks far and wide. Their skill as horsemen made them legendary. They could shoot their powerful bows while riding full tilt, and they could also stay mounted for days, sleeping atop their horses and carrying raw meat snacks between their thighs and the animals' backs. Hunnic warriors' appearance terrified their enemies: skulls elongated from having been bound between boards in infancy, faces grooved with decorative scars, and arms crawling with elaborate tattoos.

The eastern emperors paid the Huns large bribes to spare their territories. The nomads then decided to change their wandering way of life. They turned themselves into landlords, cooperating to create an empire outside of Roman territory north of the Danube. They subjected local farmers there and siphoned off their agricultural surplus. The Huns' most ambitious leader, Attila (ruled A.D. 440–453), extended his domains from the Alps to the Caspian Sea. In A.D. 452, Attila led his forces all the way to the gates of Rome before Pope Leo I ransomed the city. At Attila's death in A.D. 453, the Huns lost their fragile political cohesiveness and soon faded from history as a recognizable state. By this time, however, the damage had long been done: they had set in motion the barbarian migrations that transformed the Western Roman Empire.

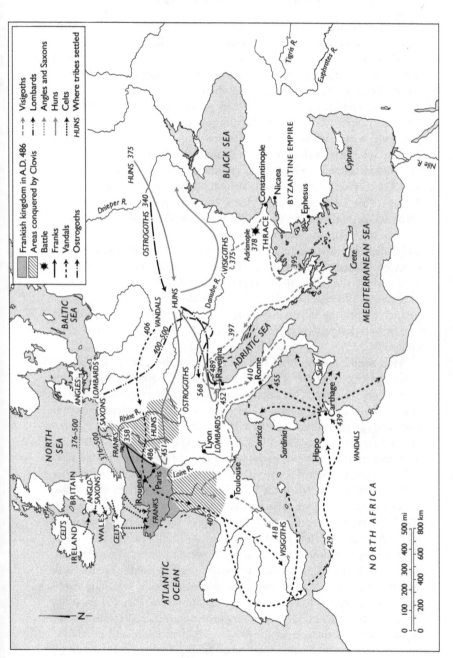

Map 12. Germanic Migrations and Invasions, Fourth and Fifth Centuries A.D.

The first Germanic barbarians to flee across the frontier into the Roman Empire came to be called the Visigoths ("West Goths"). Shredded by the Huns' raids, in A.D. 376 they begged the eastern emperor, Valens (ruled A.D. 364–378), to allow them to migrate into the Balkans. The Visigoths received permission on condition that their warriors enlist in the Roman army to defend against the Huns. When greedy and incompetent Roman officers charged with helping the refugees instead exploited them for profit, the barbarians were reduced to starving. The officials even forced them to sell some of their own people into slavery in return for dogs to eat. Pushed beyond their limits of endurance, the Visigoths rebelled. In A.D. 378 they defeated and killed Valens at Adrianople (today in European Turkey). They killed two-thirds of the Roman force, including the emperor, whose body was never found among the giant mounds of corpses. Valens's successor, the eastern emperor Theodosius I (ruled A.D. 379–395), then had to renegotiate the deal with the Visigoths. His concessions established the terms that other migrating bands would seek for themselves in the future: permission to settle permanently inside the empire, freedom to establish a kingdom under their own laws, large annual payments from the imperial treasury, and—so that the emperors could save face—a designation as "federates" (allies) pledged to help protect the empire.

Soon realizing they could not afford to pay the costs of this agreement, the eastern emperors decided to save themselves by forcing the newcomers westward. This became the eastern empire's enduring strategy: push the barbarians into the western empire. The eastern emperors therefore cut off subsidies to the refugees and threatened full-scale war unless they moved on. The angry Visigoths complied, and neither the western empire nor the Visigoths would ever be the same. In A.D. 410, these barbarians stunned the world by capturing Rome itself. They terrorized the population. When the Visigoths' commander Alaric demanded the city's gold, silver, movable property, and foreign slaves, the Romans asked, "What will be left to us?" "Your lives," the barbarian general replied (Zosimus, *New History* 5.40).

Too weak to defeat these invaders, the western imperial government in A.D. 418 reluctantly agreed to settle them in southwestern Gaul (present-day France), again saving the emperor's pride by calling them federates. There, to adapt to their new circumstances, they did what no Germanic group had done before: organize a state. The Visigoths gradually transformed themselves from a loosely democratic and ethnically diverse tribal society of raiders and small farmers into an organized kingdom occupying former Roman territory but with its own sense of dis-

Figure 29. Emperor Theodosius had himself depicted on this column among his fellow members of the elite being supplicated by cringing barbarians below. Like the cameo shown in figure 17, this monument expressed the emperor's exalted status and the power over foreigners that he claimed for his fellow Romans. Marsyas/Wikimedia Commons.

tinctive identity, written laws, and diverse economy. The political model they followed was the only one available, namely that of the government of the Roman Empire: monarchy emphasizing mutually beneficial relations with the social elite. The Visigoths financed their new state by taking over the tax revenue that Roman government had previously collected. They also forced landowners in Gaul to pay rent on their own property. Finding the new arrangements profitable, within a century the Visigoths had expanded into Spain.

Romans could be members of the Visigothic elite, though they had to show respect for their barbarian patrons. Sidonius Apollinaris, for example, a noble from the city of Lyon (A.D. 430–479), once purposely lost a backgammon game to the Visigothic king as a way of getting him to grant a favor. The Visigoths' contact with Romans helped the barbarians develop a stronger sense of their own separate ethnic identity. As usual in assertions of identity, clothing and cosmetics promoted this goal: Visigoths wore pants and dressed their hair with aromatic dressings made from animal fat to differentiate themselves from Romans wearing tunics and using olive oil lotions.

The western empire's concessions to the Visigoths emboldened other barbarian groups to use force in seizing Roman territory and create new identities for themselves. The most violent of these episodes began in A.D. 406 when the band known as the Vandals, who were also fleeing the Huns, crossed the Rhine River into Roman territory. This large group cut a swath through Gaul all the way to the Spanish coast. (The modern word *vandal*, meaning "destroyer of property," perpetuates the memory of their destructiveness.) In A.D. 429, eighty thousand Vandals sailed to North Africa, where they captured the Roman province, breaking their agreement to remain federates. The Vandals caused tremendous hardship for local Africans by confiscating property, rather than allowing its original owners to pay regular rent and keep working their properties. They further weakened the western emperors by seizing North Africa's tax payments in grain and vegetable oil to the central government. In A.D. 455 they destroyed the central symbol of the past glory of the western empire by plundering Rome. The Vandals also weakened the eastern empire when they manned a navy to disrupt Mediterranean trade, especially in food supplies.

Small groups took advantage of the disruption that the bigger bands caused to seize pieces of the crippled western empire. A significant small band for later European history was the Anglo-Saxons. Composed of Angles from what is now Denmark and Saxons from northwestern Germany, this group invaded Britain in the A.D. 440s after the Roman army had been recalled to defend Italy against the Visigoths. They established a kingdom in Britain by wresting territory away from the indigenous Celtic peoples and the remaining Roman inhabitants. Gradually, Anglo-Saxon culture replaced the local traditions of the island's eastern regions. The Celts in this part of the island lost most of their language and Christianity, which survived only in Wales and Ireland.

When the Ostrogoths ("East Goths") established a kingdom in Italy in the late fifth century A.D., this completed the process by which new Germanic regimes divided up the former western empire. The western emperors' failure in leadership helped the Ostrogoths take over Italy. The emperors in the early fifth century A.D., like their predecessors, hired numerous Germanic army commanders to support the defense of the Roman heartland. By the middle of the fifth century, Germanic generals, taking advantage of struggles for power among the Romans competing to be emperor, became power brokers in deciding who would serve as emperor. Since they made the emperor, they could unmake him, too, reducing the western emperor to a puppet under their control. The last such unfortunate Roman on the throne of the western empire was a boy called Romulus Augustulus, whose name eerily recalled both Rome's founder and its first emperor. In A.D. 476, after a dispute over pay, the Germanic commander Odoacer deposed Romulus Augustulus but, pitying his youth, gave him a pension to live in exile near Naples. Odoacer then appointed himself an independent king, formally ending the western empire's five-century-long run of ethnic Roman emperors. The (Western) Roman Empire had therefore finally "fallen," in the political sense. Nevertheless, Odoacer cultivated Rome's still-existent Senate and consuls to show his love for tradition and hope for prestige. In the same spirit, he sent an embassy to Constantinople to acknowledge his respect for the eastern emperor and willingness to cooperate. Suspecting a sham, the eastern emperor hired the Ostrogothic king Theodoric the Great to suppress Odoacer. After murdering the usurper, Theodoric betrayed his employer by creating his own Germanic kingdom in Italy, directing his Ostrogothic regime from the by now traditional western capital at Ravenna until his death in A.D. 526.

Like Odoacer, Theodoric and his Ostrogothic nobles wanted to enjoy the luxurious life of the empire's social elite, not destroy it. Although the eastern empire refused to accept Theodoric's kingdom, he, like other Germanic rulers, nevertheless tried to appropriate the Roman past in support of his own rule. He wanted to preserve the empire's prestigious traditions to give status to his new kingdom. The Senate and the office of consul therefore remained intact. Himself an Arian Christian, Theodoric followed Constantine's example by following a policy of religious toleration, despite his strong disagreement with those of another religion, in this case Jews in the Italian city of Genoa: "I certainly grant you permission [to repair your synagogue], but, to my praise, I condemn the prayers of erring men. I cannot command your faith, for no one is forced to believe against his will" (Cassiodorus, *Variae* 2.27).

COMBINING TRADITIONS IN THE WEST

The replacement of western imperial government by barbarian kingdoms—which amounted to the political transformation of Europe—generated equally significant social and cultural transformations. The barbarian newcomers and the former Roman provincials created new ways of life based on a combination of their traditions. Some of the changes happened unexpectedly, but others were intentional. The Visigoth king Athaulf (ruled A.D. 410–415), for one, married a Roman noblewoman and explicitly stated his goal of integrating their diverse traditions:

> At the start I wanted to erase the Romans' name and turn their land into a Gothic empire, doing myself what Augustus had done. But I have learned that the Goths' freewheeling wildness will never accept the rule of law, and that a state with no law is no state. Thus, I have more wisely chosen another path to glory: reviving the Roman name with Gothic vigor. I pray that future generations will remember me as the founder of a Roman restoration (Orosius, *Seven Books of History Against the Pagans* 7.43.4–6).

As the case of the Visigoths showed, the newcomers had to develop a more tightly structured society to be able to govern their new lands and subjects. The social and cultural traditions they originally brought with them from their homelands in northeastern Europe had ill prepared them for ruling others. There, they had lived in small settlements whose economies depended on farming tiny plots, herding, and iron working. They had no experience directing kingdoms. In their original society, lines of authority and identity were only loosely defined beyond those of the patriarchal household. Households were grouped into clans on kinship lines based on maternal as well as paternal descent. The members of a clan were supposed to keep peace among themselves; violence against a fellow clan member was the worst possible offense. Clans in turn grouped themselves into larger tribes, and then into yet larger but very loose and fluctuating multiethnic confederations, which non-Germans could also join. Different groups identified themselves primarily by their clothing, hairstyles, jewelry, weapons, religious cults, and oral stories.

Assemblies of free male warriors provided the barbarians' only traditional form of political organization. Their leaders' functions were restricted mostly to religious and military duties. Clans, tribes, and confederations often suffered internal conflicts and also frequently feuded violently with one another. Rejecting these organizational traditions, Germanic groups managed to create kingdoms with a hierarchical structure and a functioning administration because they followed Roman models in ordering their new regimes. In the end, however, none of these barbarian kingdoms ever rivaled the scope or services of earlier Roman provincial government in the Golden Age of the empire. The Germanic kingdoms remained much smaller and more local, and much territory in the former Roman provinces remained outside their control, or that of any other central authority.

Roman law was the most influential precedent for the Germanic kings in their efforts to construct stable societies. In their previous existence outside Roman territory, the barbarians had never developed written laws. Now that they had transformed themselves into monarchies ruling Romans as well as themselves, their rulers created legal codes for a system of justice to help keep order. The Visigothic kings developed the first written law code in Germanic history. Written in Latin and heavily influenced by Roman legal traditions, it made fines and compensation the primary method for resolving disputes.

A major step in developing barbarian law codes came when the Franks took over Gaul by overthrowing the Visigoths. Frankish warriors had been serving in the Roman army ever since the early fourth century A.D., when the imperial government had settled this group in a rough northern border area (now in the Netherlands). Their king Clovis (ruled A.D. 485–511) overthrew the Visigothic king in A.D. 507 with support from the eastern Roman emperor, who named Clovis an honorary consul. Clovis made his kingdom stable by following Roman models. He carefully fostered good relations with Gaul's Roman elite and bishops to serve as the regime's intermediaries with the population. He also emphasized written law. His code, published in Latin, promoted social order through clear penalties for specific crimes. In particular, he formalized a system of fines intended to defuse feuds and vendettas between individuals and clans.

The most prominent component of this system was *Wergild*, the payment a murderer had to make as compensation for his crime. Most of the money was paid to the victim's kin, but the king received around one-third of the amount. The differing compensations imposed reveal the relative values of different categories of people in the kingdom of the Franks. The murder of a woman of childbearing age, a boy under twelve, or a man in the king's inner circle brought a massive fine of 600 gold coins, enough to buy 600 cattle. A woman past childbearing age (specified as sixty years old), a young girl, or a freeborn man was valued at 200 coins. Ordinary slaves rated 35 coins.

Clovis's new state, which historians call the Merovingian Kingdom in memory of Merovech, the legendary ancestor of the Franks, foreshadowed the kingdom that would emerge much later as the forerunner of modern France. The dynasty endured for another two hundred years, far longer than most other Germanic kingdoms in the west. The Merovingians survived so long because they created a workable combination of Germanic military might and Roman social and legal traditions.

The migrations that transformed the western empire politically and culturally also transformed its economy, but in ways that failed to strengthen it. The Vandals' violent sweep severely damaged many towns in Gaul, and the urban communities there shriveled. Economic activity increasingly shifted to the countryside, becoming more isolated in the process. Wealthy Romans there built sprawling villas on extensive estates, staffed by tenants bound to the land like slaves. These estates aimed to operate as self-sufficient units by producing all they needed, defending themselves against raids, and keeping their distance from any authorities. Craving isolation, the owners shunned service in municipal office and tax collection, the public services by the social elite that had supplied the traditional lifeblood of Roman administration. When the last traces of Roman provincial administration disappeared, the new kingdoms never developed sufficiently to replace its internal structures of government and services fully.

The situation only grew rougher as the effects of these changes multiplied one another. The infrastructure of trade—roads and bridges—fell into disrepair with no public-spirited elite to pay to maintain them. Self-sufficient nobles holed up on their estates no longer had an interest in helping the central authority, Roman or Germanic, by paying or collecting taxes. They could take care of themselves and their fortress-like households because they could be astonishingly rich. The very wealthiest boasted an annual income rivaling that of an entire region in the old western empire. Naturally they faced great dangers, as they were obvious targets for raiders. Some failed, some survived for generations. It was to be another five hundred years, however, before western Europe would once again develop a civilization based on cities linked by trade. That fact alone reveals how significant the transformations were in that half of the Roman Empire.

THE FATE OF THE EASTERN EMPIRE

The Eastern Roman Empire avoided the massive transformations that reshaped the western half. It continued to be economically sound and politically united for much longer than the west. Modern historians sometimes refer to the eastern empire as the Byzantine Empire, a term derived from the ancient name of its capital, Constantinople, but contemporaries never used that name. Shrewdly employing force, diplomacy, and bribery, the emperors in Constantinople deflected the Germanic migrations westward away from their territories and also blocked the aggression of the Sasanian kingdom in Persia to their east, employing the Gassanid Arabs as federates defending the vast areas from the Euphrates River to the Sinai Peninsula and protecting the east-west caravan routes of the Spice Road along which constant long-distance trade took place. In this way, the rulers of the eastern empire largely maintained their region's ancient traditions and population. Beginning in the seventh century, its emperors lost great expanses of territory to the onslaught of Islamic armies, but they ruled in the eastern capital for eight hundred fifty years more.

The eastern emperors confidently saw themselves as the continuators of the original Roman Empire and the guardians of its culture against barbarian customs. Over time they increasingly spoke Greek as their first language, but they nevertheless continued to refer to themselves and their subjects explicitly as "Romans." The sixth-century A.D. eastern empire enjoyed an economic vitality that had vanished in the west. Its social elite spent freely on luxury goods imported from East Asia on camel caravans and ocean-going ships: silk, precious stones, and prized spices such as pepper. The markets of its large cities, such as Constantinople, Antioch, and Alexandria, teemed with merchants from east and west. Soaring churches testified to its self-confidence in its devotion to God, its divine protector. As their predecessors had done in the earlier Roman Empire, the eastern emperors sponsored religious festivals and entertainments on a massive scale to rally public support for their rule. Rich and poor alike crowded city squares and filled amphitheaters to bursting on these spirited occasions. Chariot racing aroused the hottest passions. Constantinople's residents, for instance, divided themselves into competitive factions called Blues and Greens after the racing colors of their favorite charioteers. It has even been thought that these high-energy fans fueled their disputes by mixing in religious disagreements with their sports rivalry, with Blues favoring orthodox Christian doctrines and Greens supporting Monophysite beliefs.

The eastern emperors ardently believed they had to maintain tradition to support the health and longevity of Roman civilization. They therefore did everything they could to preserve "Romanness," fearing in particular that contact with Germanic peoples would "barbarize" their empire, just as it had the western empire. Like the western emperors, they hired many Germanic and Hunnic mercenaries, but they tried to keep these warriors' customs from influencing the empire's residents. Styles of dress figured prominently in this struggle to maintain ethnic identity. Therefore, imperial regulations banned the capital's residents from wearing Germanic-style clothing (pants, heavy boots, and clothing made from animal furs) instead of traditional Roman garb (bare legs, sandals or light shoes, and robes).

Preserving any sort of unitary "Romanness" was in reality a hopeless quest because the eastern empire was thoroughly multilingual and multiethnic, as that part of the Mediterranean world had always been. Travelers in the eastern empire heard many different languages, observed many styles of dress, and encountered various ethnic groups. The everyday common language for this diverse region was Greek, but Latin continued to be used in government documents and military communication. Many Byzantine subjects retained their original local customs, but some also refashioned their ethnic identities. The Arabs of the Gassanid clan, for example, became fervent Monophysite Christians, drank wine at symposia like the ancient Greeks, and dressed their soldiers in Roman military style, while retaining their ancient customs of horse parades, feasts, and poetry recitals.

"Romanness" definitely included Christianity, but frequent and bitter controversies over doctrine continued to divide Christians and disrupt society. The emperors joined forces with church officials in trying to impose orthodoxy, with only limited success. In some cases, nonorthodox believers fled oppression by leaving the empire. Emperors preferred words to swords when possible in convincing heretics to return to orthodox theology and the hierarchy of the church, but they routinely applied violence when persuasion failed. They had to resort to such extreme measures, they believed, to save lost souls and preserve the empire's religious purity and divine goodwill. The persecution of Christian subjects by Christian emperors symbolized the disturbing consequences that the drive for a unitary identity could cause.

Society in the eastern empire continued to exhibit the characteristic patriarchy of Romans in the west, with some additional traditions stemming from eastern Mediterranean ways. Most women minimized contact with men outside their households. Law barred them from fulfilling many public functions, such as witnessing wills. Subject to the authority of their fathers and husbands, women veiled their heads (though not their faces) to show modesty. Since Christian theologians generally went beyond Roman tradition in restricting sexuality and reproduction, divorce became more difficult, and remarriage was frowned on even for widows. Stiffer legal penalties for sexual offenses also became normal. Nevertheless, female prostitutes, usually poor women desperate for income, continued to abound in the streets and inns of eastern cities, just as in earlier days. They had to break the law or starve.

Women in the royal family were the exception to the rule: they could sometimes achieve a prominence unattainable for their poorer contemporaries. Theodora, wife of the emperor Justinian, dramatically showed the influence women could achieve in the ruling dynasty. Uninhibited by her humble origins (she was the daughter of a bear trainer and had been an actress with a scandalous reputation), she came to rival anyone in influence and wealth. A contemporary who knew her well judged her to be "superior in intelligence to anyone whatsoever of her contemporaries" (John the Lydian, *On the Magistracies of the Roman Constitution* 3.69).

Until her untimely death in A.D. 548, Theodora apparently had a hand in every aspect of her husband's rule, from determining government policy to stiffening his courage at time of crisis. Her prominence and influence upset tradition-minded men, above all the imperial official and historian Procopius. He penned the controversial work today called *The Secret History* in part to accuse her of outrageous behavior, from promiscuity to sexual exhibitionism on stage as a paid performer; the truth of his claims is unrecoverable. Blaming her (in addition to Justinian) for what he saw as the cruelty and injustice of their reign, Procopius's scorching account of alleged misdeeds and scandalous personal behavior by the government's highest officials has provoked lively disputes about its accuracy that persist to this day.

The eastern empire's government worsened social divisions between rich and poor because it provided services according to people's wealth. Its complicated hierarchy required reams of paperwork and fees for countless aspects of daily life, from commercial permits to legal grievances. Getting something done required official permission; obtaining that permission required catching the ear of the right official. People with money and status found this process easy: they relied on their social connections to get a hearing and on their wealth to pay tips to move matters along quickly. Whether seeking preferential treatment or just spurring administrators to do what they were supposed to do, the rich could make the system work.

Those with limited funds, by contrast, found their poverty put them at a grave disadvantage because they had difficulty paying the generous tips that government officials routinely expected to motivate them to carry out their duties. Without tipping, nothing got done. Because interest rates were high, people could incur heavy debt trying to raise the cash to pay high officials to act on important matters. This system existed because it saved the emperors money to spend on their own projects. They could pay their civil servants pitifully low salaries because the public supplemented their incomes under this recognized system of extortion. The sixth-century administrator John the Lydian, for instance, reported that he earned thirty times his annual salary in payments from petitioners during his first year in office. To keep the system from destroying itself through unlimited greed, the emperors published an official list of the maximum tips that their employees could exact. Overall,

Figure 30. Brightly shining mosaics show Emperor Justinian and Empress Theodora attended by their courts as they make offerings to God. Placed high on the walls of the church of San Vitale in Ravenna, these images emphasized that the royal family was supremely rich and also supremely generous in worshiping God in thanks for his protection of the Romans. Wikimedia Commons.

however, this approach to government service generated hostility among poorer subjects and did nothing to encourage public support for the emperors' ambitious plans in pursuit of conquest and glory.

THE REIGN OF JUSTINIAN

The last emperor to try to resurrect the old empire was Justinian (c. A.D. 482–565), the most famous eastern emperor above all for the scholarly work he sponsored to organize and document Roman law and for the magnificent buildings that he had constructed in Constantinople. Born to a Latin-speaking family in a small Balkan town, he rose rapidly in imperial service until in A.D. 527 he succeeded his uncle as emperor. During his reign, Justinian launched military expeditions to try to sup-

Figure 30. *Continued*

press the west's Germanic kingdoms and resurrect the old empire as it had been in the time of Augustus. His goal above all was to win fame by reversing the tide of history and recapturing former Roman territory in the west. Like Augustus, Justinian longed to "restore" Roman power and glory. He also hoped to recapture the Germanic kingdoms' tax revenues and revive the seaborne shipments of food to the eastern empire that the Vandal navy had interrupted from its bases in North Africa. In the beginning he tried to make the reconquest happen with a smaller and cheaper force, but by the latter part of his reign he was financing a substantial military effort in the west. His commanders eventually recaptured Italy, the Dalmatian coast, Sicily, Sardinia, Corsica, part of southern Spain, and western North Africa from their barbarian occupiers. These victories indeed did temporarily reunite the majority of old imperial territory. (Most of Spain and Gaul remained under barbarian control.) Justinian's territory stretched from the Atlantic Ocean eastward as far inland as the border of Mesopotamia.

Unfortunately, Justinian's military victories turned out to be disastrous in the long run: they seriously damaged the western empire's infrastructure and population, and their cost emptied the eastern empire's treasury. Italy endured the most damage. The war there against the Goths spread death and destruction on a massive scale. The east suffered because Justinian squeezed even more taxes out of his already overburdened population to finance the western wars, and to bribe the Sasanians in Mesopotamia not to attack while his home defenses were depleted. The tax burden crippled the economy, leading to constant banditry in the countryside. Crowds poured into the capital from rural areas, seeking relief from poverty and robbers.

These stresses combined to provoke social violence. So heavy and so unpopular were the regime's taxes and so notorious was the ruthlessness with which officials collected them that a major riot broke out in the capital in A.D. 532. The nine days of the Nika Riot (so called from the crowd's shouts in Greek of "Win!") saw constant street battles and looting that left much of Constantinople in ashes. The catastrophe panicked Justinian, who prepared to flee the city and abandon his rule. Just as he was about to leave, Theodora (according to Procopius) sternly rebuked him along these lines: "Once born, no one can escape dying, but for one who has held imperial power it would be unbearable to be a fugitive. May I never take off my imperial robes of purple, and not live to see the day when those who meet me will not address me as their master" (Procopius, *History of the Wars* 1.24.36). Shamed by his wife's words, Justinian halted his flight and ordered troops into the streets. They ended the rampage by slaughtering thirty thousand rioters that they trapped in the racetrack.

Natural disaster compounded the Byzantine Empire's troubles in this period. In the A.D. 540s, a horrific epidemic spread by flea bites killed a third of its people. A quarter of a million died in Constantinople alone, half the capital's population. The loss of so many people created a shortage of army recruits, requiring the hiring of expensive mercenaries. It also left countless farms vacant, reducing the food supply and tax revenues. This combination of demographic and financial disaster greatly weakened the empire in the long run. Later Byzantine emperors lacked the resources to hold on to Justinian's conquests, new Germanic kingdoms emerged in the west, and the old Roman Empire was divided for the last time.

The financial pressure on the population in Justinian's reign contributed to social unrest. The emperor therefore imposed legal and religious reforms with the same aims as his polytheist and Christian predecessors on the imperial throne: to defend social order based on hierarchy and regain divine favor for himself and his subjects. The many problems threatening his regime made Justinian crave stability, and in response he increased the openly autocratic nature of his rule and emphasized his closeness to God. To promote the former goal, for example, he made senators kneel to kiss his shoe, and Theodora's, when they came before the rulers. To promote the latter goal, he had imperial artists brilliantly recast the symbols of stable rule in a Christian context. A gleaming mosaic in his church at San Vitale in Ravenna, for instance, displayed a dramatic vision of the emperor's role: Justinian standing at the center of the cosmos shoulder to shoulder with mosaics of the ancient Hebrew patriarch Abraham and Christ. Moreover, Justinian proclaimed the emperor the "living law," reviving a philosophy of law that went back to the kingdoms of the region before the arrival of the Romans.

Justinian's building program in the capital concretely communicated an image of his overpowering supremacy and religiosity. Most spectacular of all was his magnificent reconstruction of Constantine's Church of the Holy Wisdom (Hagia Sophia). Facing the palace, the church's location announced Justinian's interlacing of imperial and Christian authority. Creating a new design for churches, his architects erected a huge building on a square plan capped by a dome 107 feet across and soaring 160 feet above the floor below. Its interior walls glowed like the sun from the light reflecting off their four acres of gold mosaics. Imported marble of every color added to the sparkling effect. According to later tradition, when Justinian first entered his masterpiece, dedicated in A.D. 538, he announced, "Glory to God, who thought me worthy to complete such a work. I have conquered you, Solomon!" (*Anonymi Narratio de aedificatione Templi S. Sophiae* 28). The emperor was claiming to have surpassed the splendor of the temple in Jerusalem built by that famous ancient king of the Hebrews. His building program became the most visible reminder to later ages of the glory that Justinian strove so hard to win.

The increased autocracy of the central government more and more concentrated attention on the capital to the detriment of the provinces. Most seriously, it reduced the autonomy of the empire's cities. Their local councils ceased to govern. Imperial officials took over instead. Provincial elites still had to assure full payment of their areas' taxes, but they lost the compensating reward of deciding local matters. Now the imperial government determined all aspects of decision-making and social status. Men of property from the provinces who aspired to power and prestige knew they could only satisfy their ambitions by joining the imperial administration at the center.

To further solidify his authority, Justinian had the laws of the empire

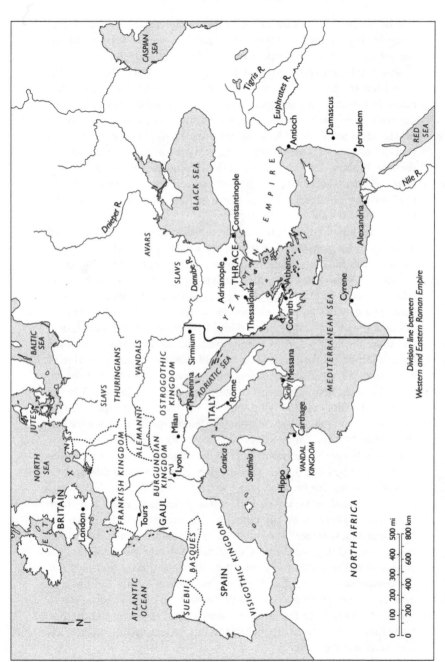

Map 13. Peoples and Kingdoms in the Roman World, Early Sixth Century A.D.

codified to bring greater uniformity to the often-confusing jumble of legal decisions that earlier emperors had enacted over the centuries. A team of scholars condensed millions of words of regulations to produce the *Digest*. This collection of laws influenced European legal scholars for centuries. His experts also compiled a textbook for students, the *Institutes*, which continued to appear in law school reading lists until modern times. Justinian's support for the production of these works of legal scholarship on both the principles and the statutes of law proved to be his most enduring legacy in western Europe.

To fulfill his sacred duty to secure the welfare of the empire, Justinian acted to guarantee its religious purity. Like the polytheist and Christian emperors before him, he believed his world could not flourish if the divine power protecting it became angered by the presence of religious offenders. As emperor, Justinian decided who the offenders were. Zealously enforcing laws against pagans, he compelled them to be baptized or forfeit their lands and official positions. Most energetically of all, he strictly purged Christians whom he could not reconcile to his version of orthodoxy. In further pursuit of purity, his laws made male homosexual relations illegal for the first time in Roman history and enforced the penalty of burning at the stake for those who did not repent and change their ways. Homosexual marriage, which may not have been unknown earlier, had been officially prohibited in A.D. 342, but civil sanctions had never before been imposed on men engaging in homosexual activity. All the previous emperors had simply taxed male prostitutes. The legal status of homosexual activity between women is less clear. It probably counted as adultery when married women were involved and was therefore a crime for that reason.

The use of legal sanctions and force against pagans, Christian heretics, and people convicted of homosexual relations expressed the emperor's official devotion to God and his concern for his future reputation as a pious and successful ruler. This motivation had roots extending far back in ancient history, but one unintended effect was further to erode popular feelings of unity. Still, emperors after Justinian fought on to maintain what they saw as Rome's mission to seek "empire without limit." They simply lacked the resources to succeed. When in the seventh and eighth centuries A.D. another new faith, Islam, motivated armies to seek a similar goal, the Eastern Roman Empire began to lose territory to the attackers that it could in the end never recover.

PRESERVING CLASSICAL LITERATURE

As it turned out, the eastern empire's most enduring contribution to the future did not come from its attempt to revive the old Roman Empire territorially. Instead, that contribution came from its preservation for much later times of the knowledge of literature from much earlier times, and of many of the physical texts on which continuing that knowledge depended. Whether intended or not, the effect of these actions was long-lasting.

The Christianization of the empire put the survival of classical Greek literature—from plays and histories to philosophical works and novels—at risk because this literature was pagan. The danger stemmed not as much from active censorship as from potential neglect. As Christians became authors, which they did copiously and with a passion, their works displaced the ancient texts of Greece and Rome as the most important literature of the age. Under these circumstances, one central reason encouraging the survival of classical texts was that elite Christian education and literature followed distinguished pagan models, Latin as well as Greek. In the eastern empire, the region's original Greek culture remained the dominant influence, but Latin literature continued to be read because the administration was bilingual, with official documents and laws published in Rome's ancient tongue (along with Greek translations). Emperor Constantius II, the son of Constantine, had decreed that any man seeking a job in the government had to be well educated in classical literature. This requirement for a comfortable position in the civil service induced families to have their sons study famous ancient pagan authors as early as possible in their education: in the village of Nessana in the Negev desert (today in Israel near the Egyptian border), archaeologists have unearthed a copy of a student's Latin vocabulary list for Vergil's *Aeneid*. It probably belonged to a local Arab boy who aimed at qualifying for a job in Roman government in the eastern empire.

Latin scholarship in the east received a boost when Justinian's Italian wars impelled Latin-speaking scholars to flee for safety to Constantinople. Their work there helped to conserve many works that might otherwise have disappeared, because conditions in the west were hardly conducive to preserving ancient learning, except in such rare instances as that of Cassiodorus (A.D. 490–585). He supported monks in Italy in the task of copying manuscripts to keep their contents alive as old ones disintegrated. His own book *Institutions* encapsulated the respect for tradition that kept classical learning alive: in prescribing the works a person of superior education should read, Cassiodorus's guide included ancient secular texts, as well as scripture and Christian literature.

Much of the classical literature available today survived because it served as schoolwork for educated Christians. They received at least a rudimentary knowledge of some pre-Christian classics as a requirement for a good career in government service, the goal of every ambitious student. In the words of an imperial decree dating back to A.D. 360, "No person shall obtain a post of the first rank unless it shall be shown that he excels in long practice of liberal studies, and that he is so polished in literary matters that words flow from his pen faultlessly" (*Theodosian Code* 14.1). Another factor promoting the preservation of knowledge of classical literature was that the principles of classical rhetoric provided the guidelines for the most effective presentation of Christian theology. When Ambrose, a bishop of Milan in the later fourth century A.D., composed the first systematic description of Christian ethics for young priests, he consciously imitated the great classical orator Cicero. Theologians employed the dialogue form pioneered by Plato to refute heretical Christian doctrines, and pagan traditions of laudatory biography survived in the wildly popular field of saints' lives. Similarly, Christian artists incorporated pagan traditions in communicating their beliefs and emotions in paintings, mosaics, and carved reliefs. A famous mosaic of Christ with a sunburst surrounding his head, for example, took its inspiration from pagan depictions of the radiant Sun as a god (see Figure 22, p. 153).

The explosion of Christian literature fostered a technological innovation whose effects also helped in the physical preservation of classical texts. Scribes had traditionally written books on sheets made of thin animal skin, or of paper made from papyrus reeds. They then glued the sheets together and attached rods at both ends to form scrolls. Readers faced a cumbersome task in unrolling them to read. For ease of use, Christians tended to follow a growing trend to produce their texts in the form of the *codex*—a book with bound pages. Eventually the codex became the standard form of book production in the Roman world. Because it was less susceptible to damage and could contain large texts more efficiently than scrolls, which were cumbersome for reading long works, the codex aided the preservation of literature. This technological innovation greatly increased the chances of survival of classical texts that were copied over into this more efficient form.

Despite the continuing importance of classical Greek and Latin texts for education and rhetorical training under the eastern empire, the survival of this knowledge from the past remained in danger in a war-torn world. Knowledge of Greek in the violence-plagued west faded so drastically that almost no one any longer had the knowledge to read the original versions of Homer's *Iliad* and *Odyssey*—for centuries and centuries the traditional foundations of a superior literary education. Classical Latin fared better, and scholars such as Augustine and Jerome knew ancient Latin literature extremely well. But they also saw the Greek and Latin classics of literature as potentially too seductive for a pious Christian. Jerome in fact once had a nightmare of being condemned on Judgment Day for having been a Ciceronian instead of a Christian.

The closing in A.D. 529 of the Academy originally founded in Athens by Plato a thousand years earlier vividly demonstrated the dangers for the survival of classical learning at this point. It is unclear whether Justinian was directly responsible for shutting down the Academy, which taught ideas from Neoplatonic philosophy that some Christians found intriguing and helpful. It is certain, however, that the emperor was outraged by the remarks of its virulently anti-Christian head, Damascius, and drove him into temporary exile in Persia. It could be dangerous to seem too connected to the pre-Christian past of the old Roman Empire.

As always, enforcement of imperial policy—though "policy" is perhaps too grand a characterization of what boiled down to the wishes of the emperor—was irregular in different regions of the empire. No action was taken against the Neoplatonist school at Alexandria. It perhaps mattered that the head of that institution of higher education, John Philoponus ("Lover of Work"), was a Christian. Nevertheless, ideas from the pagan past remained central to the school's work: Philoponus wrote commentaries on the works of Aristotle as well as works on Christian theology. Some of Philoponus's ideas on the concept of space and perspective anticipated those of Galileo a thousand years later. With his intellectual research, Philoponus achieved the kind of synthesis of old and new that was one of the fruitful possibilities in the ferment of the late Roman world: he was a Christian subject of the Roman Empire in Egypt in the sixth-century A.D., heading a school founded long before by pagans, studying the works of an ancient Greek philosopher as the inspiration for forward-looking scholarship. Philoponus's example provides a fitting end to this overview of ancient Roman history because it makes clear the value—to say nothing of the personal satisfaction—that can be added in any time and place by learning from the knowledge encoded in the past of human experience.

SUGGESTED READINGS

These items, all in English, have been selected from the vast and international bibliography on Roman history to suit, it is hoped, the needs and interests of readers new to the subject. The lists include, first, primary sources ("Ancient Texts" and "Collections of Ancient Sources") and, then, secondary sources ("Modern Studies"). Some of the modern studies assume that readers have substantially more than an introductory knowledge of Roman history, but they are included because their main interpretative conclusions should be accessible to readers willing to persevere.

The ancient texts available in English translation and the modern works cited in parentheses in the text are also included.

ANCIENT TEXTS

Titles of works listed are those of the translations listed here, which often are not word-for-word translations of the original titles. The translations have been selected for readability and, when possible, price.

Acts of Paul and Thecla. In J. K. Elliott, *The Apocryphal New Testament: A Collection of Apocryphal Christian Literature in English Translation.* Oxford: Clarendon Press, 1993.

Ammianus Marcellinus. *The Later Roman Empire: A.D. 354–378.* Trans. Walter Hamilton. New York: Penguin, 1986.

Apicius. *Cookery and Dining in Imperial Rome.* Trans. Joseph Dommers Vehling. Mineola: Dover, 1977.

Appian. *The Civil Wars.* Trans. John Carter. New York: Penguin, 1996.

Apuleius. *The Golden Ass.* Trans. P. G. Walsh. Oxford: Oxford University Press, 2008.

Athanasius. *The Life of Antony and the Letter to Marcellinus.* Trans. Robert C. Gregg. New York: Paulist Press, 1980.

Athenaeus. *The Learned Banqueters.* Trans. S. Douglas Olson. 7 vols. Cambridge, Mass.: Harvard University Press, 2006–2010.

Augustine. *City of God.* Trans. Henry Bettenson. New York: Penguin, 2003.

———. *Confessions.* Trans. Henry Chadwick. Oxford: Oxford University Press, 2009.

———. *Letters. The Works of St. Augustine: A Translation for the 21st Century.* Vol. 4. *Letters* 211-270, 1*–29*. Brooklyn: New City Press, 2005.

———. *Sermons on Selected Lessons of the New Testament.* In *A Select Library of Nicene and Post-Nicene Fathers of the Christian Church.* Vol. 6. New York: The Christian Literature Co., 1888.

Augustus. *Res Gestae Divi Augusti: Text, Translation, and Commentary.* Trans. Alison E. Cooley. Cambridge: Cambridge University Press, 2009.

Babcock, Charles L. "An Inscription of Trajan Decius from Cosa." *American Journal of Philology* 83 (1962): 147–158.

Caesar, Julius. *The Civil War.* Trans. J. M. Carter. Oxford: Oxford University Press, 2008.

———. *The Gallic War.* Trans. Carolyn Hammond. Oxford: Oxford University Press, 2008.

Cassiodorus. *Variae.* Trans. S. J. B. Barnish. Liverpool: Liverpool University Press, 1992.

Cassius Dio. *The Reign of Augustus.* Trans. Ian Scott-Kilvert. New York: Penguin, 1987.

———. *Roman History.* Trans. Earnest Cary. 9 vols. Cambridge, Mass.: Harvard University Press, 1914–1927.

Catullus. *The Complete Poems.* Trans. Guy Lee. Oxford: Oxford University Press, 2009.

Celsus. *On the True Doctrine: A Discourse Against the Christians.* Trans. R. Joseph Hoffman. Oxford: Oxford University Press, 1987.

Cicero. *Letters to Quintus and Brutus; Letter Fragments; Letter to Octavian; Invectives; Handbook of Electioneering.* Trans. D. R. Shackleton Bailey. Cambridge, Mass.: Harvard University Press, 2002.

———. *The Nature of the Gods.* Trans. P. G. Walsh. Oxford: Oxford University Press, 2008.

———. *On the Good Life.* Trans. Michael Grant. New York: Penguin, 1971.

———. *On Government (Against Verres II.5, For Murena, For Balbus, On the State III, On Laws III, Brutus, Philippics IV,V, X).* Trans. Michael Grant. New York: Penguin, 1993.

———. *On Obligations: De Officiis.* Trans. P. G. Walsh. Oxford: Oxford University Press, 2008.

———. *Political Speeches.* Trans. D. H. Berry. Oxford: Oxford University Press, 2009.

———. *The Republic and The Laws.* Trans. Niall Rudd. Oxford: Oxford University Press, 2008.

———. *Selected Letters.* Trans. P. G. Walsh. Oxford: Oxford University Press, 2008.

Cyprian. *On the Church: Select Letters. St. Cyprian of Carthage.* Trans. Allen Brent. Crestwood: St. Vladimir's Seminary Press, 2006.

Dionysius of Halicarnassus. *Roman Antiquities.* Trans. Earnest Cary. 7 vols. Cambridge, Mass.: Harvard University Press, 1937–1950.

Eusebius. *The Church History.* Trans. Paul L. Maier. Grand Rapids: Kregel, 2007.

————. *Life of Constantine*. Trans. Averil Cameron and Stuart G. Hall. Oxford: Oxford University Press, 1999.

Gaius. *Institutes*. Trans. W. M. Gordon and O. F. Robinson. London: Duckworth, 1997.

Herodian. *History of the Roman Empire since Marcus Aurelius*. Trans. Edward C. Echols. Berkeley: University of California Press, 1961.

Horace. *The Complete Odes and Epodes*. Trans. David West. Oxford: Oxford University Press, 2008.

————. *The Satires of Horace and Persius*. Trans. Niall Rudd. New York: Penguin, 2005.

Ignatius of Antioch. *The Epistles of St. Clement of Rome and St. Ignatius of Antioch*. Trans. James A. Kleist, S.J. Westminster, MD.: The Newman Bookshop, 1946.

Jerome. *Letters and Select Works. A Select Library of Nicene and Post-Nicene Fathers of the Christian Church*. Second series, vol. 6. New York: The Christian Literature Co., 1893.

John the Lydian. *De Magistratibus: On the Magistracies of the Roman Constitution*. Trans. T. F. Carney. Lawrence: Coronado, 1971.

John Philoponus. *Against Aristotle, on the Eternity of the World*. Trans. Christian Wildberg. London: Duckworth, 1987.

Josephus. *The Jewish War*. Trans. G. A. Williamson. Rev. ed. New York: Penguin, 1981.

Julian. *The Works of the Emperor Julian*. Trans. Wilmer Cave Wright. 3 vols. Cambridge, Mass.: Harvard University Press, 1962–1980.

Justinian. *The Digest of Justinian*. Ed. Alan Watson. Rev. ed. 4 vols. Philadelphia: University of Pennsylvania Press, 2009.

————. *Justinian's Institutes*. Trans. Peter Birks and Grant McLeod. Ithaca: Cornell University Press, 1987.

Juvenal. *The Satires*. Trans. Niall Rudd. Oxford: Oxford University Press, 2008.

Lactantius. *Divine Institutes*. Trans. Anthony Bowen and Peter Garnsey. Liverpool: Liverpool University Press, 2003.

Lives of the Later Caesars: The First Part of the Augustan History, with Newly Compiled Lives of Nerva and Trajan. Trans. Anthony Birley. New York: Penguin, 1976.

Livy. *The Early History of Rome: Books I–V of From the Foundation of the City*. Trans. Aubrey de Sélincourt. New York: Penguin, 2002.

————. *Hannibal's War (Books Twenty-One to Thirty of From the Foundation of the City)*. Trans. J. C. Yardley. Oxford: Oxford University Press, 2006.

————. *Rome and Italy, Books VI–X of From the Foundation of the City*. Trans. Betty Radice. New York: Penguin, 1982.

————. *Rome and the Mediterranean, Books XXXI–XLV of From the Foundation of the City*. Trans. Henry Bettenson. New York: Penguin, 1976.

Lucan. *Civil War*. Trans. Susan Braund. Oxford: Oxford University Press, 2008.

Macrobius. *Saturnalia*. Trans. Robert A. Kaster. Cambridge, Mass.: Harvard University Press, 2011.

Marcus Aurelius. *Meditations*. Trans. Martin Hammond. New York: Penguin, 2006.

Origen. *Contra Celsum*. Trans. Henry Chadwick. Cambridge: Cambridge University Press, 1980.

Orosius. *Seven Books of History Against the Pagans*. Trans. A. T. Fear. Liverpool: Liverpool University Press, 2010.

Ovid. *The Erotic Poems*. Trans. Peter Green. New York: Penguin, 1982.

———. *Metamorphoses*. Trans. A. D. Melville. Oxford: Oxford University Press, 2009.

Perpetua. *What Would You Die For? Perpetua's Passion*. Ed. Joseph J. Walsh. Baltimore: Apprentice House, 2006.

Petronius. *The Satyricon*. Trans. P. G. Walsh. Oxford: Oxford University Press, 2009.

Pliny the Younger. *Complete Letters*. Trans. P. G. Walsh. Oxford: Oxford University Press, 2009.

Plotinus. *The Essential Plotinus: Representative Treatises from the Enneads*. Trans. Elmer O'Brien. Indianapolis: Hackett, 1964.

Plutarch. *The Fall of the Roman Republic*. Trans. Rex Warner. New York: Penguin, 2006.

———. *The Makers of Rome*. Trans. Ian Scott-Kilvert. New York: Penguin, 2004.

———. *Roman Lives*. Trans. Robin Waterfield. Oxford: Oxford University Press, 2009.

Polybius. *The Histories*. Trans. Robin Waterfield. Oxford: Oxford University Press, 2010.

Procopius. *History of the Wars, Secret History, and Buildings*. Trans. H. B. Dewing. 7 vols. Cambridge, Mass.: Harvard University Press, 1914–1940.

———. *The Secret History*. Trans. G. A. Williamson and Peter Sarris. Rev. ed. New York: Penguin, 2007.

Sallust. *Catiline's Conspiracy, The Jugurthine War, Histories*. Trans. William W. Batstone. Oxford: Oxford University Press, 2010.

Seneca. *Moral and Political Essays*. Trans. J. F. Procopé and John M. Cooper. Oxford: Oxford University Press, 1995.

Sima Qian. *Records of the Grand Historian: Han Dynasty II*. Trans. Burton Watson. Rev. ed. Hong Kong: Columbia University Press, 1993.

Socrates. *Church History*. A Select Library of Nicene and Post-Nicene Fathers of the Christian Church. Second series, vol. 2. New York: The Christian Literature Co., 1890.

Suetonius. *Lives of the Caesars*. Trans. Catharine Edwards. Oxford: Oxford University Press, 2009.

Symmachus. *Prefect and Emperor: The Relationes of Symmachus, A.D. 384*. Trans. R. H. Barrow. Oxford: Clarendon Press, 1973.

Tacitus. *Agricola and Germany*. Trans. Anthony Birley. Oxford: Oxford University Press, 2009.

———. *Agricola, Germany, and the Dialogue on Orators*. Trans. Herbert W. Benario. Norman: University of Oklahoma Press, 1991.

———. *The Annals: The Reigns of Tiberius, Claudius, and Nero*. Trans. J. C. Yardley. Oxford: Oxford University Press, 2008.

———. *The Histories*. Trans. W. H. Fyfe and D. S. Levene. Oxford: Oxford University Press, 2008.

Tertullian. *Apology, De spectaculis*. Trans. T. R. Glover. Cambridge, Mass.: Harvard University Press, 1931.

The Theodosian Code and Novels, and the Sirmondian Constitutions. Trans. Clyde Pharr. Princeton: Princeton University Press, 1952.

Valerius Maximus. *Memorable Deeds and Sayings: A Thousand Tales from Ancient Rome*. Trans. Henry John Walker. Indianapolis: Hackett, 2004.

Vegetius. *Epitome of Military Science*. Trans. N. P. Milner. 2d. ed. Liverpool: Liverpool University Press, 1996.

Velleius Paterculus. *The Roman History: From Romulus and the Foundation of Rome to the Reign of the Emperor Tiberius*. Trans. J. C. Yardley and Anthony A. Barrett. Indianapolis: Hackett, 2011.

Vergil. *The Aeneid of Vergil*. Trans. Sarah Ruden. New Haven: Yale University Press, 2009.

Zosimus. *New History*. Trans. Ronald T. Ridley. Canberra: Australian Association for Byzantine Studies, 1982.

COLLECTIONS OF ANCIENT SOURCES

Beard, Mary, John North, and Simon Price, eds. *Religions of Rome*. Vol. 2. Oxford: Oxford University Press, 1998.

Burstein, Stanley M., trans. *The Hellenistic Age from the Battle of Ipsos to the Death of Kleopatra VII*. Cambridge: Cambridge University Press, 1985.

Campbell, Brian, ed. *The Roman Army 31 BC–AD 337: A Sourcebook*. London: Routledge, 1994.

Cherry, David, ed. *The Roman World: A Sourcebook*. Malden: Blackwell, 2001.

Dillon, Matthew and Lynda Garland, eds. *Ancient Rome: From the Early Republic to the Assassination of Julius Caesar*. London: Routledge, 2005.

Drew, Katherine Fischer, trans. *The Laws of the Salian Franks*. Philadelphia: University of Pennsylvania Press, 1991.

Frier, Bruce W. and Thomas A. J. McGinn, eds. *A Casebook on Roman Family Law*. Oxford: Oxford University Press, 2004.

Grubbs, Judith Evans, ed. *Women and the Law in the Roman Empire: A Sourcebook on Marriage, Divorce and Widowhood*. London: Routledge, 2002.

Futrell, Alison, ed. *The Roman Games: A Sourcebook*. Malden: Blackwell, 2006.

Hope, Valerie M., ed. *Death in Ancient Rome: A Sourcebook*. London: Routledge, 2007.

Hyamson, H. *Mosaicarum et romanarum legum collatio*. London: Oxford University Press, 1913.

Kraemer, Ross Shepard, ed. *Women's Religions in the Greco-Roman World: A Sourcebook*. Oxford: Oxford University Press, 2004.

Lee, A. D., ed. *Pagans and Christians in Late Antiquity: A Sourcebook*. London: Routledge, 2000.

Levick, Barbara, ed. *The Government of the Roman Empire: A Sourcebook*. London: Routledge, 2000.

Lewis, Naphtali and Meyer Reinhold, eds. *Roman Civilization: Selected Readings*. 3d. ed. Vol. 1: *The Republic and The Augustan Age*. Vol. 2: *The Empire*. New York: Columbia University Press, 1990.

Maas, Michael, ed. *Readings in Late Antiquity: A Sourcebook*. 2d. ed. London: Routledge, 2010.

MacMullen, Ramsay and Eugene N. Lane, eds. *Paganism and Christianity, 100–425 C.E.: A Sourcebook*. Minneapolis: Fortress, 1992.

Mahoney, Anne, ed. *Roman Sports and Spectacles: A Sourcebook*. Newburyport: Focus, 2001.

Musurillo, Herbert, trans. *The Acts of the Christian Martyrs*. Oxford: Clarendon Press, 1972.

Pollitt, J. J., ed. *The Art of Rome, c. 753 B.C.–A.D. 337*. Cambridge: Cambridge University Press, 1983.

Ridley, Ronald T. *History of Rome: A Documented Analysis*. Rome: L'Erma di Bretschneider, 1987.

Roberts, C. H. and E. G. Turner, eds. *Catalogue of the Greek and Latin Papyri in the John Rylands Library, Manchester*. 4 vols. Manchester: Manchester University Press, 1911–1952.

Sage, Michael M., ed. *The Republican Roman Army: A Sourcebook*. London: Routledge, 2008.

Shelton, Jo-Ann, ed. *As The Romans Did: A Sourcebook in Roman Social History*. 2d. ed. Oxford: Oxford University Press, 1998.

Warmington, E. H., trans. *Remains of Old Latin*. 4 vols. Cambridge, Mass.: Harvard University Press, 1956–1961.

MODERN STUDIES

Adkins, Lesley and Roy A. Adkins. *Handbook to Life in Ancient Rome*. Oxford: Oxford University Press, 2004.

Ando, Clifford. *Imperial Ideology and Provincial Loyalty in the Roman Empire*. Berkeley: University of California Press, 2000.

———. *The Matter of the Gods: Religion and the Roman Empire*. Berkeley: University of California Press, 2008.

Badian, Ernst. *Foreign Clientelae (264–70 B.C.)*. Oxford: Oxford University Press, 1958; reprint with corrections, 1984.

Barrett, Anthony. *Caligula: The Corruption of Power*. New York: Simon and Schuster, 1990.

Beard, Mary. *The Roman Triumph*. Cambridge, Mass.: Harvard University Press, 2007.

Bennett, Julian. *Trajan: Optimus Princeps*. London: Routledge, 2001.

Birley, Anthony R. *Marcus Aurelius, A Biography*. New Haven: Yale University Press, 1987.

———. *Hadrian: The Restless Emperor*. London: Routledge, 1997.

———. *Septimius Severus: The African Emperor*. London: Routledge, 1999.

Bishop, M. C. and J. C. N. Coulson. *Roman Military Equipment: From the Punic Wars to the Fall of Rome*. Oxford: Oxbow Books, 2006.

Bonfante, Larissa, ed. *Etruscan Life and Afterlife: A Handbook of Etruscan Studies*. Detroit: Wayne State University Press, 1986.

Boswell, John. *Same-Sex Unions in Premodern Europe*. New York: Villard Books, 1994.

Bowersock, G. W., Peter Brown, and Oleg Grabar, eds. *Late Antiquity: A Guide to the Postclassical World*. Cambridge, Mass.: Harvard University Press, 1999.

Bradley, Keith. *Slavery and Society at Rome.* Cambridge: Cambridge University Press, 1994.

Brown, Peter. *The World of Late Antiquity: AD 150–750.* New York: W. W. Norton, 1971.

———. *The Body and Society: Men, Women, and Sexual Renunciation in Early Christianity.* New York: Columbia University Press, 1988.

Browning, Robert. *Justinian and Theodora.* Rev. ed. London: Thames and Hudson, 1987.

Brunt, P. A. *The Fall of the Roman Republic and Related Essays.* Oxford: Oxford University Press, 1988.

Cameron, Alan. *The Last Pagans of Rome.* Oxford: Oxford University Press, 2010.

Champlin, Edward. *Nero.* Cambridge, Mass.: Harvard University Press, 2003.

Clarke, John R. *Roman Life 100 B.C. to A.D. 200.* New York: Harry H. Abrams, 2007.

Conte, Gian Biagio. *Latin Literature: A History.* Trans. Joseph B. Solodow, rev. Don Fowler and Glenn W. Most. Baltimore: The Johns Hopkins University Press, 1994.

Cornell, Tim. *The Beginnings of Rome: Italy and Rome from the Bronze Age to the Punic Wars* (c. 1000–264 B.C.). London: Routledge, 1995.

Crawford, Michael H. *Roman Republican Coinage.* 2 vols. Cambridge: Cambridge University Press, 1974; reprint with corrections, 2001.

Crossan, Dominic and Jonathan L. Reed. *In Search of Paul: How Jesus' Apostle Opposed Rome's Empire with God's Kingdom.* New York: Harper, 2005.

Cruse, Audrey. *Roman Medicine.* Stroud: Tempus, 2004.

De Jong, Mayke. *In Samuel's Image: Child Oblation in the Early Medieval West.* Leiden: Brill, 1996.

Dennison, Matthew. *Livia, Empress of Rome: A Biography.* New York: St. Martin's, 2011.

DiMaio, Michael, Jr. and Richard Weigel, eds. *De Imperatoribus Romanis: An Online Encyclopedia of Roman Emperors:* http://www.roman-emperors.org/.

Dodge, Hazel. *Spectacle in the Roman World.* London: Duckworth, 2011.

Dupont, Florence. *Daily Life in Ancient Rome.* Trans. Christopher Woodall. Malden: Blackwell, 1989.

Dyson, Stephen L. *Rome: A Living Portrait of an Ancient City.* Baltimore: The Johns Hopkins University Press, 2010.

Earl, Donald C. *The Moral and Political Tradition of Rome.* Ithaca: Cornell University Press, 1967.

Eckstein, Arthur M. *Rome Enters the Greek East: From Anarchy to Hierarchy in the Hellenistic Mediterranean, 230–170 B.C..* Malden: Blackwell, 2008.

Edmondson, Jonathan, ed. *Augustus: Edinburgh Readings on the Ancient World.* Edinburgh: Edinburgh University Press, 2009.

Elsner, Jas. *Imperial Rome and Christian Triumph: The Art of the Roman Empire, A.D. 100–450.* Oxford: Oxford University Press, 1998.

Erdkamp, Paul, ed. *A Companion to the Roman Army.* Malden: Blackwell, 2007.

Evans, J. A. S. *The Empress Theodora: Partner of Justinian.* Austin: University of Texas Press, 2002.

———. *The Emperor Justinian and the Byzantine Empire.* Westport: Greenwood, 2005.

Fagan, Garrett G. *Bathing in Public in the Roman World*. Ann Arbor: University of Michigan Press, 1999.

————. *The Lure of the Arena: Social Psychology and the Crowd at the Roman Games*. Cambridge: Cambridge University Press, 2011.

Flower, Harriet I., ed. *The Cambridge Companion to the Roman Republic*. Cambridge: Cambridge University Press, 2004.

————. *Roman Republics*. Princeton: Princeton University Press, 2010.

Forsythe, Gary. *A Critical History of Early Rome: From Prehistory to the First Punic War*. Berkeley: University of California Press, 2005.

Frank, Tenney, ed. *An Economic Survey of Ancient Rome*. 6 vols. Baltimore: The Johns Hopkins University Press, 1933–1940.

Freisenbruch, Annelise. *Caesars' Wives: Sex, Power, and Politics in the Roman Empire*. New York: Free Press, 2010.

Frend, W. H. C. *The Rise of Christianity*. Philadelphia: Fortress, 1986.

Futrell, Allison. *Blood in the Arena: The Spectacle of Roman Power*. Austin: University of Texas Press, 1997.

Galinsky, Karl. *Augustan Culture*. Princeton: Princeton University Press, 1996.

————, ed. *The Cambridge Companion to the Age of Augustus*. Cambridge: Cambridge University Press, 2005.

Gardner, Jane. *Women in Roman Law and Society*. London: Routledge, 1986.

Garland, Robert. *Hannibal*. London: Duckworth, 2010.

Garnsey, Peter and Richard Saller. *The Roman Empire: Economy, Society, and Culture*. Berkeley: University of California Press, 1987.

Gelzer, Matthias. *The Roman Nobility*. Trans. Robin Seager. Oxford: Blackwell, 1969.

Goldsworthy, Adrian. *The Complete Roman Army*. London: Thames and Hudson, 2003.

————. *Caesar: The Life of a Colossus*. London: Weidenfeld and Nicolson, 2006.

————. *How Rome Fell: Death of a Superpower*. New Haven: Yale University Press, 2009.

Green, Bernard. *Christianity in Ancient Rome: The First Three Centuries*. London: T. and T. Clark, 2010.

Greene, Kevin. *The Archaeology of the Roman Economy*. Berkeley: University of California Press, 1986.

Grubs, Judith Evans. *Law and Family in Late Antiquity: The Emperor Constantine's Marriage Legislation*. Oxford: Clarendon Press, 1995.

Gruen, Erich S. *The Last Generation of the Roman Republic*. Berkeley: University of California Press, 1974.

Harl, Kenneth W. *Coinage in the Roman Economy, 300 B.C. to A.D. 700*. Baltimore: The Johns Hopkins University Press, 1996.

Harris, William V. *War and Imperialism in Republican Rome*. Oxford: Clarendon Press, 1985.

————. *Rome's Imperial Economy: Twelve Essays*. Oxford: Oxford University Press, 2010.

Heather, P. J. *The Goths*. Oxford: Blackwell, 1996.

————. *Empires and Barbarians: The Fall of Rome and the Birth of Europe*. Oxford: Oxford University Press, 2010.

Hezser, Catherine. *The Oxford Handbook of Jewish Daily Life in Roman Palestine*. New York: Oxford University Press, 2010.

Hopkins, Keith and Mary Beard. *The Colosseum*. London: Profile, 2005.

Isaac, Benjamin H. *The Limits of Empire: The Roman Army in the East*. Rev. ed. Oxford: Clarendon Press, 2000.

Johns, Catherine and Timothy Potter. *The Thetford Treasure: Roman Jewellery and Silver*. London: Trustees of the British Museum, 1983.

Joshel, Sandra R. *Slavery in the Roman World*. Cambridge: Cambridge University Press, 2010.

Kelly, Christopher. *The End of Empire: Attila the Hun and the Fall of Rome*. New York: W. W. Norton, 2009.

Köhne, Eckart and Ewigleben, Cornelia, eds.; Ralph Jackson, ed. English edition. *Gladiators and Caesars: The Power of Spectacle in Ancient Rome*. Berkeley: University of California Press, 2000.

Kraemer, Ross Shepard. *Her Share of the Blessings: Women's Religions among Pagans, Jews, and Christians in the Greco-Roman World*. New York: Oxford University Press, 1992.

Kulikowski, Michael. *Rome's Gothic Wars: From the Third Century to Alaric*. New York: Cambridge University Press, 2007.

Laes, Christian. *Children in the Roman Empire: Outsiders Within*. Cambridge: Cambridge University Press, 2011.

Lanciani, R. A. *Ancient Rome in the Light of Recent Discoveries*. Boston: Houghton Mifflin, 1888.

Lenski, Noel, ed. *The Cambridge Companion to the Age of Constantine*. Cambridge: Cambridge University Press, 2006.

Levick, Barbara. *Claudius*. New Haven: Yale University Press, 1990.

———. *Tiberius the Politician*. London: Routledge, 1999.

———. *Vespasian*. London: Routledge, 1999.

———. *Augustus: Image and Substance*. Harlow: Longman, 2010.

Lintott, A. W. *The Constitution of the Roman Republic*. Oxford: Clarendon Press, 1999.

———. *Violence in Republican Rome*. Oxford: Oxford University Press, 1999.

Maas, Michael, ed. *The Cambridge Companion to the Age of Justinian*. Cambridge: Cambridge University Press, 2005.

MacMullen, Ramsay. *Christianizing the Roman Empire (A.D. 100–400)*. New Haven: Yale University Press, 1984.

———. *The Second Church: Popular Christianity A.D. 200–400*. Atlanta: Society of Biblical Literature, 2009.

Marincola, John. *Greek and Roman Historiography*. Oxford: Oxford University Press, 2011.

Matthews, John. *Laying Down the Law: A Study of the Theodosian Code*. New Haven: Yale University Press, 2000.

———. *Roman Perspectives: Studies in the Social, Political and Cultural History of the First to Fifth Centuries*. Swansea: Classical Press of Wales, 2010.

Mattingly, David J. *Imperialism, Power, and Identity: Experiencing the Roman Empire*. Princeton: Princeton University Press, 2010.

Matyszak, Philip. *Chronicle of the Roman Republic: The Rulers of Ancient Rome from Romulus to Augustus*. London: Thames and Hudson, 2003.

Millar, Fergus. *The Emperor in the Roman World*. 2d ed. Ithaca: Cornell University Press, 1992.

Mitchell, Stephen. *A History of the Later Roman Empire, AD 284–641: The Transformation of the Ancient World*. Malden: Blackwell, 2007.

———. *One God: Pagan Monotheism in the Roman Empire*. Cambridge: Cambridge University Press, 2010.

Morgan, Gwyn. *69 A.D.: The Year of Four Emperors*. Oxford: Oxford University Press, 2006.

Murphy, Frederick. *An Introduction to Jesus and the Gospels*. Nashville: Abingdon, 2005.

Nicolet, Claude. *The World of the Citizen in Republican Rome*. Trans. P. S. Falla. Berkeley: University of California Press, 1980.

North, J. A. and S. R. F. Price, eds. *The Religious History of the Roman Empire: Pagans, Jews, and Christians*. Oxford: Oxford University Press, 2011.

Odahl, Charles M. *Constantine and the Christian Empire*. 2d ed. London: Routledge, 2010.

O'Donnell, James J. *Augustine: A New Biography*. New York: Echo, 2005.

Pavkovic, Michael F. *The Army of Imperial Rome*. Aldershot: Ashgate, 2008.

———. *The Army of the Roman Republic*. Aldershot: Ashgate, 2011.

Peachin, Michael, ed. *The Oxford Handbook of Social Relations in the Roman World*. Oxford: Oxford University Press, 2011.

Potter, David. S. *The Roman Empire at Bay*. London: Routledge, 2004.

———, ed. *A Companion to the Roman Empire*. Malden: Blackwell, 2006.

Potter, David S. and David J. Mattingly, eds. *Life, Death, and Entertainment in the Roman Empire*. Ann Arbor: University of Michigan Press, 2010.

Pulleyblank, E. G. "The Roman Empire as Known to Han China." *Journal of the American Oriental Society* 119 (1999): 71–79.

Rawson, Elizabeth. *Cicero: A Portrait*. Rev. ed. Bristol: Bristol Classical, 1983.

Roller, Duane W. *Cleopatra: A Biography*. Oxford: Oxford University Press, 2010.

Rosen, William. *Justinian's Flea: Plague, Empire, and the Birth of Europe*. New York: Viking, 2007.

Rosenstein, Nathan. *Rome at War: Farms, Families, and Death in the Middle Republic*. Chapel Hill: University of North Carolina Press, 2004.

Rosenstein, Nathan and Robert Morstein-Marx, eds. *A Companion to the Roman Republic*. Malden: Blackwell, 2006.

Roth, Jonathan P. *Roman Warfare*. Cambridge: Cambridge University Press, 2009.

Rousseau, Philip. *Ascetics, Authority, and the Church in the Age of Jerome and Cassian*. 2d ed. Notre Dame: University of Notre Dame Press, 2010.

Saller, Richard P. *Patriarchy, Property, and Death in the Roman Family*. Cambridge: Cambridge University Press, 1994.

Scarre, Christopher. *Chronicle of the Roman Emperors: The Reign-by-Reign Record of the Rulers of Imperial Rome*. London: Thames and Hudson, 1995.

Scheid, John. *An Introduction to Roman Religion*. Trans. Janet Lloyd. Bloomington: Indiana University Press, 2003.

Schoff, Wilfred H. *The Periplus of Hanno: A Voyage of Discovery Down the West African Coast, by a Carthaginian Admiral of the Fifth Century* B.C. Philadelphia: Commercial Museum, 1912.

Seager, Robin. *Pompey the Great: A Political Biography.* Oxford: Blackwell, 2002.

Shahîd, Irfan. *Byzantium and the Arabs in the Sixth Century.* 4 vols. Washington: Dumbarton Oaks Research Library and Collection, 1995–2009.

Smith, Christopher John. *Early Rome and Latium: Economy and Society c. 1000 to 500* BC. Oxford: Oxford University Press, 1996.

Sorek, Susan. *The Jews Against Rome.* London: Continuum, 2008.

Southern, Pat. *Domitian: Tragic Tyrant.* London: Routledge, 1997.

———. *Empress Zenobia: Palmyra's Rebel Queen.* London: Hambledon Continuum, 2008.

Southern, Pat and Karen R. Dixon. *The Late Roman Army.* London: B. T. Batsford, 1996.

Stark, Rodney. *The Rise of Christianity: A Sociologist Reconsiders History.* Princeton: Princeton University Press, 1996.

Stephenson, Paul. *Constantine: Unconquered Emperor, Christian Victor.* London: Quercus, 2009.

Stewart, Peter. *The Social History of Roman Art.* Cambridge: Cambridge University Press, 2008.

Stewart, Roberta. *Public Office in Early Rome: Ritual Procedure and Political Practice.* Ann Arbor: University of Michigan Press, 1998.

Stockton, D. L. *The Gracchi.* Oxford: Clarendon Press, 1979.

Strauss, Barry S. *The Spartacus War.* New York: Simon and Schuster, 2009.

Strong, Donald. *Roman Art.* 2nd ed. New Haven: Yale University Press, 1995.

Syme, Ronald. *The Roman Revolution.* Oxford: Clarendon Press, 1939; reprint with corrections, 1952 and later.

Toner, Jerry. *Popular Culture in Ancient Rome.* Cambridge: Polity, 2009.

Tougher, Shaun. *Julian the Apostate.* Edinburgh: Edinburgh University Press, 2007.

Treggiari, Susan. *Roman Marriage: Iusti Coniuges from the Time of Cicero to the Time of Ulpian.* Oxford: Clarendon Press, 1991.

Tsafir, Yoran. "Nessana." In Bowersock et al., *Late Antiquity,* pp. 601–602.

Wallace-Hadrill, Andrew. *Herculaneum: Past and Future.* London: Frances Lincoln, 2011.

Wells, Peter. *The Battle That Stopped Rome: Emperor Augustus, Arminius, and the Slaughter of the Legions in the Teutoburg Forest.* New York: W. W. Norton, 2004.

Wickham, Chris. *Framing the Early Middle Ages: Europe and the Mediterranean, 400–800.* Oxford: Oxford University Press, 2005.

Williams, Stephen. *Diocletian and the Roman Recovery.* New York: Routledge, 1997.

Williamson, Callie. *The Laws of the Roman People: Public Law in the Expansion and Decline of the Roman Republic.* Ann Arbor: University of Michigan Press, 2005.

Wiseman, T. P. *The Myths of Rome.* Exeter: University of Exeter Press, 2004.

Woolf, Greg. *Tales of the Barbarians: Ethnography and Empire in the Roman West.* Malden: Wiley-Blackwell, 2011.

Zanker, Paul. *The Power of Images in the Age of Augustus.* Trans. by Alan Shapiro. Ann Arbor: University of Michigan Press, 1988.

———. *Pompeii: Public and Private Life.* Trans. Deborah Lucas Schneider. Cambridge, Mass.: Harvard University Press, 1998.

INDEX

Page numbers in bold refer to illustrations.